What Research Says to the Science Teacher

Volume Seven

The Science, Technology, Society Movement

Robert E. Yager, editor

National Science Teachers Association

Copyright © 1993 by the National Science Teachers Association,
1742 Connecticut Ave., NW, Washington, DC 20009.

This book has been edited and produced by the staff of NSTA Special
Publications. Shirley Watt Ireton, managing editor; Christine M. Pearce,
associate editor; Andrew Saindon, associate editor; Anne Calmes, editorial
assistant; and Daniel Shannon, editorial assistant. Christine M. Pearce
was project editor for this book. The cover of this volume was designed by
Sharon H. Wolfgang of AURAS Design. The book was printed by
Reproductions, Incorporated.

Library of Congress Catalog Number 93–83059

Stock Number #PB–37/7

ISBN Number 0–87355–113–3

Printed in the United States of America

The Science, Technology, Society Movement

Part III. STS in Broader Perspectives

Part IV. Results of STS Instruction

Acknowledgements

Many persons contributed to this volume in addition to the 28 authors, many of whom are internationally recognized. The authors are recognized by their written words which will benefit many professionals and ultimately the students they are privileged to touch. However, this volume would not have been possible without the wisdom, support, and encouragement of three NSTA presidents, namely LaMoine Motz, who initiated the effort, Hans Andersen, and Bonnie J. Brunkhorst. The work and support of the NSTA Special Publications committee is also acknowledged. Finally, the great support and assistance of the NSTA STS Task Force on Initiatives has been most significant. These persons include: Gary Appel, Life Lab Science Program, Santa Cruz, California; Herbert K. Brunkhorst, California State University, San Bernardino, California; Sam Crowell, California State University, San Bernardino, California; Carolyn S. Graham, State Education Department, Albany, New York; Jon L. Harkness, Wausau West High School, Wausau, Wisconsin; Phillip A. Heath, The Ohio State University at Lima, Lima, Ohio; Mattie Jefferson, Cardozo Senior High School, Washington, DC; Michael G. Lang, Arizona Department of Education, Phoenix, Arizona; Morgan L. Masters, Chariton Community High School, Chariton, Iowa; Donald E. Maxwell, Biological Sciences Curriculum Study, Colorado Springs, Colorado; E. Joseph Piel, Professor Emeritus, State University of New York, Stony Brook, New York; Roger Spratt, Mesa Public Schools, Mesa, Arizona; and JoAnne Wolf, Mesa Public Schools, Mesa, Arizona.

A special note of thanks must also go to our reviewers: Shannon Cde Baca, science teacher at Thomas Jefferson High School in Council Bluffs, Iowa; Patricia Blosser, professor of science education at The Ohio State University; Delmar Janke, associate professor of science education at Texas A&M University, College Station, Texas; Florence Juillerat, associate professor of biology at Indiana University Purdue University at Indianapolis; David Kennedy, director of curriculum for the Office of the Superintendent of Public Instruction for the state of Washington; Dan Ochs, professor of science education at the University of Louisville, Louisville, Kentucky; and David Stronck, professor of science education at California State University, Hayward.

Thanks also goes to Grace Newby, secretary in the Science Education Center at The University of Iowa, who corresponded with authors and typed drafts of the entire monograph for review by the Task Force members and other reviewers. Certainly the fine NSTA Special Publications staff headed by Shirley Watt Ireton and the diligent work of Christine Pearce, associate editor, are to be commended. Without their work, this effort could not have been completed.

All who contributed and supported this effort look forward to the judgment of the readers concerning the sincere efforts of so many.

Robert E. Yager,
Editor and Task Force Chair

Foreword

This monograph takes the same view of science, technology, society as the National Science Teachers Association's position statement (see p. 5). In this definition, the context for teaching is more important for teaching and learning than are the concepts and processes that often define science in school programs. For many, the emergence of context as a major factor to consider for teaching and learning is counter to their own experiences, and yet, the research evidence is most convincing. Most contributors believe that such a definition ensures that STS is something more than a curriculum organizer, a content strand, or a set of special themes which can be infused into science courses. Nonetheless, it should be noted that this more macro-view of STS is not universally accepted. Definitions that restrict it to a kind of specialized content—content quite different from the concepts and processes traditionally used as the basic ingredients to courses and curriculum planning—often encounter stiff criticism, skepticism, and even anger. Too often the inclusion of STS themes means the exclusion of more common, comfortable, or important information.

At times some authors who have contributed to this volume use STS as content and talk of STS topics, themes, vignettes, and ideas. Some see such content as important supplements or replacements to typical concepts and processes. This dichotomy reflects one of our current problems with STS.

Part I
An Overview of STS

NATIONAL SCIENCE TEACHERS ASSOCIATION

Science/Technology/Society: A New Effort for Providing Appropriate Science for All

National Science Teachers Association

A statement prepared by the NSTA Task Force on STS Initiatives. Unanimously approved by NSTA Board of Directors, July, 1990.

NSTA views STS as the teaching and learning of science in the context of human experience. It represents an appropriate science education context for all learners. The emerging research is clear in illustrating that learning science in an STS context results in students with more sophisticated concept mastery and ability to use process skills. All students improve in terms of creativity skills, attitude toward science, use of science concepts and processes in their daily living, and in responsible personal decision-making.

There are no concepts and/or processes unique to STS; instead STS provides a setting and a reason for considering basic science and technology concepts and processes. STS means determining and experiencing ways that these basic ideas and skills can be observed in society. STS means focusing on real-world problems which have science and technology components from the students' perspectives, instead of starting with concepts and processes. This allows students to instigate, analyze, and apply concepts and processes to real situations. A good program will have built-in opportunities for the students to extend beyond the classroom to their local communities. These activities should be appropriate for the age of the students and be learner-centered. STS should help lay the basis for empowering students so that as future citizens they realize they have the power to make changes and the responsibility to do so.

STS: How to Recognize Program

Basic to STS efforts is the production of an informed citizenry capable of making crucial decisions about current problems and issues and taking personal actions as a result of these decisions. STS means focusing upon current issues and attempts at their resolution as the best way of preparing students for current and future citizenship roles. This means identifying local, regional, national, and international problems with students, planning for individual and group activities which address them, and moving to actions designed to resolve the issues investigated. The emphasis is on responsible decision making in the real world of the student. STS provides direction for achieving scientific and technological literacy for all. The emphasis is on responsible decision making in the real world of the student where science and technology are components. Curricular and instructional processes might consider the following:

- Is it a problem or issue?
- How did it become a problem or issue?
- What are some alternative approaches to its solution?
- What are the potential effects of applying the alternatives on individuals and/or Society?

STS programs are characterized as those with many of the following characteristics:

- student identification of problems with local interest and impact;
- the use of local resources (human and material) to locate information that can be used in problem resolution;
- the active involvement of students in seeking information that can be applied to solve real-life problems;
- the extension of learning going beyond the class period, the classroom, the school;
- a focus upon the impact of science and technology on individual students;
- a view that science content is more than concepts which exist for students to master on tests;
- an emphasis upon process skills which students can use in their own problem resolution;
- an emphasis upon career awareness—especially careers related to science and technology;
- opportunities for students to experience citizenship roles as they attempt to resolve issues they have identified;
- identification of ways that science and technology are likely to impact the future;
- some autonomy in the learning process (as individual issues are identified).

STS: A Way of Producing Scientific and Technological Literacy

The major goal for STS efforts is the production of scientifically and technologically literate persons after 13 years of involvement with science in school. The scientifically and technologically literate person:

- uses concepts of science and of technology as well as an informed reflection of ethical values in solving everyday problems and making responsible decisions in everyday life, including work and leisure
- engages in responsible personal and civic actions after weighing the possible consequences of alternative options
- defends decisions and actions using rational arguments based on evidence
- engages in science and technology for the excitement and the explanations they provide
- displays curiosity about and appreciation of the natural and human-made world
- applies skepticism, careful methods, logical reasoning, and creativity in investigating the observable universe
- values scientific research and technological problem solving
- locates, collects, analyzes, and evaluates sources of scientific and technological information and uses these sources in solving problems, making decisions, and taking actions

- distinguishes between scientific and technological evidence and personal opinion and between reliable and unreliable information
- remains open to new evidence and the tentativeness of scientific/technological knowledge
- recognizes that science and technology are human endeavors
- weighs the benefits and burdens of scientific and technological development
- recognizes the strengths and limitations of science and technology for advancing human welfare
- analyzes interactions among science, technology, and society
- connects science and technology to other human endeavors, e.g., history, mathematics, the arts, and the humanities
- considers the political, economic, moral, and ethical aspects of science and technology as they relate to personal and global issues
- offers explanations of natural phenomena which may be tested for their validity

Summary

STS requires that we rethink, restructure, reorganize, rewrite, and revise current materials (e.g., curriculum, texts, audiovisuals) used to teach science.

STS will require a realignment of goals and objectives and a reallocation of resources. STS will require re-education on all levels from policy makers to teachers to parents. Such reform of science education is essential.

The bottom line in STS is the involvement of learners in experiences and issues which are directly related to their lives. STS empowers students with skills which allow them to become active, responsible citizens by responding to issues which impact their lives. The experience of science education through STS strategies will create a scientifically literate citizenry for the 21st century.

References

National Science Teachers Association. (1992–1993). In *National Science Teachers Association Handbook, 1992–93* (pp. 168–169). Washington, DC: Author.

STS: Most Pervasive and Most Radical of Reform Approaches to "Science" Education

Robert E. Yager and Rustum Roy
The University of Iowa and Pennsylvania State University

A remarkable phenomenon has occurred in American education since 1970. A hundred years of continuous fissioning of the body of knowledge into increasingly narrow specialties gradually halted and a trend towards integrating disciplines began. This epistemological turning point took place under the banner of a new interdisciplinary thrust called Science, Technology, and Society (STS).

STS has become a movement. As the name suggests, STS aims to integrate science and technology, the quintessential and pervasive characteristics of our culture, into all the traditional learnings of society. STS mimics life and reality in relating civil engineering to ethics, physical chemistry to philosophy, and technological decline to political choice; STS is unavoidable as the core of integrative general education.

STS is a major reassertion by the university of one of its principal functions—the unifying function. Discovering and proclaiming great unities should be the university's direct service to society. Which other institution could possibly be appropriate to unite the grand traditions of humankind handed down from one generation to the next with the latest knowledge, insights, deep truths, and indeed, problems and challenges which confront contemporary humans? And in a culture where the incredibly seductive and powerful forces of technology and science literally define what is characteristic and unique about our own culture, the unifying of Western values with the meanings of science and technology must surely be the focal point of the intellectual *raison d'etre* of the modern university.

General education, presumably, is the place in the curriculum where unification could be done. The spate of general education reforms is testimony to the universal awareness that, on most campuses, general education remains a pork barrel for distribution of large-enrollment "service" courses. For the first time, in STS, a set of integrative principles has emerged which forms an intellectual core for much of general education decisively different from the "course distribution" requirements of a Chinese dinner. It is the genuine fusion of ideas, knowledge, and values which counters the fissioning of knowledge over the last century. Moreover, this integrative style also helps, by contagion, to render more porous the walls between the higher reaches of the disciplines. And conversely, it demands a radically different approach to teaching both technology and science in grades K–12.

A Short History of STS

Starting in 1970, a few U.S. universities—Cornell, Penn State, Stanford, and SUNY-Stony Brook—officially started programs that offered courses on subject matter which we today call STS. A consortium of British universities did the same. Gradually, across the country, other institutions joined in: small, elite four-year colleges (Wesleyan, Vassar), major research universities (MIT, RPI), scattered primary and secondary schools, and hundreds of institutions in between launched STS as an academic field.

By 1977, STS had gathered enough momentum to emerge as one of the five focal points of Norris Harms' Project Synthesis (Harms, 1977). An STS task force for Project Synthesis outlined the goals of STS projects.

- Prepare students to use science for improving their own lives and for coping in an increasingly technological world.
- Teach students to deal responsibly with technology/society issues.
- Identify a body of fundamental knowledge that students should master to deal intelligently with STS issues.
- Give students an accurate picture of the requirements of and opportunities in the many careers available in the STS field.

After the Project Synthesis report in 1981 (Harms & Yager, 1981) the National Science Teachers Association initiated its Search for Excellence in Science Education program. STS was included as one of the initial search areas in 1982–83 and again in 1986.

Nationally, since the initial efforts, STS has flourished as a focus for school science—as an area for identifying new goals, new curriculum modules, new instructional strategies, and new forms for evaluation. It has been used as such for science education reform in Iowa since the initiation of the NSTA-NSF Chautauqua Program in 1983. Today, as a result of that program, more than 1,700 teachers, especially in grades 4–9, have developed and introduced STS modules into their science classrooms. Other state initiatives are found in Arizona, Florida, New York, and Wisconsin. In 1984, the NSTA Board unanimously adopted a statement recommending that all students in American high schools receive formal exposure to STS courses varying from 15 percent in the lower grades to 25 percent in the higher ones. The movement was well accepted throughout the K–12 system and was soon to be institutionalized in a number of state departments of education. Thus by 1990 in the United States, STS was present in about 2,000 colleges in the form of STS courses, about 100 formal departments, divisions, or official interdisciplinary programs in most of the leading institutions, and thousands of high schools.

Comparing STS to Traditional Science Courses

STS programs have changed considerably since they were identified in NSTA's *Search for Excellence* (Penick & Meinhard-Pellens, 1984). Table 1 identifies 12 points of contrast between standard science programs (as revealed by the NSF status studies and Project Synthesis) and many experimental STS programs found throughout the United States.

Table 1

Standard	STS
Surveys major concepts found in standard textbooks	Identifies problems with local interest/impact
Uses labs and activities suggested in textbook and accompanying lab manual	Uses local resources (human and material) to resolve problems
Students passively assimilate information provided by teacher and textbook	Students actively seek information to use
Focuses on information proclaimed important for students to master	Focuses on personal impact, making use of students' own natural curiosity and concerns
Views science as the information in textbooks and teacher lectures	Views science content *not* as something that merely exists for student mastery because it is recorded in print
Students practice basic process skills—but don't apply them for evaluation purposes	De-emphasizes process skills which can be seen as the glamorized tools of practicing scientists
Pays little attention to career awareness, other than an occasional reference to a scientist (most of whom are dead) and his/her discoveries	Focuses on career awareness, emphasizing careers in science and technology that students might pursue, especially in areas other than scientific research, medicine, and engineering
Students concentrate on problems provided by teachers and text	Students become aware of their responsibilities as citizens as they attempt to resolve issues they have identified
Science occurs only in the science classroom as a part of the school's science curriculum	Students learn what role science can play in a given institution and in a specific community
Science is a body of information that students are expected to acquire	Science is an experience students are encouraged to enjoy
Science class focuses on what is previously known	Science class focuses on what the future may be like

Table 1 illustrates the conditions that exemplify STS classrooms as advanced by the NSTA position on STS. It also contrasts each of these conditions with the descriptions provided in the Project Synthesis final report of what typical conditions are like, especially pertaining to instruction. The Project Synthesis report included such contrasts in the areas of goals, curricula, assessment, and teacher education with respect to instruction. In general, all the Synthesis features called "Desired States" apply to classrooms where STS approaches are used.

The assessment of STS has often centered on the five domains of science teaching: concepts, process, connections and applications, creativity, and attitude. These domains were advanced by Yager and McCormack (1989) as a way of broadening science beyond a unidimensional structure that is often used in textbooks, curriculum guides, and state frameworks labelled "science." Unfortunately, this limited view that science is an organization of concepts comprising a given discipline (e.g., biology, chemistry, Earth science, and physics) makes science seem unrelated to any human enterprise and to the daily living of most students. A look at each of the five domains provides another means for contrasting traditional science classrooms to STS classrooms. These contrasts relate to the features of STS described earlier, to the nature of instruction, and to instructional outcomes. Table 2 illustrates the differences between students involved in an STS program with respect to these domains. The differences are based upon the reports of the nature of traditional classrooms, including instructional techniques used, and the assessment of student learning from Project Synthesis. The situation for the STS classrooms arises from analyses of the features of STS (from NSTA definition) as well as the emerging research reports that are summarized in subsequent chapters.

Table 2

Traditional	STS
Concepts	
Students learn concepts so as to do well on a test	Students find science concepts useful in their own lives
Concepts are seen as results of teaching	Concepts are seen as a needed commodity for dealing with problems
The focus of science class is on students learning concepts	Learning concepts occurs because of activity; it is important, but not a focus in and of itself
Students do not retain concepts for long	Students who learn by experience retain concepts and can often relate them to new situations
Process	
Science processes are skills scientists possess	Science processes are skills students themselves can use
Students see processes as something to practice as a course requirement	Students see processes as skills they need to refine and develop themselves more fully
Teacher emphasis on process skills is not understood by students, because these skills rarely contribute to actions outside class or even to the course grade	Students readily see the relationship of science processes to their own actions

Traditional	STS
Students see science processes as abstract, glorified, unattainable skills	Students see processes as a vital part of what they do in science classes

Connections and Applications

Traditional	STS
Students see no value or use for the material studied in science class	Students can relate their science studies to their daily lives
Students see no value in their science studies for resolving current societal problems	Students become involved in resolving social issues; they see science as a way of fulfilling their responsibilities as citizens
Students recite information they studied	Students seek out science information and apply it
Students cannot relate the science they study to any current technology	Students are engrossed in current technological developments and through them see the importance and relevance of scientific concepts

Creativity

Traditional	STS
Students' ability to question declines because the questions they raise that do not conform to the course outline are often ignored	Students ask more questions, and these questions are used to develop science activities and materials
Students rarely ask thought-provoking questions	Students frequently ask unique questions that excite their own interests, that of other students, and that of the teacher
Students are ineffective in identifying possible causes and effects in specific situations	Students are skilled in identifying possible causes and effects of certain observations and actions
Students have few original ideas	Students have a plenitude of ideas

Attitude

Traditional	STS
Student interest in science declines at all grade levels (as evidenced by the 3rd, 4th, and 5th science assessments of the National Assessment of Educational Progress)	Student interest increases from grade level to grade level and in specific courses (see chapter 22)
Student curiosity about science seems to decrease	Students become more curious about the material world
Students see the science teacher as a purveyor of information	Students see the science teacher as a facilitator/guide
Students see science as information to learn	Students see science as a way of dealing with problems

It is apparent from Table 2 that STS instruction aims to affect students in radically different ways in each of the five domains. Teachers in traditional science classrooms would probably find the desired features of STS as worthy, however, the tradtional view of teaching (i.e., transmitting to learners what is known) results in few improvements except for the seeming mastery of basic science concepts. And attitudes typically become more negative as students progress through the required K–12 sequence of science courses (Hueftle, Rakow, & Welch, 1983; NAEP, 1978; Weiss, 1987). The more positive conditions in the Connections and Applica-tions processes and Creativity domains are illustrated specifically in the section of this volume which focuses on specific research results. The results provide evidence that STS instruction is successful in producing results described in Table 2.

Moving Towards STS Approaches

It is the present science education system, with its own epistemology, its own selection of subjects, its scope and sequence of courses, if you will, that has brought us to the present situation. We have a population turned off from science. We have an anti-technology bias in society. We have manifest technological illiteracy as a result of whatever we are doing now. Three years of the same chemistry and two years of the same physics cannot do anything at all to address the needs of the mainstream citizens in learning "appropriate science and technology."

STS does not equal science education, but neither does physics or chemistry equal science education. Each of these is part of contemporary science education. STS is the matrix of every citizen's science education within which various specializations may be added. STS means focusing on problems, on questions, on unknowns. It means searching for answers and explanations. The searching means that students encounter many new questions and problems. Science is a never-ending process. In fact, the best STS modules (and teacher experiences with STS) result in teacher comments like: "I never imagined that we would investigate so many questions . . ."; "I had no idea that STS would result in so much student initiative, enthusiasm, action . . ."; "The students did the work. They identified problems, proposed actions—they wouldn't let it stop!"

All of these experiences with STS by teachers and students are hastening its spread. Unfortunately, such experiences are not universal, and word-of-mouth testimony is inadequate to sustain a reform effort. Moving beyond personal experience and testimony is possible. Still, the emerging results stimulate greater interest and agreement that STS exemplifies needed reform for most learners.

All reasonable projections agree on the universal penetration of STS as a K–12 and college-level approach to course structure and teaching approach throughout formal academia. There is little data on which to base a guess at the speed STS will penetrate all education. However, it is not unreasonable to project the goal that by the year 2000, more than one-half of all students in the K–Ph.D. pipeline will encounter STS in formal courses at some point in their education.

That would be a wonderful goal to attain, Sut it implies a challenging responsibility for all of us in academia, K–12 teachers, agency personnel, and others, to guide this innovation-in-education carefully. Federal and state agencies must be fully aware that the resources allocated to the burgeoning STS field are minuscule compared to those allocated to the traditional disciplines. STS is a great opportunity to reorient the American citizenry towards a new, healthy, balanced perspective on science.

STS has become more and more widely used during the ten years that have passed since Project Synthesis. STS activities provide excitement. Some STS developments have occurred in every state; many are used to illustrate what reform should be like. Many STS programs are affecting entire school curriculua not just the nature of science courses and teaching. Perhaps it is time for a second Synthesis study to note with certainty the extent that STS programs have addressed the science education issues so clearly identified in 1978.

References

Harms, N. C. (1977). *Project Synthesis: An interpretative consolidation of research identifying needs in natural science education.* (A proposal prepared for the National Science Foundation.) Boulder, CO: University of Colorado.

Harms, N. C., & Yager, R. E. (Eds.). (1981). *What research says to the science teacher, Vol. 3.* Washington, DC: National Science Teachers Association.

Hueftle, S. J., Rakow, S. S., & Welch, W. W. (1983). *Images of science: A summary of results from the 1981–1982 National Assessmemt in Science.* Minneapolis, MN: The Minnesota Research and Evaluation Center at the University of Minnesota.

National Assessment of Educational Progress. (1978). *The Third Assessment of Science, 1976–1977.* Denver, CO: Author.

Penick, J. E., & Meinhard-Pellens, R. (Eds.). (1984). *Focus on excellence: Science/technology/society* (Vol. 1, No. 5). Washington, DC: National Science Teachers Association.

Weiss, I. (1987). *Report of the 1985–1986 National Survey of Science and Mathematics Education.* Research Triangle Park, NC: Center for Educational Research and Evaluation, Research Triangle Institute.

Yager, R. E., & McCormack, A. J. (1989). Assessing teaching/learning successes in multiple domains of science and science education. *Science Education, 73*(1), 45–58.

Part II
STS in the Classroom

Almost every report discussing failures of schools includes a listing of what students don't know and what misconceptions they hold. Many of these misconceptions stand in the way of students' decision-making abilities, necessary for a democracy to work. The decisions to be made in the next century call for an informed citizenry. STS is seen by many as a necessity if we want to amply prepare the next generation to make the decisions that will affect the well-being of our planet. Alan Voelker stated the problem well in his Volume 4 report:

> . . . if we want a science program that is truly responsive and responsible to the citizen in a scientifically and technologically oriented society, we must elevate current and future citizen concerns. We cannot assume that curricula which emphasize traditional cognitive knowledge and an understanding of the scientific process will lead to an understanding of the science-related issues confronting society. Neither can we assume that such traditional curricula will assist our student-citizens in applying their scientific knowledge and processes to these issues. Some sacred cows of the science curriculum must be eliminated. But the short-term trauma this sacrifice may elicit will be replaced by long-term gains for all citizens. (Voelker, 1981)

Unfortunately, studies concerning what teachers know and believe are as alarming as the situation with their students. The exciting work of Glen Aikenhead and his colleagues in Canada provides insight concerning the extent of these problems and some approaches to resolving them.

Other chapters of this Part II of our monograph deal with science textbooks. We know that a huge majority of science teachers depend almost wholly on the textbook for the material and the strategies used for teaching and testing. We know that these textbooks do not build from STS questions and experiences, nor do they suggest STS/constructivist teaching strategies. Also addressed in Part II is what we know about the behaviors of STS teachers and what the features are of exemplary science teachers.

References

Voelker, A. M. (1981). The development of an attentive public for science: Implications for science teaching. In R. E. Yager (Ed.), *What research says to the science teacher, Vol. 4* (pp. 65–79). Washington, DC: National Science Teachers Association.

3

STS Issues: A Perspective

Jon E. Pedersen
University of Arkansas

A common argument against teaching STS issues is that it interferes with the teaching of science content. As one teacher responded in a survey by Bybee and Bonnstetter (1985), "Don't water down science courses. Present social science problems should be secondary to science content. Students must know science content before one can solve the problems of society." This philosophy, to make science rigorous because "this might be the last science course students will take," is contrary to data that indicates students do not pursue science because their last course was rugged (Leyden, 1984). Leyden asserted that eight years after teaching high school freshman about science, twice as many will have been in jail as have bachelor's degrees in biology, chemistry, physics, Earth science, or science education.

Across the nation, science teachers are agreeing that STS issues are important to study. Bybee and Bonnstetter (1985) indicate that 85.3 percent of high school teachers and 90.1 percent of college teachers feel that STS issues are important to study. They also state that one-half of the educators polled deemed it very important to study STS issues in middle or junior high school. Over 96 percent considered the study of STS issues at least fairly important at each level above the elementary school level and 77.3 percent considered it at least fairly important in elementary school. These statistics are surprising considering that in the same study Bybee and Bonnstetter state that science teachers express some hesitation to take on the STS themes that require new materials and sometimes new approaches to teaching. Even though most teachers express a variety of goals, in practice most consider only the academic preparation goals (Harms & Yager, 1981; Stake & Easley, 1978; Yager & Stodghill, 1979). This lends credence to the notion that science educators are consistently teaching to the top one percent of their classes. The other 99 percent, those neglected by the science education community, represent students who are poorly equipped to deal with the realities of our technologically complex world (Roy, 1985).

The STS Philosophy

Ideas for outlining criteria for implementing and designing STS modules are explained by Yager (1988). There are seven steps or criteria that a curriculum must meet to fit the STS philosophy. The curriculum should:

1. Present the relations of technological or scientific developments to socially relevant issues clearly, early, and in compelling ways to capture attention

2. Consider the mutual influences of technology, science, and society on each other
3. Develop learners' understanding of themselves as interdependent members of society and society as a responsible agent within the ecosystem
4. Include a balance of differing viewpoints about the issues and options without necessarily striving to hide the author's perspective
5. Help learners to venture beyond the specific subject matter to broader considerations of science, technology, and society such as those of personal and societal values/ethics
6. Engage learners in developing problem-solving and decision-making skills
7. Encourage learners to become involved in a societal or personal course of action after weighing the tradeoffs among values and effects drawn from various scenarios or alternative options

A key component of the STS module, according to Yager (1988), is that the material uses the STS linkage to foster learners' confidence in handling and understanding at least one (limited) "science" area, and/or handling and using some quantification as a basis for judgment in the STS area.

Implementing STS Themes

Hickman, Patrick, and Bybee (1987) delivered a similar scenario for their guidelines on curriculum reform for STS themes. Three primary categories (acquisition of knowledge, use of cognitive process skills, and development of values and attitudes) highlight the curriculum framework for reform which is central to implementing STS materials and strategies.

> "Each of these three categories is a guide to formulation or selection of educational goals, means of instruction, content, and learning activities." (Hickman, Patrick, & Bybee, 1987)

Knowledge acquisition centers around the development of the three fundamental concepts—science, technology, and society—and the interrelationships among these such as the symbiotic connection of science and technology that occurs in a social context. Other aspects emphasized include: knowledge of major concepts in science and technology that are associated with significant social changes and scientific issues; major concepts and topics in history and the social sciences that are associated with significant social changes and scientific issues rooted in science/technology; STS issues in history and contemporary society that illuminate and enhance comprehension of STS interactions; and understanding the uses, limits, abuses, and various social consequences of scientific and technological endeavors.

Several areas are emphasized in using cognitive process skills. First, there is an emphasis in developing the cognitive process skills involved in scientific/technological inquiry, including information processing and problem solving, as a way of producing and applying knowledge about nature and society. Cognitive process skills involved in civic decision-making, which require a rational means of assessing, judging, and choosing options and resolving issues about the uses of science and technology in society, are also stressed. Direct, didactic teaching to introduce skills and an emphasis on practicing skills are typical components of knowledge acquisition; however, there is growing evidence that real learning rarely results from this approach. Finally, learning activities for cognitive process skills in science/technology/society should be developed systematically and extensively in all social studies and science courses, in a manner consistent with the intellectual development and prior learning experiences of students.

Hickman, Patrick, and Bybee (1987) also emphasized guidelines for values and attitudes in STS. Primarily, the focus is to foster an appreciation of science and technology as worthwhile human endeavors. But there is also a sense of developing an understanding and intelligent commitment to values, attitudes, and assumptions of a democratic or free society, which are compatible with the premises and precepts undergirding scientific inquiry. To tackle this goal, a curriculum should: emphasize the critical importance of ethical questions about the uses of science and technology in society; develop a commitment to rationally evaluate, with regard to democratic values, issues about applications of science and technology in society; and finally, teach values and attitudes of science and democracy in combination with the knowledge and cognitive process skills that are central to studies of STS.

Attitudes, Anxiety, Problem-Solving, and Achievement in Science

A major study was initiated in the fall of 1989 to examine the effects of STS issues on four areas (Pedersen, 1990). Attitudes towards science, anxiety towards science, problem-solving perceptions, and achievement (objective testing of content) were compared for students participating in STS study and those in traditional study settings. The study used the past decade of research on the theoretical and philosophical constructs of STS issues to develop the model for instruction (Pedersen, 1991). For three of the four variables (attitude, anxiety, and problem-solving perceptions) significant differences were found between the experimental and control groups.

The significant difference in attitudes between the two groups suggested that the STS learning structure provided students with the necessary components to change their attitudes towards science (Pedersen, 1990). Peer tutoring, active participation, and social interaction are all keys to attitudinal change and are all part of the learning environment. Yager's conclusion (1990) that students involved in the study of STS issues had more positive attitudes towards science further supports these results. Yager observed that students continually offered ideas, student interest increased from grade level to grade level, students saw their teacher as a facilitator, and students saw science as a way of dealing with problems.

There are indications that anxiety towards science may be as important a factor in learning science as attitudes towards science. Yet there is a dearth of information on how to reduce the level of anxiety towards science (Okebukola, 1986). Pedersen showed that students involved in the study of STS issues reduced their anxiety levels. He attributed this to several factors.

1. Students had the opportunity to share information and, more importantly, discuss the information that the group was studying.
2. Students worked together in cooperative groups, sharing information and tasks to accomplish a goal.
3. Students relied on each other for information and did not have to be preoccupied with the fear of knowing all.
4. Students were provided tasks, allowing them to research, discuss, and report in cooperative groups in an organized manner (Pedersen, 1990, p. 84).

Pedersen (1990) also examined the problem-solving perceptions of the students involved in the study of STS issues. Kahl and Harms (1981) suggested that science education should foster attitudes in individuals such that they would use science in making everyday decisions and solving problems. It is the application of science to problems of personal and societal relevance that exemplifies the goals of STS education.

Heppner et al. (1982) suggested that students' perceptions of how they solve problems may be important in determining their success at solving problems. And Lochhead (1983) found that if students believed they were incapable of solving problems, it was because they thought that there was nothing they could do to solve the problems.

But research indicates that there are ways of improving students' perceptions of their problem-solving abilities; for example, involving students in discussions and role play about STS issues, as well as involving students in cooperative activities to solve problems pertaining to STS issues (Pedersen, 1990). These results do not indicate that the students are better problem-solvers, but that they have better perceptions of their ability to solve problems. However, McClure, Chinsky, and Larcen (1978) found evidence that involvement in discussions and role-playing did increase students' problem-solving skills, complementing Pedersen's study. Piaget (1964) also stated that peer interaction is considered a necessary form of behavior to develop critical thinking and objectivity in students.

One of the key components to being a successful problem-solver is the ability to recognize a problem. It is only when students realize that they can be successful problem-solvers that they are able to recognize that there is a problem to solve (Bloom & Broder, 1950). By using hands-on-experiences to solve problems, students change their perceptions about their abilities to solve problems (Pedersen, 1990).

Of the four variables examined by Pedersen (1990), only achievement showed no significant difference between STS and traditional instruction. Studying STS issues prepared students equally well as traditional instruction to take a teacher-made objective exam. Pedersen (1990) indicated that the only reason achievement testing was included in the study was because this is the only outcome with which many science teachers are concerned. This raises a fundamental question: What is the value of the information gained from the tests given by teachers? Current trends suggest that studying less content in science is important so that what is studied can be made meaningful (AAAS, 1989b). How does a teacher objectively "measure" how meaningful content is? If science is taught by incorporating social and technological issues within the fabric of the curriculum, will traditional means of evaluation be appropriate? To overcome the inadequacies of current classroom teaching, a new structure of teaching and evaluation must develop. For if teachers continue to evaluate in traditional ways, the value of STS will be lost in the dogmatism of grading.

National Assessment of Educational Progress data conclude that "students are losing interest in science at an alarming rate" (Mullis & Jenkins, 1988). Current NAEP data also indicate that students are poorly equipped for informed citizenship and productive performance in the workplace, let alone postsecondary studies in science. Project 2061 (AAAS, 1989a), as well as Project Synthesis (Kahl & Harms, 1981), suggested that a greater emphasis must be placed on student learning which is relevant to the student's personal life and his or her environment.

In light of the current trends in science education, the results of Pedersen's (1990) study are encouraging. By placing students in a situation in which they must share information cooperatively, present their perspective of the STS issue being studied, and come to a group consensus on the issue, anxiety towards science is reduced, a more positive attitude towards science is taken, and the perceptions of the students' own problem-solving abilities are enhanced. The implications of this seem direct. Students find that studying societal issues in a structured manner is less stressful, more interesting and worthwhile, and they feel more confident to solve problems.

References

American Association for the Advancement of Science. (1989a). *Science for all Americans: Summary—Project 2061*. Washington, DC: Author.

American Association for the Advancement of Science. (1989b). *Science for all Americans: A Project 2061 report on literacy goals in science, mathematics, and technology.* Washington, DC: Author.

Bloom, B. S., & Broder, L. J. (1950). *Problem solving processes of college students: An exploratory investigation.* Chicago, IL: The University of Chicago Press.

Bybee, R. W., & Bonnstetter, R. J. (1985). STS: What do the teachers think? In R. W. Bybee (Ed.), *NSTA yearbook: Science/technology/society* (pp. 117–127). Washington, DC: National Science Teachers Association.

Harms, N. C., & Yager, R. E. (Eds.). (1981). *What research says to the science teacher Vol. 3.* Washington, DC: National Science Teachers Association.

Heppner, P. P., Hibel, J. H., Neal, G. W., Weinstein, C. L., & Rabinowitz, F. E. (1982). Personal problem solving: A descriptive study of individual differences. *Journal of Counseling Psychology, 39,* 580–590.

Hickman, F. M., Patrick, J. J., & Bybee, R. W. (1987). *Science/technology/society: A framework for curriculum reform in secondary school science and social studies.* (p. 8). Boulder, CO: Social Science Education Consortium, Inc.

Kahl, S. & Harms. N. (1981). Project synthesis: Purpose, organization and procedures. In N. Harms & R. Yager (Eds.), *What research says to the science teacher, Vol. 3,* (pp. 5–11). Washington, DC: National Science Teachers Association.

Leyden, M. B. (1984). You graduate more criminals than scientists. *The Science Teacher, 51*(3), 27–30.

Lochhead, J. (1983). Thinking about learning: Improving intelligence through pair problem solving. *The Journal of Learning Skills, 2*(1), 3–15.

McClure, L. F., Chinsky, J. M., & Larcen, S. W. (1978). Enhancing social problem-solving performance in an elementary school setting. *Journal of Educational Psychology, 70(4),* 501–513.

Mullis, I. V. S., & Jenkins, L. B. (Eds.). (1988). *The science report card: Elements of risk and recovery.* (p. 10). Princeton, NJ: NAEP Educational Testing Service.

Okebukola, P. A. O. (1986). Reducing anxiety in science classes: An experiment involving some models of class interaction. *Educational Research, 28*(2), 146–149.

Pedersen, J. E. (1990). *The effects of science, technology and societal issues, implemented as a cooperative controversy, on attitudes toward science, anxiety toward science, problem solving perceptions and achievements in secondary science.* Unpublished doctoral dissertation, University of Nebraska, Lincoln.

Pedersen, J. E. (1991). Take issue with science. *Science Scope, 15*(8), 34–37.

Piaget, J. (1964). Three lectures. In R. E. Ripple & V. N. Rockcastle (Eds.), *Piaget rediscovered* (pp. 7–39). Ithaca, NY: Cornell University Press.

Roy, R. (1985). The science/technology/society connection. *Curriculum Review, 24*(3), 13–16.

Stake, R. E., & Easley, J. (1978). *Case studies in science education* (Vols. 1 and 2). Urbana, IL: Center for Instructional Research and Curriculum Evaluation, University of Illinois at Urbana-Champaign.

Yager, R. E. (1990). Instructional outcomes change with STS. *Iowa Science Teachers Journal, 27*(1), 2–20.

Yager, R. E. (1988). STS: The place to begin. *Chautauqua Notes, 3*(8), 1–2.

Yager, R. E., & Stodghill, R. (1979). School science in an age of science. *Educational Leadership, 36*(6), 439–445.

Evaluation of Views of High School Graduates on STS Topics

Glen S. Aikenhead and Alan G. Ryan
University of Saskatchewan

A new evaluation instrument, *Views on Science-Technology-Society (VOSTS)* (Aikenhead, Ryan, & Fleming, 1989) is actually a pool of 114 multiple-choice items which were developed over the past five years through extensive research with students in grades 11 and 12. VOSTS allows teachers to select items relevant to their STS lessons and use them in various ways to monitor students' reasoned beliefs on that STS content. VOSTS items may also be used to stimulate and structure student discussions on STS topics.

The Research

Over the past 25 years, several standardized instruments have been developed to assess student understanding of STS topics. However, these instruments have, by and large, been used with the erroneous assumption that students perceive and interpret the test statements in the same way as science educators do (Aikenhead, Fleming, & Ryan, 1987). For instance, a test item may state, "Science gives us objective knowledge." To the science educator, this item addresses the idea of value-free knowledge. But we have found that a large number of students will believe that it means "People have certain objectives in mind when they make scientific discoveries." When a student responds to such a test item, the science educator has no way of realizing that the student's response is based on an alternative interpretation. This has been a traditional problem for science education evaluators (Gardner, 1987). A significant resolution to the problem uses multiple-choice STS items that were empirically derived from students' own writing (Aikenhead, 1988).

How were we able to use students' ideas to produce a multiple-choice instrument? An overview of this research is provided here. In Phase 1 of a three-phase research project, 17-year-olds wrote paragraph responses to statements which described an STS topic, for example:

"Few scientists and technologists would choose to work on military research and development." (VOSTS item 20321)

The students' paragraph responses were analyzed to determine their understanding of an STS topic. The topic of the statement cited above is the influence of society on science/technology through the allocation of human resources. The analysis of the responses yielded a list of commonly held positions. This list of typical student positions on the topic was a crude multiple-choice. Here are some responses for item 20321:

- I agree, because most scientists would rather work in other fields which are a benefit to human life and the environment.
- I disagree, because many scientists work for the military. That's where the money is.
- I can't tell, because some scientists find military projects interesting. But others might not want to work on projects related to war.

Phase 2 investigated how well the students' responses matched what they really believed (as determined by interviews). It was discovered that students conveyed their beliefs more accurately, not by composing a paragraph response, but by selecting a response from a crude multiple-choice list derived from the paragraph analyses of Phase 1 (Aikenhead, 1988). The list of responses allowed students to consider a wider selection of viewpoints, thereby making it easier for them to express their particular view on the topic.

Finally, in Phase 3, the crude multiple-choice items were polished to create an inventory of STS items, relying heavily on several types of empirical feedback from students (Aikenhead, Ryan, & Desautels, 1989). The resultant item pool is called *Views on Science-Technology-Society (VOSTS)*. A national survey of Canadian twelfth-grade students provides baseline data on the typical responses one can expect from students *before* they have received systematic instruction on the STS topics. These results are reported following a brief description of the content of VOSTS.

The Domain of STS Content

The STS topics covered by the VOSTS inventory correspond to content appropriate for high school students. The STS topics included are limited to those emphasizing student thinking rather than student attitude. Attention is not given to feelings about global or regional issues. Instead, VOSTS focuses on the reasons students give to justify a viewpoint. Consequently VOSTS consists mainly of *informed* viewpoints; that is, cognitive beliefs.

VOSTS content is based on recent literature concerning the social and technological aspects of science; for example, journals such as *Science, Technology & Human Values*, or *Bulletin of Science, Technology & Society*, and articles and books such as those by Aikenhead (1985), Barnes and Edge (1982), Bybee (1985), Fleming (1989), Gauld (1982), Snow (1987), and Ziman (1980, 1984). The topics in VOSTS are shown in Table 1. In the future, the number of topics can expand. In fact, at the present time, section three has been left blank in order to leave room for future development emphasizing the area of technological literacy. Currently, the VOSTS item pool emphasizes STS content associated with *scientific* literacy.

Table 1

VOSTS Conceptual Scheme

Definitions
I. ***Science and Technology***
1. Defining science (e.g., instrumentalism, curiosity satisfaction, social enterprise)
2. Defining technology (e.g., social and human purposes, hardware, socio-economic and cultural components)
3. Defining research and development (R&D)
4. Interdependence of science and technology (e.g., rejection that technology is simply applied science)

External Sociology of Science

II. *Influence of Society on Science/Technology*

1. Government (e.g., control over funding, policy, and science activities; influence of politics)
2. Industry (e.g., corporate control dictated by profits)
3. Military (e.g., use of scientific human resources)
4. Ethics (e.g., influence on research program)
5. Education institutions (e.g., mandatory science education)
6. Special interest groups (e.g., health societies, non-government, and non-industrial groups)
7. Public influence on scientists (e.g., upbringing, social interactions)

III. *(future category)*

IV. *Influence of Science/Technology on Society*

1. Social responsibility of scientists/technologists (e.g., communicating with public, concern, and accountability for risks and pollution, "whistle blowing")
2. Contribution to social decisions (e.g., technocratic vs. democratic decision-making, moral and legal decisions, expert testimony, lobbying for funds)
3. Creation of social problems (e.g., trade-offs between positive and negative consequences, competition for funds)
4. Resolution of social and practical problems (e.g., technological fix, everyday type of problems)
5. Contribution to economic well-being (e.g., wealth and jobs)
6. Contribution to military power
7. Contribution to social thinking (e.g., lexicon, metaphors)

V. *Influence of School Science on Society*

1. Bridging C. P. Snow's two cultures
2. Social empowerment (e.g., consumer decisions)
3. Social characterization of science

Internal Sociology of Science

VI. *Characteristics of Scientists*

1. Personal motivation of scientists
2. Standards/values that guide scientists at work and home (e.g., open-mindedness, logicality, honesty, objectivity, skepticism, suspension of belief; as well as the opposite values: closed-mindedness, subjectivity, etc.)
3. Ideologies of scientists (e.g., religious views)
4. Abilities needed to do science (e.g., commitment, patience)
5. Gender effect on the process and product of science
6. Underrepresentation of females

VII. *Social Construction of Scientific Knowledge*

1. Collectivization of science (e.g., loyalties to research team and employer)
2. Scientific decisions (e.g., disagreements among scientists, consensus-making)
3. Professional communication among scientists (e.g., peer review, journals, press conferences)
4. Professional interaction in the face of competition (e.g., politics, secrecy, plagiarism)
5. Social interactions
6. Individual's influence on scientific knowledge
7. National influence on scientific knowledge and technique
8. Private vs. public science

VIII. *Social Construction of Technology*
1. Technological decisions
2. Autonomous technology (e.g., technological imperative)

Epistemology
IX. *Nature of Scientific Knowledge*
1. Nature of observations (e.g., theory-ladenness, perception-bound)
2. Nature of scientific models
3. Nature of classification schemes
4. Tentativeness of scientific knowledge
5. Hypotheses, theories, and laws (e.g., definition, role of assumptions, criteria for belief)
6. Scientific approach to investigations (e.g., nonlinearity, rejection of a stepwise procedure, "the scientific method" as a writing style)
7. Precision and uncertainty in scientific/technological knowledge (e.g., probabilistic reasoning)
8. Logical reasoning (e.g., cause/effect problems, epistemology, and etiology)
9. Fundamental assumptions for all science (e.g., uniformitarianism)
10. Epistemological status of scientific knowledge (e.g., ontology as an assumption, questioning logical positivism)
11. Paradigms vs. coherence of concepts across disciplines

The VOSTS Item Pool

Teaching science through STS means that STS content is taught *in conjunction with* the normal science discipline complement of facts, principles, concepts and problem-solving skills. Thus, VOSTS by itself does not assess all components of an STS course, but does assess some of the STS course objectives or goals. VOSTS items allow students to express their reasons for holding particular viewpoints on STS topics. These reasoned views include misconceptions, naive or idealistic conceptions, as well as an authentic conception of an STS topic.

Unlike the typical multiple-choice question, VOSTS items have no absolutely "right" answers among the choices. One must examine the choices ahead of time and decide which choice students should pick if they have attained the objectives. In some cases, there may be more than one appropriate choice. Teachers must also identify which choices are incorrect, naive, or inappropriate. Students selecting these options are indicating that they have not attained the teacher's objectives for the course. Strictly speaking, while there are no "right" answers to VOSTS items, the literature on STS mentioned earlier does lead us to the "more accurate" choices for most VOSTS items.

Current VOSTS items were developed with responses from 16- and 17-year-olds. Teachers can modify the language and complexity of VOSTS items to meet the level of their own students. By editing the choices, one can be confident of starting with a set of choices that students themselves find sensible.

Some Survey Results

A Canadian national survey sampled the views of students in grades 11 and 12 (Aikenhead & Ryan, 1989). Included in the survey were about 1,750 English-speaking students from across Canada, and about 580 French-speaking students from the province of Quebec. The sample represented a cross section of student abilities and rural/urban settings. For the purposes of this paper, only the responses from the English-speaking students will be analyzed.

Almost every VOSTS item received a diversity of responses. There are seldom typical answers on which students agree. In the absence of STS instruction, students tend to be influenced by what they glean from the media (Aikenhead, 1988). Thus, the media itself can be a useful starting point when one approaches an STS topic in class.

   Responses to three VOSTS items are analyzed in detail here to show how one can analyze the answers of one's own students. Following these three examples, the results of a number of other VOSTS topics are described.

Science and Technology: Defining Science

Definitions of science in the literature vary widely depending on an author's perspective and philosophy. High school students, too, express a wide variety of definitions, as shown in Table 2. Table 2 presents item 10111 along with the frequency of student responses obtained in our Canadian survey. Percent responses are indicated for the English-speaking students.

Table 2

VOSTS Item 10111 **Defining science is difficult because science is complex and does many things. But *mainly* science is:**		
% Responding		**Your position, basically:**
7	A.	a study of fields such as biology, chemistry, and physics
28	B.	a body of knowledge, such as principles, laws, and theories, which explain the world around us (matter, energy, and life)
24	C.	exploring the unknown and discovering new things about our world and universe and how they work
3	D.	carrying out experiments to solve problems of interest about the world around us
2	E.	inventing or designing things (for example: artificial hearts, computers, space vehicles)
10	F.	finding and using knowledge to make this world a better place to live in (for example: curing diseases, solving pollution, and improving agriculture)
2	G.	an organization of people (called scientists) who have ideas and techniques for discovering new knowledge
19	H.	No one can define science.
1	I.	I don't understand.
0	J.	I don't know enough about this subject to make a choice.
4	K.	None of these choices fits my basic viewpoint.

   Choices A and B represent definitions which conceptualize science as a body of knowledge. This view of science received the largest student response; 7 percent for the more simplistic choice A, and 28 percent for choice B. The idea that science is a body of knowledge is consistent with teaching practices that emphasize: (1) getting the right answer, or (2) preparing students for external exams (e.g., college boards) or for post-secondary science courses. The definition of science as a body of knowledge, however, is at odds with most of the professional literature dealing with science education, especially STS science.

   Choices C and D define science more as a *process* than a body of knowledge. The proportion of students expressing this perspective on science was relatively high (27 percent). Position D (receiving a 3 percent response) describes science as systematic puzzle-solving, a description Kuhn (1970) claims is the essence of "normal" science. Position C paints a broader picture of science, a picture which 24 percent of the students chose as the best definition of science. (In our research, we discovered through interviewing students that most believed there was a clear difference between choices C and D.) The professional literature on science education goals has often described science as an active process, as captured by choices C and D. If this definition were the accepted goal of Canadian science teachers, they would have grounds for feeling disappointed that only a quarter of Canadian students defined science in those terms.

According to research by Fleming (1987), students tend to confuse science with technology. Choice E, a simplistic notion of technology, offers students the chance to reveal such a confusion. Only a negligible number of students confused science with technology in the context of item 10111. The confusion, however, is more widespread in some responses to other VOSTS items.

Some students (10 percent in this case) subscribe to a vision of science as something which "makes the world a better place to live in," choice F. This view is known as an "instrumentalist" view (i.e., science is an instrument of society). This instrumentalist view shows up more strongly in other VOSTS items.

Choice G takes this concept one step further, viewing science as a social institution. In STS science, the social dynamics within science are usually studied to better understand how scientific knowledge itself is influenced by technology and society. STS science instruction, therefore, adopts a definition of science broader in scope than any of the definitions listed above. Science is what scientists do, and the doing of science is as much a social process as it is an intellectual process. John Ziman's book, *An Introduction to Science Studies: The Philosophical and Social Aspects of Science and Technology* (1984), is one of the most authoritative sources for STS science. In it he explores the following statement:

> Academic science is a social institution devoted to the construction of a rational consensus of opinion over the widest possible field. (Ziman, 1984)

A "system of science" was defined by Snow (1987) in terms of an elaborate conceptual map, initially organized into three dimensions: cognitive, personal, and sociological. The map gives a clear view of science as a social institution. Thus, one would expect that choice G (Table 2) is the best definition of science for an STS science course. The choice was selected by only 2 percent of the students.

It is interesting to note that 19 percent of the students thought that science is undefinable, choice H. Choices I, J, and K are for students who find that none of the positions matches their own, for the reasons stated. All VOSTS items end with these three choices.

The data from this item strongly suggest that Canadian students have not gained an authentic view of science, but instead are holding on to various definitions of science they learned in school science courses.

Influence of School Science on Society: Science Classes Versus the Media

Both the media and science classes convey images of science to students. The caricature of the bespectacled, bald-headed old man in a white lab coat is a media image, for instance, that is deeply etched into students' minds and which influences their career decisions, especially those of young females (Aikenhead, 1988). Unless science classes deal systematically with STS topics, students get their STS view predominantly from the media. But how do students compare the media with their science classes in terms of which one gives them a more accurate view of science as it really is? Table 3 shows the frequency of English responses to VOSTS item 50313.

Table 3

VOSTS Item 50313
The mass media in general (TV, newspapers, magazines, movies, etc.) give a *more* accurate picture of what science really is in Canada, compared to the picture offered by science classes.

% Responses		Your position, basically:
		The mass media give a more accurate picture:
5	A.	because the media show all sides of science. In science classes, you may not get the whole picture because of the teacher's bias
9	B.	because the media are more up-to-date in their coverage
3	C.	because the media use pictures. Pictures usually describe events more clearly than words do.
12	D.	because the media concentrate more on new developments which show how science is put to use in the real world. Science classes *only* give you notes, problems, laws, and theories that do not apply to everyday life.
41	E.	*Both* the media and science classes give accurate pictures of science. The media concentrate more on new developments which show how science is put to use in the real world. Science classes concentrate more on the underlying principles that help explain what the media are reporting on.
6	F.	*Neither* the media nor science classes give accurate pictures of science. The media exaggerate, distort, and oversimplify. Science classes only give you notes, problems, and details that do not apply to everyday life.
		Science classes give a *more* accurate picture because classes give the facts, the explanations, and the chances to do it yourself through studying science step by step (i.e., you learn how science really happens). The media:
7	G.	only give specific or simple examples, though they may be interesting to look at. These examples produce a narrow view of science.
13	H.	basically give people what they want to see: controversy, opinions, exaggerations, and simple explanations.
0	I.	I don't understand
2	J.	I don't know enough about this subject to make a choice.
3	K.	None of these choices fits my basic viewpoint.

Overall, 29 percent of the students thought that the media gave a more accurate picture of science (choices A–D), while 20 percent thought that science classes did (choices G and H). However, the largest group of students (41 percent) believed that each offered a complementary image of science.

The reasons which support the view that science classes offer a *less* accurate picture of science include: teacher bias (choice A), out-of-date material (B), and irrelevant content (D). A small number of students selected choice F which paints a negative image of both science classes and the media.

The reasons for students believing that science classes offer the *most* accurate image of science include: science classes help explain the media coverage (E), and science classes involve you in science while the media reports are narrowly focused (G) or are exaggerated (H).

Epistemology: Nature of Observations

A number of philosophers of science (e.g., Kuhn, 1970) consider scientific observations to be theory-laden because a theory influences: (1) the perceptions of a scientist, (2) the significance of a potential observation, and (3) the design of an experiment. VOSTS item 90111 addresses this topic. Table 4 presents item 90111 along with the students' response frequencies for each choice.

Table 4

VOSTS Item 90111
Scientific observations made by competent scientists will usually be different if the scientists believe different theories.

% Responses		Your position, basically:
21	A.	Yes, because scientists will *experiment* in different ways and will notice different things.
16	B.	Yes, because scientists will *think* differently and this will *alter their observations*.
28	C.	Scientific observations will *not differ* very much even though scientists believe different theories. If the scientists are indeed *competent* their observations will be similar.
10	D.	No, because observations are as exact as possible. This is how science has been able to advance.
11	E.	No, observations are exactly what we see and nothing more; they are the facts.
4	F.	I don't understand.
6	G.	I don't know enough about this subject to make a choice.
4	H.	None of these choices fits my basic viewpoint.

A relatively large proportion (37 percent) of students believed that observations are theory-laden (choices A and B). Choice A mentions the effect of a theory on experimental design and on the significance of an observation. Choice B more generally addresses the idea that observations depend on one's thinking, which is influenced by one's theory. Choosing either A or B would correspond to achieving an objective of teaching science through STS.

A second group of students (choice C, 28 percent) entertained the possibility that a theory might affect an observation. The competency of scientists, however, would almost ensure that identical observations are made by scientists who believe different theories.

Students who rejected theory-laden observations supported their position by: (1) pointing to the historical evidence of science's success with exactness (choice D, 10 percent), or (2) equating observations with absolute facts (choice E, 11 percent). Another 10 percent of the students did not understand or did not know enough about observations and theories to make a choice (choices F and G).

An Overview of the National Survey Findings

The detailed analysis of the three items in this chapter illustrates the kind of information that can be obtained from VOSTS items. Space does not permit a full analysis of the other VOSTS items, but a few other observations are worth mentioning.

The results of our research reinforce the common knowledge that little or no organized, consistent instruction teaches Canadian students a coherent, authentic view of the nature of science. Preliminary studies in the United States indicate that Canadian and American students are very similar in their responses to VOSTS items (Brunkhorst, 1987).

Our Canadian study has shown that students had difficulty adequately describing science and technology. They tended to give an outdated idea about the relationship between science and technology—technology is applied science. Although many students recognized that scientists themselves could not readily apply their theoretical knowledge to practical problem-solving situations, students nevertheless tended to expect that technologists should be able somehow to apply scientific knowledge to their professional problem-solving situations. Students were also less than secure in their understanding of an authentic view of scientific observation, models, hypotheses, theories, laws, methods, assumptions, tentativeness, fundamental tenets of science, and how research programs unfold.

One fear arising from this observation is that many students would have difficulty understanding or rationally discussing news stories that touch on topics related to the nature of science. Since many science-related social issues do implicitly revolve around such topics, most high school graduates will likely appear to be less than scientifically literate when they deal with science-related social issues.

On the other hand, the evidence suggests that students do have a realistic grasp of R&D, classification schemes, probability, correlations versus cause/effects, and the problem of coherence across disciplines. Relatively large proportions of students seemed to grasp the idea that science and technology exert an influence on other areas of society, particularly when it comes to making science-related social decisions.

High school students tend to be extremely interested in, and quite well informed about, issues which both affect them directly and strike a chord with their idealistic streak. Consequently, items that address environmental issues elicited socially responsible and informed responses.

The social scene is a familiar context for many students. When asked to make inferences about the social nature of science and scientists, many students seemed to be relatively competent. The influence of ideologies on science, for instance, was handled realistically by many students. Stereotypical images of scientists were seldom evident in the students' responses. This is further reflected in students' strongly held position that men and women make equally competent scientists and in students' consistent view that scientists, technologists, and the public should work cooperatively on many matters. Student sophistication on these topics would seem to outstrip the portrayal of scientists generally found in television dramas.

Topics related to the social construction of scientific knowledge, however, appeared to be less familiar to students. Consequently, about one-half of the students consistently gave idealistic responses. When dealing with topics such as the social responsibility of scientists or the investment of money in research, students gave more emphasis to an instrumentalist view of science (science is an instrument of society). Such shifts in emphasis can lead to apparent inconsistencies among student responses to various VOSTS items. Perhaps such shifts in emphasis reflect student idealism gaining the upper hand on rational or realistic viewpoints.

Students' ideas about technology are difficult to discuss because a student's view depends so much on the particular technology he or she is considering. Decisions about nuclear missiles are very different in the minds of students than decisions about pollution standards. Therefore, one can expect that students will be vulnerable to, and uncritical of, vivid presentations of scientific information, unless those students have also received an education that addresses the realistic and logical role of science in technology and society.

Conclusion

The VOSTS item pool is a new tool for evaluating students and for initiating class discussions. Because the choices for each item were derived empirically from students' views on STS topics (rather than from science educators' philosophical positions), a teacher can feel secure in knowing that the meaning that teachers read into each choice is likely the same meaning which students read into each choice.

A teacher can select those VOSTS items that suit his or her particular instruction. Although the 114 VOSTS items cover the domain of STS topics pertaining to reasoned beliefs, the item pool does not address all possible STS topics. Consequently, teachers can modify or develop their own items and add them to their personally selected pool of VOSTS items.

Obtaining the VOSTS Item Pool

The Canadian version of VOSTS (English or French) is available on a cost-recovery basis. For further details, write to: The VOSTS Project, Curriculum Studies, University of Saskatchewan, Saskatoon, S7N 0W0, Canada.

Acknowledgements

The research was funded by Grant Number 410-87-1051 from the Social Science and Humanities Research Council of Canada. The work and advice of Pat Thomas, research assistant, is greatly appreciated.

References

Aikenhead, G. S. (1985). Collective decision making in the social context of science. *Science Education, 69*(4), 453–475.

Aikenhead, G. S. (1988). An analysis of four ways of assessing student beliefs about STS topics. *Journal of Research in Science Teaching, 25*(8), 607–627.

Aikenhead, G. S., Fleming, R. W., & Ryan, A. G. (1987). High school graduates' beliefs about science-technology-society. I. Methods and issues in monitoring students' views. *Science Education, 71*(2), 145–161.

Aikenhead, G. S., & Ryan, A. G. (1989). *The development of a multiple-choice instrument for monitoring views on science-technology-society topics.* Ottawa, Quebec, Canada: Social Sciences and Humanities Research Council of Canada.

Aikenhead, G. S., Ryan, A. G., & Desautels, J. (1989, April). *Monitoring student views on science-technology-society topics: The development of multiple-choice items.* Paper presented at the annual meeting of the National Association for Research in Science Teaching, San Francisco, California.

Aikenhead, G. S., Ryan, A. G., & Fleming, R. W. (1989). *Views on science-technology-society.* Saskatoon, Saskatchewan: University of Saskatchewan.

Barnes, B., & Edge, D. (1982). *Science in context.* Cambridge, MA: Massachusetts Institute of Technology Press.

Brunkhorst, H. K. (1987). A comparison of student/teacher positions on selected STS topics: A preliminary study. In K. Riquarts (Ed.), *Science and technology education and the quality of life* (Vol. II) (pp. 613–622). Kiel, Germany: Institute for Science Education.

Bybee, R. W. (Ed.). (1985). *NSTA yearbook: Science/technology/society.* Washington, DC: National Science Teachers Association.

Fleming, R. W. (1987). High school graduates' beliefs about science-technology-society. II. The interaction among science, technology and society. *Science Education, 71*(2), 163–186.

Fleming, R. W. (1989). Literacy for a technological age. *Science Education, 73*(4), 391–404.

Gardner, P. L. (1987). Measuring ambivalence to science. *Journal of Research in Science Teaching, 24*(3), 241–247.

Gauld, C. (1982). The scientific attitude and science education: A critical reappraisal. *Science Education, 66*(1), 109–121.

Kuhn, T. (1970). *The structure of scientific revolutions* (2nd ed.). Chicago, IL: The University of Chicago Press.

Snow, R. E. (1987). Core concepts for science and technology literacy. *Bulletin of Science-Technology-Society, 7*(5/6), 720–729.

Ziman, J. (1980). *Teaching and learning about science and society.* Cambridge, MA: Cambridge University Press.

Ziman, J. (1984). *An introduction to science studies: The philosophical and social aspects of science and technology.* (p. 10). Cambridge, MA: Cambridge University Press.

Science Teachers Rely on the Textbook

Iris R. Weiss
Horizon Research, Inc.

T he dominant role of the textbook in determining what science is taught was well documented in the major NSF-supported needs assessment conducted in the mid-1970s. In summarizing the findings of the series of case studies conducted as part of the needs assessment, Stake and Easley noted the pervasiveness of what they called "text-bound teaching":

> As we saw it, teachers relied on, teachers believed in, the textbook. Textbooks and other learning materials were *the instrument* of teaching and learning. Learning was a matter of developing skills, of acquiring information. The guide and the source was the textbook. *Information* is pretty much what many of the courses are about. (1978a, emphasis in original)

The other two components of the needs assessment (a comprehensive literature review and a major national survey of science education) painted a similar picture of the centrality of the textbook in science instruction (Helgeson, Blosser, & Howe, 1977; Weiss, 1978). After synthesizing a wealth of information about science teaching from the needs assessment and other sources, a research team focusing on the middle/junior high school concluded that "Typically, a science course is bound to a single textbook, which the teacher views as the subject matter authority and the heart of the instructional program" (Hurd, Robinson, McConnell, & Ross, 1981, p. 13). The same could have been said for science instruction at other grade levels as well.

More recent evidence indicates that the textbook continues to play a dominant role in science teaching. The 1985–86 National Survey of Science and Mathematics Education found that, except in grades K–3, more than 90 percent of elementary and secondary science classes use published textbooks/programs. Moreover, it is clear that textbooks are used as more than a reference: the majority of science teachers report "covering" 75 percent or more of the textbook in their classes (Weiss, 1987). Student-reported data confirm the picture of heavy reliance on textbooks. Roughly one-half of all eleventh-grade students and two-thirds of those in the seventh grade reported reading their science textbooks in science class at least several times a week (Mullis & Jenkins, 1988).

The 1985–86 National Survey of Science and Mathematics Education also asked teachers to rate the science textbooks they used. While most science teachers believe their textbooks are clear and well-organized and most are satisfied with the way science concepts are explained, many teachers would like the textbooks to include more examples to help reinforce the concepts.

Similarly, sizable numbers of teachers expressed dissatisfaction with the treatment of applications in their textbooks, indicating, for example, that the textbooks lack examples of the use of science in daily life and do not adequately show the application of science in careers (Weiss, 1987).

Interestingly, in a nation that prides itself on local autonomy in determining what is taught, a small number of textbook publishers dominate the science textbook market. In 1985–86, four publishers (D.C. Heath; Merrill; Holt, Rinehart & Winston; and Silver Burdett) for grades K–6 accounted for two-thirds of the textbooks used. At the secondary level, two publishers (Holt, Rinehart & Winston; Merrill) accounted for more than half of the market, with Merrill dominant in grades 7–9 and Holt in grades 10–12 (Weiss, 1987).

Objectives of Science Instruction

While the textbook is an important determinant of the curriculum in science classes, teachers typically have considerable latitude in the amount of time they spend on particular topics and the types of instructional activities they use with their classes. In the 1985–86 National Survey of Science and Mathematics Education, teachers were given a list of possible objectives of science instruction and asked how much emphasis each receives in a randomly selected class. Table 1 shows the percent of science classes in three grade ranges whose teachers indicated heavy emphasis for each objective.

Table 1

Objectives of Science Instruction

Objective	Percent of Classes with Heavy Emphasis*		
	K–6	7–9	10–12
Learn basic science concepts	67	85	86
Become aware of the importance of science in daily life	68	68	59
Develop a systematic approach to solving problems	48	63	67
Develop inquiry skills	55	62	57
Prepare for further study in science	42	52	56
Become interested in science	54	51	45
Learn to effectively communicate ideas in science	45	46	47
Develop awareness of safety issues in lab	23	52	54
Develop skills in lab techniques	15	45	55
Learn about applications of science in technology	27	40	39
Learn about the career relevance of science	22	30	31
Learn about the history of science	9	12	12

*Teachers were given a 6-point scale for each objective, with 1 labeled "none," 2 "minimal emphasis," 4 "moderate emphasis," and 6 "very heavy emphasis." These numbers represent the total circling either 5 or 6.

There is a marked congruity in instructional objectives between 7–9 and 10–12 science classes, but substantial differences between these and K–6 classes. By far the most heavily emphasized objective of science instruction at the secondary level is having students learn basic science concepts, with roughly 85 percent of 7–9 and 10–12 science classes giving heavy emphasis to this objective. Far fewer classes emphasize learning about the applications of these concepts—in daily life, in technology, and in careers. Again, we see a pattern in secondary science classes of conveying basic information, with much less attention to the uses of that information. At the elementary level, having the students become aware of the importance of science in daily life receives as much emphasis as does having them learn basic science concepts (Weiss, 1987).

It is particularly discouraging to note that, at all levels, relatively few teachers emphasize having the students become interested in science. It would seem reasonable to assume that the goal of having students learn more science would be more readily achieved if teachers paid more attention to sparking interest in the subject, including showing students how the science they are studying relates to the world around them.

Class Activities

The case studies conducted in the 1970s, and survey studies conducted then and more recently, consistently found that lecture and discussion are the prevalent techniques of science instruction (Stake & Easley, 1978b; Weiss, 1978, 1987). Teachers were given a list of ten activities and asked to indicate which ones took place during their most recent lesson in a particular class. As can be seen in Figure 1, use of hands-on activities is more common in elementary science than in secondary science. Moreover, the use of hands-on science has declined since a similar survey in 1977. For example, in 1977, 72 percent of junior high school science classes had lectures in their most recent science lesson, and 59 percent used hands-on activities, a difference of 13 percent. In comparison, in 1985–86, 83 percent of junior high school science lessons included lecture and 43 percent included hands-on activities, a difference of 40 percent (Weiss, 1987).

Figure 1

Science Classroom Activities Reported by Teachers (1985–1986)

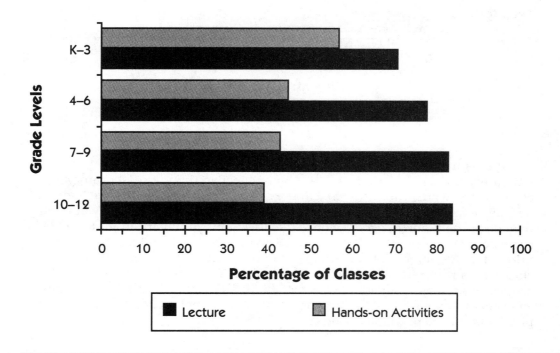

Lecture and Hands-On Activities

Student-reported data collected as part of the 1986 National Assessment of Educational Progress also indicate that hands-on activities are infrequently used. At the third-grade level, 33 percent of students report reading their science textbooks on a daily basis, three times as many who report doing science experiments that often. Similarly, as can be seen in Figure 2, two-thirds of seventh-graders and more than half of eleventh-graders reported reading their science textbooks at least several times a week; fewer than one in five said they did experiments with other students that frequently (Weiss, 1989). These same items were administered to 13-year-old students in a number of countries as part of the 1988 International Assessment of Educational Progress. The United States tied for first in frequency of textbook reading, with 70 percent of students reporting reading their science textbook at least several times a week. The U.S. ranked eighth out of 12 countries/provinces in frequency of science experiments (LaPointe, Mead, & Phillips, 1989).

Figure 2

Frequent Science Classroom Activities Reported by Students

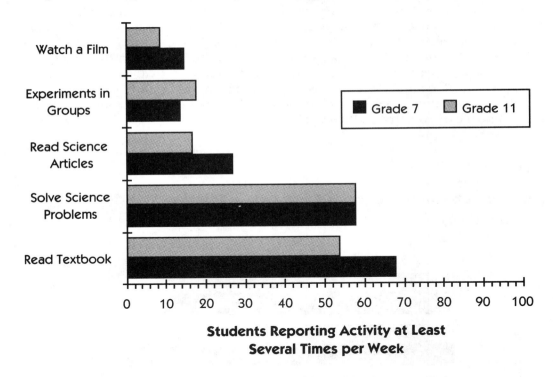

Students Reporting Activity at Least Several Times per Week

Interestingly, the majority of science teachers report a belief that laboratory-based science classes are more effective than non-laboratory classes, well worth the extra time and expense they typically involve. One possible explanation for the discrepancy between what teachers say and what they do is the inadequacy of science facilities and equipment in many schools. For example, in the 1985–86 National Survey of Science and Mathematics Education, 38 percent of elementary teachers reported teaching science in classrooms with *no* science facilities or materials. Similarly, resource problems such as inadequate facilities and insufficient funds for purchasing equipment and supplies, are among the most frequently cited "serious problems" in science instruction (Weiss, 1987).

Student Attitudes Towards Science

As part of the 1986 National Assessment of Educational Progress, students in grades 3, 7, and 11 were asked to respond to the question, "When you have science in school, do you like it?" Roughly 70 percent of third- and seventh-graders said they liked science. By eleventh grade, the percentage of students saying they enjoyed science dropped to 62 percent. Third-grade male and female students are equally disposed to liking science; however, by eleventh grade, females are much less likely to say they find science enjoyable (see Figure 3). Seventh- and eleventh-graders were also asked how often they found their science classes boring. Roughly one-third of seventh- and eleventh-graders described their science classes as often or always boring. There were no differences between seventh-grade male and female students; however, by eleventh grade, a greater proportion of females found their science classes boring (Mullis & Jenkins, 1988).

Figure 3

Students Finding Science Enjoyable by Gender

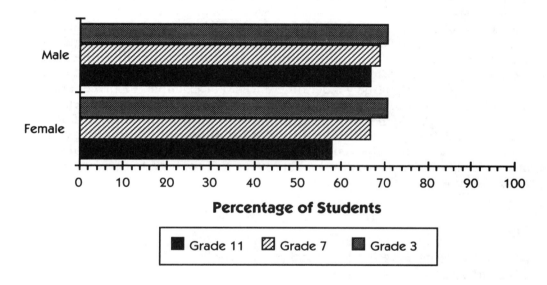

Students can use scientific knowledge for decision-making in their everyday lives. Whether they choose to do so may be some indication of how useful they find science, and whether they think they can personally benefit from scientific research and learning. As part of the 1986 National Assessment of Educational Progress, students in grade 11 were asked to report on whether or not they or their family used scientific information to make decisions relating to a number of activities: what foods to eat, how to stay healthy, vitamins used, choice of toothpaste, and cigarette smoking. As can be seen in Table 2, the majority of students (70 percent) reported using scientific information to stay healthy. Percentages were lower for the more specific uses, ranging from 57 percent in the case of cigarette use to 37 percent for choosing a toothpaste (Mullis & Jenkins, 1988).

Table 2

Students' Use of Scientific Information
Grade 11

Do you use science information to . . .	Percentage of Students Agreeing
Stay healthy?	70
Decide whether or not to smoke?	57
Decide what foods to eat?	46
Choose a toothpaste?	37

Additional information about student interaction with science in daily life comes from a series of questions where students in grades 7 and 11 were asked how often they had tried to fix something electrical, fix something mechanical, or figure out what was wrong with an unhealthy plant or animal. The results are shown in Figures 4 and 5. Note that while most seventh- and eleventh-graders reported having tried to fix electrical and mechanical things, there were extremely large gender differences. For example, 87 percent of seventh-grade males, but only 61 percent of seventh-grade females, reported having tried to "fix something electrical" at least once. Only about half of seventh- and eleventh-graders had tried to figure out what was wrong with an unhealthy plant. Here the gender differences were reversed, with female students significantly more likely than males to have tried to determine what ailed an unhealthy plant (Mullis & Jenkins, 1988).

Figure 4

Applications of Science Knowledge
Electrical/Mechanical, Grade 7

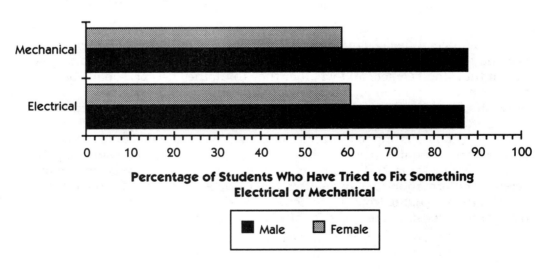

Percentage of Students Who Have Tried to Fix Something Electrical or Mechanical

■ Male   ▨ Female

Figure 5

Applications of Science Knowledge
Plants/Animals, Grade 7

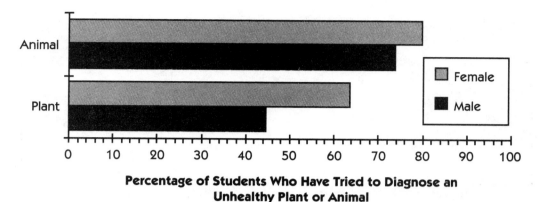

Percentage of Students Who Have Tried to Diagnose an Unhealthy Plant or Animal

Finally, students were asked a number of questions about the utility of the science they learned in school. While two out of three third-graders thought that science was useful outside of school, only about half of seventh- and eleventh-graders agreed. This finding is consistent with the data provided by teachers, indicating that having students become aware of the importance of science in daily life is emphasized considerably more in the lower grades (Mullis & Jenkins, 1988).

References

Helgeson, S. L., Blosser, P. E., & Howe, R. W. (1977). *The status of pre-college science, mathematics, and social science education: 1955–75.* Columbus, OH: Center for Science and Mathematics Education, The Ohio State University.

Hurd, P. DeH., Robinson, J. T., McConnell, M. C., & Ross, N. M., Jr. (1981). *The status of middle school and junior high school science; Technical Report* (Vol. 1). Louisville, CO: Center for Educational Research & Evaluation.

Lapointe, A., Mead, N. A., & Phillips, G. W. (1989). *A world of differences: An international assessment of mathematics and science.* Princeton, NJ: National Assessment of Educational Progress, Educational Testing Service.

Mullis, I. V. S., & Jenkins, L. B. (Eds.). (1988). *The science report card: Elements of risk and recovery.* Princeton, NJ: NAEP Educational Testing Service.

Stake, R. E., & Easley, J. (1978a). *Case studies in science education* (Vol. 19, p. 6). Urbana, IL: Center for Instructional Research and Curriculum Evaluation, University of Illinois at Urbana-Champaign.

Stake, R. E., & Easley, J. (1978b). *Case studies in science education* (Vols. 1 and 2). Urbana, IL: Center for Instructional Research and Curriculum Evaluation, University of Illinois at Urbana-Champaign.

Weiss, I. R. (1978). *Report of the 1977 national survey of science, mathematics, and social studies education: Center for educational research and evaluation.* Washington, DC: U.S. Government Printing Office.

Weiss, I. R. (1987). *Report of the 1985–86 national survey of science and mathematics education.* Research Triangle Park, NC: Center for Educational Research and Evaluation, Research Triangle Institute.

STS in Most Frequently Used Textbooks in U.S. Secondary Schools

Betty Chiang-Soong
National Taiwan Normal University, R. O. C.

Many science educators were astonished to find how important the textbook was in determining what students experienced in their science classes (Harms & Yager, 1981; Helgeson, Blosser, & Howe, 1977; Stake & Easley, 1978; Weiss, 1978). Ninety percent of all science teachers used their textbooks more than 90 percent of the time. Further, students expected the textbook to be used as the source of nearly all information and as the determinant of the content for each course. Even parents considered the textbook as central and expressed concern if textbooks were not issued and used for assignments. Textbooks provided an accurate record of what constitutes science study for nearly all students in the United States (and perhaps around the world). In addition, it has been found that relatively few textbooks represent the science studied. Hurd, Bybee, Kahle, and Yager (1980) reported that there was less than ten percent variation in content from one text for a given discipline or grade level to another text. Further, these investigators found that just three textbooks for a given grade level (or discipline in high school) characterized the study of science for 85 percent of all U.S. students.

Interrelationship of Science/Technology/Society
The STS Focus Group of Project Synthesis identified eight specific areas of concern that characterized STS. Piel (1981), the Chair of the STS Panel for Project Synthesis, identified eight conceptual domains for STS. These areas are: (1) energy, (2) population, (3) human genetic engineering, (4) environmental quality, (5) use of natural resources, (6) national defense and space, (7) sociology of science, and (8) effects of technological development. Two broad areas of goals, namely (1) personal needs and (2) societal needs, were identified as central to STS programs. These two goal areas and the eight topic areas provided a definition of STS learning objectives derived from where topics and personal or societal goals were both judged as being present. Piel (1981) pointed out one of the problems of STS and textbooks when he stated:

> There is little or nothing of STS in currently available textbooks. Our group reviewed a number of widely used textbooks and found virtually no references to technology in general, or to our eight specific areas of concern. (p. 106)

A New Search of Textbook Content

Four science textbooks most frequently used at the junior high level and seven used at the high school level were examined with regard to STS coverage. Of the seven, three were biology, two chemistry, and two were physics texts. (In each category, i.e., junior high, biology, chemistry, and physics textbooks, at least one of the NSF-supported programs was included for analysis.) Comparisons were made for the textbooks within and across disciplines and grade levels, and between NSF-supported and publisher-funded series.

Although textbook coverage is not a recommended teaching strategy, it is apparently a most common one. Ideally STS cannot be defined in terms of curriculum or in terms of coverage in textbooks. Nonetheless, the complete dominance of the textbook as a teaching tool makes a careful study of commonly used textbooks important in terms of STS emphasis in typical classrooms.

The major question raised was: How do the eleven books compare as to the treatment of "the interrelationship of science, technology, and society?" Three other related questions were also raised: How much space in terms of percentage of the total narration included in each textbook is devoted to the interrelationship of science, technology, and society? What are the differences from textbook to textbook concerning STS treatment in a given discipline? and How do the textbooks vary across the grade levels with respect to attention to STS?

The eleven textbooks analyzed were selected from Weiss's (1978) listing of the most frequently used ones in the secondary schools in the United States. They included the following at the indicated grade level and for the various disciplines:

Middle School/Junior High (Grades 7–9)
1. Sutherland, B., White, S. E., Davis, J. M., Shepherd, D., and Wood, L. (1984). *Focus on Earth Science.* Columbus, OH: Charles E. Merrill.
2. Heimler, C. H., and Neal, C. D. (1986). *Principles of Science, Book 1.* Columbus, OH: Charles E. Merrill.
3. Heimler, C. H., and Neal, C. D. (1986). *Principles of Science, Book 2.* Columbus, OH: Charles E. Merrill.
4. Intermediate Sciences Curriculum Study (ISCS). (1981). *The Natural World, Vol. 1.* Morristown, NJ: Silver Burdett. (NSF-sponsored program)

High School (Grades 10–12) Biology
5. Otto, J. H., and Towle, A. (1985). *Modern Biology.* New York, NY: Holt, Rinehart, and Winston.
6. Biological Sciences Curriculum Study (BSCS). (1982). *Biological Science: An Ecological Approach.* Boston, MA: Houghton Mifflin. (NSF-sponsored program) (hereinafter called BSCS Green Version)
7. Biological Sciences Curriculum Study (BSCS). (1980). *Biological Science: An Enquiry into Life.* New York, NY: Harcourt Brace Jovanovich. (NSF-sponsored program) (hereinafter called BSCS Yellow Version)

High School (Grades 10–12) Chemistry
8. Metcalfe, H. C., Williams, J. E., and Castka, J. F. (1986). *Modern Chemistry.* New York, NY: Holt, Rinehart and Winston.
9. Parry, R. W., Bassow, H., Merrill, P., and Tellefsen, R. L. (1982). *Chemistry: Experimental Foundations.* Englewood Cliffs, NJ: Prentice-Hall. (NSF-sponsored program)

High School (Grades 10–12) Physics
10. Williams, J. E., Trinklein, F. E., and Metcalfe, H. C. (1984). *Modern Physics.* New York, NY: Holt, Rinehart and Winston.

11. Haber-Schaim, U., Dodge, J. H., and Walter, J. A. (1986). *PSSC Physics*. Lexington, MA: D. C. Heath. (NSF-sponsored program)

Results

Table 1 provides the results in percentage of the total narrative page space devoted to each STS topic. Table 2 summarizes the total number of full pages and the total percentage of the narrative devoted to each aspect of STS. Since the data were collected from every page of the textbook, the results presented in the tables provide actual values both in full pages and in percentages of the narrative devoted to each STS goal or topic. The differences indicate the actual differences. Since all the data collected were based on STS notions that Piel summarized in Project Synthesis (Piel, 1981) the data should be interpreted in such a light. All emphasize the curricular/topical definitions of STS—the ones easiest and most useful in analyzing instructional materials such as textbooks. The goals can more often be less tangible in the narrative and more a matter of teacher concern in the act of instruction.

Table 1

Comparison of the Average Percentages of the Total Narrative Page Space Devoted to Science/Technology/Society in Eleven Science Textbooks

STS Topic	Four Junior High Texts	Three Biology Texts	Two Chemistry Texts	Two Physics Texts
Energy	1.07	0.57	0.05	0.19
Population	0.09	0.67	0.00	0.00
Human Engineering	0.04	0.34	0.08	0.00
Environmental Quality & Natural Resources	4.29	2.38	0.67	0.03
Space Research & National Defense	0.30	0.00	0.01	0.02
Sociology of Science	0.18	0.64	0.01	0.02
Effects of Technological Developments	1.57	0.49	0.46	0.69
Total	7.54	5.09	1.28	0.95

Table 2

Comparison of the Total Narrative Page Space Devoted to Science/Technology/Society in Eleven Science Textbooks

Textbook	Number of Full Pages of Narrative		
	Devoted to STS	**Total**	**Percentage**
Junior High			
Focus on Earth Science	8.02	122.26	6.56
Principles of Science (I)	6.71	141.66	4.74
Principles of Science (II)	16.71	154.19	11.51
The Natural World (I)	0.15	8.53	1.76
High School			
Biology			
Modern Biology	11.29	305.74	3.69
BSCS Green Version	12.06	223.51	5.40
BSCS Yellow Version	13.91	204.42	6.80
Chemistry			
Modern Chemistry	1.94	324.53	0.60
Chem: Expt. Foundation	4.97	214.88	2.31
Physics			
Modern Physics	3.75	311.30	1.20
PSSC Physics	0.83	171.05	0.49

Discussion

As the results reveal, major science textbooks are deficient in their treatment of STS topics. They include very little STS information. Further, the data show that as the grade level increases, the percentage of the total narrative page space devoted to STS passages decreases. This may result from the addition of more facts/content information in the specific discipline as the grade level increases. Although the quality of the STS passages was not examined, it was noticed that, usually, the STS information in the texts was presented as facts; debatable social issues were rarely discussed. In general, the students were offered very few opportunities through science textbooks to familiarize themselves with the science-related problems existing in society or to be introduced to the possible alternatives for solving these problems.

Suggestions for Improving Textbooks

What aspects of science textbooks need to be improved? How shall such improvement be undertaken? Certainly much must occur if STS topics and instructional strategies are going to characterize the classroom where students experience science. In-depth passages concerning the interrelationship of science, technology, and society need to be added to the content. Science-related issues or problems need to be identified and addressed, pros and cons need to be discussed, and possible outcomes and developments in the future need to be suggested. Possible actions, decisions, or choices in daily life that may lead to the solution of the problems need to be encouraged or used to encourage group or individual citizenship actions.

References

Harms, N. C., & Yager, R. E. (Eds.). (1981). *What research says to the science teacher, Vol. 3.* Washington, DC: National Science Teachers Association.

Helgeson, S. L., Blosser, P. E., & Howe, R. W. (1977). *The status of pre-college science, mathematics, and social science education: 1955–75.* Columbus, OH: Center for Science and Mathematics Education, The Ohio State University.

Hurd, P. DeH., Bybee, R. W., Kahle, J. B., & Yager, R. E. (1980). Biology education in secondary schools of the United States. *The American Biology Teacher, 42*(7), 388–404.

Piel, E. J. (1981). Interaction of science, technology, and society in secondary schools. In N. C. Harms & R. E. Yager, (Eds.), *What research says to the science teacher, Vol. 3* (pp. 94–112). Washington, DC: National Science Teachers Association.

Stake, R. E., & Easley, J. (1978). *Case studies in science education* (Vols. 1 and 2). Urbana, IL: Center for Instructional Research and Curriculum Evaluation, University of Illinois at Urbana-Champaign.

Weiss, I. R. (1978). *Report of the 1977 national survey of science, mathematics, and social studies education: Center for educational research and evaluation.* Washington, DC: U.S. Government Printing Office.

Teacher Strategies Used by Exemplary STS Teachers

Durojaiye A. Ajeyalemi
University of Lagos, Nigeria

Planning, in the traditional approach to science teaching, involves the teacher deciding on the topic based on a sequence suggested in the curriculum guide or textbook, defining the objectives of the lesson, consulting the standard textbook or workbook to identify the main concepts to be emphasized, deciding the appropriate procedure to follow in the classroom presentation of the topic, writing the lesson notes, and possibly practicing any activities students will engage in beforehand. The student is rarely involved in determining the goals or procedures for achieving them.

However, teaching in an STS classroom is often not a one-lesson affair. It invariably involves many lessons on an identified problem topic. The STS module is most often derived by both the students and the teacher working cooperatively together, or from suggestions offered by students alone based on their personal experience. Such modules evolve from the consideration of real-life issues confronting students, the local community, or society in general. These issues may or may not relate directly to topics in the textbook. Common sources for STS modules include the home, student experiences, newspapers, journals, magazines, radio and television programs, the library, textbooks, and local, national, or international debates/issues. The lesson is then planned as investigations designed to solve real-life problems. Thus, the main planning takes place in the classroom and is not premeditated as in traditional instruction. The students must take ownership of the topic for them to be enthusiastic in carrying out the investigations. This likely occurs if they see the relevance of the topic to their everyday lives, or if they can convince themselves of the rationale for the investigation.

After agreement on the topic, students select the aspect of it to address, either individually or in groups, and plan their investigations accordingly. The planning often involves further reading and consulting about the problem, designing the appropriate procedures for investigations, identifying the sources of necessary equipment/materials/contacts, and getting these and other supporting items ready.

Let us consider how Morgan Masters maneuvered his ninth-grade students to begin investigating the various properties of water, study pollution, and make decisions concerning whether or not to set up landfills. The textbook unit was on "Water as a Universal Solvent." The question posed by Morgan was "How many drops of water could you place on a penny before it slides off?" Each student hypothesized on the number of drops and all agreed that this could be tested by dropping water on a penny using a dropper. Students raised various questions arising from their observations. Questions concerning what makes the water stay on the penny, how it forms a bigger drop, surface tension, polarity, solubility, and changes in properties as soap is added to water were all raised. Students planned investigations to answer their questions. These included arranging themselves in groups, designing experiments and other activities, further reading, and collecting needed equipment and materials to investigate the properties of water.

Similarly, from a student's problem with toilet blockage at home and his hypothesis that this was caused by the type of toilet paper used, Joan McShane started a project with her sixth-grade students on a study of locally available toilet paper. Ultimately, she was able to link this with a one month unit on ecology. This is an example of a topic generated and an investigation designed by the class from an issue arising from a student's experience. In a brainstorming session on what to do, the teacher and students concluded that they would need a toilet in the classroom in order to test various toilet papers. They then decided to seek help and resources from the local community. One person from the community, in collaboration with the teacher, helped to design and build a suitable full-sized, but portable, commode in the classroom; a plumber donated a toilet bowl; and the Parent-Teacher Association bought a sump pump so the water could be recycled. Students, on their own, gathered packages of toilet papers from various sources including homes, supermarkets, friends, and teachers.

Common strategies employed in the traditional classroom teaching of science include lecturing, questioning, describing, explaining, outlining and illustrating on the chalkboard, demonstrating, and directing students to sources of information during lessons or to textbooks for homework. All these are planned, led, and most often, executed by the teacher. For instance, questions to be asked of students are planned in advance, and most often they require "yes," "no," or one word answers. Experimental activities are often demonstrated by the teacher while students watch. Students are rarely involved in direct, practical, problem-solving activities or encouraged to verbalize their thoughts by asking questions or answering them or in discussions.

While some of the above strategies may be useful in teaching an STS topic, certain other strategies are much more typical of an STS class. Cooperative learning strategies are usually employed and are more effective in STS teaching, and these involve student action rather than teacher action. Actually, there is no apparent demarcation between the planning and implementation phase. Students in STS classes have been involved with the following: field experiences; practical laboratory activities; case studies; simulations; role-playing; debates; library searches; brainstorming; panel discussions; individual or group projects; problem-solving; class discussions and presentations; displays, fairs and exhibitions; peer tutoring; designing and constructing equipment, models, and other learning aids; interviewing, audio/video recording, letter writing, and other survey methods; invited guest lecturing/discussion/demonstration; and decision-making. All these involve continuous planning and re-evaluation and most often may go on beyond the normal class time and extend outside the school.

Through such strategies, students come to acquire and use the processes of science which are appropriate to the solution of particular problems or needed for acquiring particular information, understand and learn how to accommodate each other's needs, strengths, and weaknesses, and learn meaningful, interesting, and socially relevant concepts (science and non-science). The result is that students are better informed on science and technology issues affecting them and society as a whole. Further, their experiences with an STS unit may lead them to take some relevant social action such as protesting ground water pollution or leading a boycott of an offending industry's products.

Joan McShane's students, for example, worked as a cooperative group on their toilet-tissue testing project, with sub-groups carrying out specific duties—some were weighing the tissue before and after use, some were recording procedures and results, and others were flushing and cleaning the toilet or drying the used tissues. In a unit on toothpastes, these same students worked individually to determine, among other things, which of the available brands would clean teeth best and which foods leave the most stains on teeth or cause the worst decay. The students later published their findings on these two issues and communicated these to individuals and organizations who contributed resources towards the activities as well as to the companies whose products were tested.

To return to Morgan Master's students, they worked in groups—some carried out experimental activities on the properties of water with or without soap, some investigated water pollution in the local environment, and the whole class later engaged in panel discussions, role-playing, and decision-making in order to reach a decision on whether or not to build a landfill in the community.

The Iowa Chautauqua Program was a nine-year project to develop an inservice model for assisting teachers with change in terms of their teaching behaviors and the curriculum selected to meet new instructional goals. The program provided an opportunity to study classrooms taught in an STS format versus a more typical textbook format. It is characterized by the following facets:

- a two-week leadership conference for 25 of the most successful teachers from previous years who want to become a part of the instructional team for future workshops
- a three-week summer workshop at each new site for 30 new teachers electing to try STS modules and strategies; the workshop provides experience with STS (teachers and students) and time to plan a five-day STS unit to be used with students in the fall
- a two-and-a-half day fall short course for 30–50 teachers (including the 30 enrolled during the summer); the focus is on developing a month-long STS module and an extensive assessment plan
- an interim communication with central staff, lead teachers, and fellow participants, including a newsletter, special memoranda, monthly telephone contacts, and school/classroom visits
- a two-and-a-half day spring short course for the same 30–50 teachers who participated in the fall; this session focuses on reports by participants on their STS experience and the results of the assessment program

After viewing more than 50 video tapes of two classrooms taught by the same teacher and more than 100 direct observations in classrooms, the following contrasts between the two situations were evident.

Standard	Exemplary
Teachers work in their classroom with several sections of students assigned to them.	Teachers work as part of a staff team working towards common goals.
Teachers feel tied to a textbook or a curriculum guide.	Teachers look beyond the boundaries of a textbook or curriculum guide; they minimally define the concepts and activities used.

Standard	Exemplary
Teachers are discipline-bound; they rarely work competently with teachers from other curriculum areas—or science teachers from disciplines other than their own.	Teacher are constantly seeking linkages with others in the rest of the school; they also seek linkages with other teachers in the state and nation.
Teachers tend to distrust the use of experts from the community (external to the school).	Teachers see themselves (and their students) as reaching into the community for information, expertise, ideas, and materials.
Teachers are seen as dispensers of the information that they possess.	Teachers are seen as learners themselves and as facilitators and collaborators in student learning.
Teachers rarely think about goals for themselves; they rarely enter into debate or meaningful dialogue about their teaching.	Teachers are anxious to share their philosophies as they seek ways of expanding their thinking; they seek information that will help them improve teaching.
Teachers complain about inservice learning opportunities.	Teachers seek out inservice assistance as they seek to grow and improve.

Teachers who are armed with a vast quantity of strategies for effective teaching are able to perform in ways that permit instructional goals to be met. Their students are able to use the concepts and processes of the science they encounter better than students found in traditional classes. In addition, their students have superior attitudes concerning science and science learning. Further, the students demonstrate significantly better creativity skills related to questioning, suggestions of causes, and predictions of consequences. Such student growth is encouraging as they are related to teacher traits that produce them.

Learning Science by Doing Science*

Joseph S. Krajcik
The University of Michigan

I t is critical that science education prepare our youth for an increasingly scientific and technological world where citizens will need to learn and apply knowledge to solve real-world problems. Unfortunately, our youth are not learning the nature of science or developing deep conceptual understandings of scientific concepts, nor do they find science interesting. Sharp contrasts exist between what research and theory have established about effective learning of science and the teaching practices seen in the vast majority of elementary, middle, and senior high schools (Boyer, 1983; Goodlad, 1984; Mullis & Jenkins, 1988; National Assessment of Educational Progress, 1979; Stake & Easley, 1978; Weiss, 1978).

The research suggests that science teachers use a limited set of instructional strategies to teach a packed curriculum to passive students. Scientific facts and algorithmic problem solving are the essence of the science curriculum taught in United States schools. Moreover, science education research (Champagne, Klopfer, & Gunstone, 1985; Nakhleh & Krajcik, 1991; Novick & Nussbaum, 1981; Osborne & Freyberg, 1986) indicates that students at the elementary, middle, and high school levels: (a) do not understand fundamental science concepts, (b) do not relate science concepts to phenomena, (c) memorize science terms without understanding, and (d) memorize how to solve problems (Eylon & Linn, 1988; Osborne & Freyberg, 1986). Students learn bits of factual information; however, they do not develop a meaningful understanding of science that can help them understand other science concepts and phenomena and apply such understanding to solve real-world problems. The science education research also indicates that students hold negative attitudes towards science and are not motivated to continue their learning of science. Yager and Penick (1986) summarized the data from the various national studies and concluded that the more years our students enroll in science courses, the less they like it.

What can be done to help students develop a meaningful understanding of science? What can be done to help students apply scientific concepts and principles to solve real-world problems? What can be done to help learners experience what doing science is all about? In this chapter, the focus is on students' understanding of physical science phenomena. It makes

*The ideas expressed in this paper on project-based science were developed collaboratively with the Science Education Research Team at the University of Michigan. The team consists of Carl Berger, Phyllis Blumenfeld, Joe Krajcik, Marty Maehr, Ron Marx, Annmarie Palincsar, and Elliot Soloway.

recommendations for the improvement of the teaching of physical science through the use of project-based science and discusses implications for curriculum development. In the next section, some of the problems in science education are illustrated by presenting examples of students' alternative conceptual systems for two fundamental physical science concepts.

Personal Knowledge and School Knowledge

It is important to distinguish between personal knowledge and school knowledge to understand the difference between students developing meaningful understanding, that is, understanding that can be used to predict and explain natural phenomena and be applied to solve real-world problems, versus knowledge of terms and formulas that can be recalled for tests (Pines & West, 1986). Personal knowledge is one's creative and personal attempt to make sense and meaning of the world. A learner constructs personal knowledge as he or she interacts with individuals and the environment. Parents, friends, teachers, books, television, movies, and cultural customs all impact on the construction of personal knowledge. School knowledge is someone else's interpretation of the world and is a product of planned instruction in school settings. It is what we find in textbooks and what students frequently memorize for examinations.

Unfortunately, schools for the most part have failed to help learners integrate their personal knowledge with school knowledge, and as a result, students fail to develop meaningful understanding of some important scientific concepts and to understand the essence of doing science. As a result of instruction, science concepts become a list of memorized facts that students recall for examinations. Using school knowledge, students can solve algorithms and give definitions, but they cannot describe qualitative phenomenon, ask meaningful questions, or apply their knowledge to solve real-world problems. Ignoring the personal understanding that students bring with them to the science classroom and "telling" students the scientist's models and methods leads to students memorizing "school knowledge" without the development of meaningful understanding. For some, memorization leads to success on classroom and standardized examinations; however, memorization does not lead to students applying science concepts and developing personal knowledge of science.

What can teachers do to help learners develop meaningful understanding of science concepts? What can teachers do to get students involved in investigations that emulate what scientists actually do, to experience what it is like to do science? What can teachers do to help students actively construct meaningful knowledge of science?

Project-Based Science

Fortunately, science educators have made progress on designing instruction based on constructivist conceptions of learning. The current view of learning pictures students as actively constructing their knowledge by working with and using ideas. Moreover, educational researchers argue that knowledge is contextualized and that learners construct knowledge by solving complex, meaningful problems (Brown, Collins, & Duguid, 1989; Resnick, 1987). Using these theoretical frameworks, science educators are creating exciting opportunities for students to learn science by doing project-based science (Blumenfeld et al., 1991; Tinker, 1991).

Project-based science allows students to learn science by doing science and, as a consequence, actively construct their understanding of science by working with and using their ideas. In project-based science, students are engaged in real, meaningful problems that emulate what scientists do. A project-based science classroom will allow students to freely discuss their ideas, challenge the ideas of others, and try out their ideas.

NATIONAL SCIENCE TEACHERS ASSOCIATION

Effective science projects have five characteristics.

- **They encourage active engagement.** Project-based science creates a classroom environment in which students can find answers to non-trivial problems by asking and refining questions, making predictions, designing plans and/or experiments, collecting and analyzing data or information, debating ideas, communicating their ideas and findings to others, drawing conclusions, and asking new questions. As such, project-based science is collaborative, giving students opportunities to share and debate ideas, questions, results, and conclusions. Students must be willing to challenge each other's ideas, and by doing so they help clarify their own understanding. Hence, the collaborative nature of project-based science gives students opportunities to construct an understanding of science concepts by doing science.

- **They extend over time.** Projects take considerable time and effort, emulating the work of scientists. Hence, students must hold commitment and motivation towards resolving their questions. Projects are distinguished from performing exercises or activities designed to illustrate a single science concept. Activities and/or exercises are typically not driven by the resolution of a question or problem. Student projects, however, might include a series of activities or exercises designed to help students learn concepts or processes relevant to completing the project.

- **They provide realistic, contextualized problem solving.** Projects attempt to build bridges between scientific phenomena in the classroom and real life experiences. The questions that arise in the daily experiences of students are given value and are open to investigation. Everyday, important questions from students serve both to drive the project and give it the needed coherence over time. Project-based learning can be interdisciplinary so that students use ideas from many areas simultaneously, helping to eliminate artificial distinctions between subject matter areas.

- **They include key scientific concepts and processes.** As students investigate a problem, they develop meaningful understanding of key scientific concepts such as acids and bases or solar energy. The concepts students develop from taking part in project-based science helps determine the worth of the project (Ruopp, 1993). However, the science processes a student uses in answering the questions must also be considered. Undertaking a project should help students develop understandings of some key science concepts and an understanding of the processes of science.

- **They result in a series of artifacts or products.** As a result of completing a project, students often develop a series of artifacts or products that culminate in a final product that addresses the driving question. These products can be shared with other class members, teachers, parents, and members of the community. The creation and sharing of artifacts makes doing project-based science more like doing real science (Blumenfeld et al., 1991).

Projects have been created and distributed by publishers of educational materials. Bob Tinker and his colleagues at the Technical Education Research Center (TERC) have pioneered the effort to develop project-based science curriculum. TERC and National Geographic have developed projects for upper elementary students on science topics such as acid rain and solar energy. These particular projects focus on important environmental problems and involve students in gathering and analyzing data and in examining local industry and laws. A key feature of the projects developed by National Geographic and TERC has been the use of telecommunications which allow students to gain and share information with students at other schools throughout the United States and in other countries. The use of telecommunications helps create a collaborative environment by allowing students access to a wider community in which they can communicate with knowledgeable individuals, take advantage of resources others have to offer, communicate with other students in different communities, and share data with other student scientists and professional scientists. Other forms of new technology, such as the use of microcomputer-based laboratories, also hold great promise in helping to enhance project-based science environments (Blumenfeld et al., 1991; Tinker, 1991).

One of the projects, *Acid Rain*, developed by National Geographic and TERC as part of Kids Network, can serve as an example. In *Acid Rain*, students investigate the pH of local, regional, and global rainfall. Students predict the pH of their local rainfall by collecting information about factors that effect the pH of rain including the number of acid-gas producing factories, the number of cars, and the number of people. They then study the effect of acid rain on the environment and make predictions about the pH of other regions throughout the country from information they receive from other students through telecommunications. In the process of exploring relevant questions, students perform activities to learn about acids and bases and how to measure pH. Concepts will often cut across science disciplines as well as social science issues. For instance, in *Acid Rain*, students can study acid and base concepts and meteorology concepts, as well as issues regarding the environment. Students practice data collection, analysis, and presentation of data, learning how to find patterns in data and draw conclusions from the data that they collected and the data that was given to them by other student scientists through telecommunications. In the process of finding out about acid rain, students learn important science concepts and processes by doing science. *Acid Rain* is one of several units published by the National Geographic Society that affords opportunities for children to investigate authentic questions and share data and ideas with other student scientists in geographically diverse classrooms throughout the United States and in other countries through telecommunications.

Project Ideas

Where do ideas for projects come from? Teachers do not have to use published projects to have students engage in meaningful, long-term investigations. Classroom teachers, teams of teachers, or teachers working collaboratively with their students can develop projects. Some excellent projects can come from students' own ideas. Listen to students; they have a number of questions to explore. Although a teacher may need to help students refine and modify questions, student-generated questions provide a powerful starting point. When students ask questions, refine and modify questions, design procedures, carry-out their design, and debate the data, they are doing science.

How do students learn to ask good questions? Most often we do not give students the opportunity to ask and investigate. Providing opportunities is a start, but teachers need to help students focus and refine their questions. Unfortunately, students' creativity to ask questions has not been promoted in the schools. We need to provide opportunities and build on them. Begin a subject by brainstorming ideas to investigate, then help students to refine these questions and to design procedures. Once a project is started, it will often lead to other investigations.

A water quality project performed by a bilingual, middle-school Haitian Creole class serves as a good model of how student-generated questions can lead to performing meaningful projects (Warren, Rosebery, & Conant, 1989). As a result of a teacher-led brainstorming activity that was conducted at the close of a unit on the chemistry, biology, and ecology of local water, students decided to investigate the water quality of drinking water in their schools. Their investigation began by determining whether they actually preferred the water from the water fountain on their floor to other fountains at school.

When their "blind taste test" indicated that they preferred the water from a fountain on another floor, they decided to expand their population of taste testers. When this second test further substantiated their earlier findings, it led them to investigate the reasons behind the taste test results. They planned and performed quantitative tests of temperature, bacteria level, and pH concentration. In pursuing the answer to their question, students were engaged in learning science by doing science. Students asked questions, refined their questions, planned experiments, and discussed and debated their results.

Implications for Science Curriculum Development

Project-based science affords many possibilities for science teaching by providing students with the opportunity to construct their knowledge by being engaged in meaningful problem-solving. Projects involve students in solving authentic problems, in working with others, and in formulating plans, tracking progress, evaluating solutions, and building real solutions; hence, projects allow learners to construct personal knowledge of doing science. Project-based science does not teach learners "about" science; rather it allows students to "do" science. However, such an approach to science teaching will call on teachers to evaluate their teaching style and explore new methods of teaching as their students explore new science concepts.

References

Blumenfeld, P., Soloway, E., Marx, R., Krajcik, J. S., Guzdial, M., & Palincsar, A. (1991). Motivating project-based learning. *Educational Psychologist, 26*(3&4), 369–398.

Boyer, E. L. (1983). *High school: A report on secondary education in America.* New York, NY: Harper and Row.

Brown, J. S., Collins, A., & Duguid, P. (1989). Situated cognition of learning. *Educational Researcher, 18,* 32–42.

Champagne, A. B., Klopfer, L. E., & Gunstone, R. F. (1985). Instructional consequences of students' knowledge about physical phenomena. In A. L. Pines & L. H. T. West (Eds.), *Cognitive Structure and Conceptual Change* (pp. 61–88). New York, NY: Academic Press.

Eylon, B., & Linn, M. C. (1988). Learning and instruction: An examination of our research perspectives in science education. *Review of Educational Research, 58*(3), 251–302.

Goodlad, J. I. (1984). *A place called school—Prospects for the future.* New York, NY: McGraw Hill Book Co.

Mullis, I. V. S., & Jenkins, L. B. (Eds.). (1988). *The science report card: Elements of risk and recovery.* Princeton, NJ: NAEP Educational Testing Service.

Nakhleh, M. B., & Krajcik, J. S. (1991, April). *The effect of level of information as presented by different technologies on students' understanding of acid, base, and pH concepts.* Paper presented at the 64th Annual Meeting of the National Association for Research in Science Teaching, Lake Geneva, WI.

National Assessment of Educational Progress. (1979). *Attitudes toward science: A summary of results from the 1976–77 National Assessment of Science.* Denver, CO: Educational Commission of the States.

Novick, S., & Nussbaum, J. (1981). Pupils' understanding of the particulate nature of matter: A cross-age study. *Science Education, 65*(2), 187–196.

Osborne, R. J., & Freyberg, P. (1986). *Learning in science: The implications of children's science.* London, England: Heinemann.

Pines, A. L., & West, L. H. T. (1986). Conceptual understanding and science learning: An interpretation of research within a sources-of-knowledge framework. *Science Education, 70*(5), 583–604.

Resnick, L. B. (1987). Learning in school and out. *Educational Researcher, 16,* 13–20.

Ruopp, R. (1993). Agenda for an uncertain future. In R. Ruopp, S. Gal, B. Drayton, & M. Pfister (Eds.), *LabNet: Toward a Community of Practice* (pp. 291–310). Hillsdale, NJ: Lawrence Erlbaum Associates.

Stake, R. E., & Easley, J. (1978). *Case studies in science education* (Vol. 2). Urbana, IL: Center for Instructional Research and Curriculum Evaluation, University of Illinois at Urbana-Champaign.

Tinker, R. (1991). *Thinking about science.* Unpublished manuscript, Technical Educational Research Center, Cambridge, MA.

Warren, B., Rosebery, A. S., & Conant, F. R. (1989). *Cheche Konnen: Science and literacy in language minority classrooms.* Unpublished manuscript, Bolt, Beranek, and Newman, Inc.

Weiss, I. R. (1978). *Report of the 1977 national survey of science, mathematics, and social studies education: Center for educational research and evaluation.* Washington, DC: U.S. Government Printing Office.

Yager, R. E., & Penick, J. E. (1986). Perceptions of four age groups toward science classes, teachers, and the value of science. *Science Education, 70*(4), 355–363.

The Jurisprudential Inquiry Model for STS

Ronald J. Bonnstetter and Jon E. Pedersen
University of Nebraska and University of Arkansas

How does one teach using an STS approach? Where is the curriculum material to accomplish the task? The answer to these and many other related questions may come as a surprise. For example, we may never see a transportable STS national curriculum; because by definition the material must focus on local issues and build from the roots of student interest. In addition, some of the strategies that are most effective require innovative teaching skills that go well beyond just dispensing information. But if teachers are willing to meet the challenge, all could find themselves involved in a teaching model that will guide students to new heights of understanding and rejuvenate early teaching ideals. A properly orchestrated STS unit can be an exciting learning experience for both student and teacher.

Successful STS teaching is not a teaching recipe. It is the interaction of numerous facilitative strategies, all directed towards the STS teaching philosophy—a philosophy that expands our current goals for teaching science to include: the development of investigative skills, opportunities for greater awareness of beliefs and cultural values, and ultimately an understanding of basic citizenship and the strategies needed for taking action to make a difference in the world.

Teaching Prerequisites for Maximum Success

The model presented in this chapter is somewhat complex and assumes that a number of teaching skills are understood, if not used by, the teacher. These include: cooperative learning strategies of Johnson, Grooker, Stutzman, Hultman, and Johnson (1985) and Slavin (1989); higher-order questioning skills; wait time; and classroom organization and management skills. In addition, it helps to understand a constructivist approach to teaching and the need for student empowerment as both an approach to teaching and as an outcome of education. Also, the teacher must have enough content knowledge of the subject being taught so that he or she can concentrate on how to teach and not spend preparation time on what to teach. All of these characteristics must be blended with an understanding of how children learn and when to intercede for maximum learning.

The Jurisprudential STS Model of Teaching

Pedersen (1990) modified the original Joyce and Weil Jurisprudential Model (1986) to create a jurisprudential inquiry STS model of teaching that effectively lends itself to the study of science, technology, and societal issues in the classroom. The jurisprudential inquiry STS model approaches teaching issues by dividing a class into the issue viewpoints. Through the use of information-acquisition strategies and classmate interactions, students present their views to a class-selected board of arbiters. It is the board's responsibility to listen to the student arguments in a public hearing and render a decision on the issue.

The final phase of this and many other STS teaching strategies involves the creation and assessment of action plans. In many ways the actual action plans developed by students are just as important an outcome as the related science concepts they learned. What follows is an outline of the six phases of the jurisprudential inquiry model applied to STS.

Phase I: Orientation to the Issue

The initial step of this model introduces students to the selected issue. This occurs on the very first day that the topic is being studied. During this initial stage, the teacher must accomplish several tasks. They include:

1. Divide the class into teams of two or three students. Each team will be assigned a side of the issue to represent in their respective group. The purpose of the team is to cooperate in reading, researching, and interacting on the side of the issue that they have been assigned.
2. Now arrange the teams into groups so that the number of teams in a group equals the number of sides to the issue. For example, a recycling issue may have two sides—recycling and nonrecycling. Therefore each group would have two teams of two (or three) members, a total of four (six) in the group.
3. Assign each team within a group one side of the issue to represent. It is important to do this randomly. Inevitably some students will be assigned to a side of an issue that they do not believe in, but this is perhaps desirable.

It is important to remember that the issue selected becomes the focus of the curriculum. The content becomes the support for the issue.

Phase II: Identifying and Defining the Issue

Students begin to use the content during the second phase of the model. The students, working in their cooperative teams, use the library and other resources to gather, clarify, and synthesize facts about the issue. The students begin to identify values and value conflicts and raise questions about opposing views. The following should be considered when entering Phase II.

1. Prepare for an adequate number of days in the library or for working with other resources. The teacher should be prepared to give guidance to both the students and resource people when necessary. For example, the teacher may need to address interview techniques, help students learn to read for fact versus opinion, or assist with questionnaire design. The teacher may also find it necessary to touch base with resource personnel such as librarians to ensure that students get the information they need. (The reader will find Hungerford, Litherland, Peyton, Ramsey, and Volk, 1988, especially useful in developing this phase of the project.)
2. Allow time for the teams to be together to research, read, interview, survey, telephone, meet, discuss the issues and what they have found, and prepare each other for a public meeting.
3. Students can use encyclopedias, magazines, journal articles,

government publications, people, special interest groups, and a host of other resources. Probably the most overlooked resource will be the local or regional newspaper. It is important for the students to understand, when reading the newspaper, the difference between fact and opinion. Students may assume that an editorial, because it is in the paper, is fact.

Phase III: Synthesizing the Research Information into Arguments

At least one day prior to the public meeting, the students get back together as an intact class. At this point, the teacher will allow all of the teams representing the same side of the issue to get together to share information and prepare for the public discussion. It is during this time that the students need to plan a strategy for the public meeting. The following can be used as a guide for the students when in the large groups.

- Establish a stance based on factual information.
- Point out the undesirable or desirable consequences of a position.
- Clarify the value conflict with analogies.
- Set priorities; assert priority of one value over another.
- Identify factual assumptions and determine if they are relevant.
- Determine the predicted consequences and examine their factual validity (will they occur?).

During Phase III, the teacher will also select from the class a board of arbiters, two newspaper reporters, and two camera crew members. Each of these positions should be represented by both or all sides of the issue if possible. The following instructions are used to guide each of these roles in the debate.

Board of Arbiters

1. Prepare questions to ask each of the presenters. (These questions should be used for clarifying points.)
2. Plan a strategy for initiating and running the public meeting. This would include who will talk first, who will talk last, and how much time will be allotted for each side and each person. (It is suggested that each student present a part of the argument for their side of the issue. Approximately 2–3 minutes per student is adequate for this purpose.)
3. Be able to summarize those points that persuaded you in making your decision.

Newspaper and Camera Crew

1. Prepare questions to ask selected members of the groups involved in the debate. (It will also be necessary to decide who to interview.)
2. Be able to summarize the comments made during the interview.
3. Be able to summarize the comments made during the meeting. (For the camera crew, the comments will be summarized by editing the videotape and/or adding comments of their own.)

Phase IV: The Public Meeting

The fourth phase of the jurisprudential inquiry STS model involves the students in a mock public meeting. This meeting involves all students in presenting the different sides of the issue being studied. During the debate it is important that the students on the board of arbiters initiate and oversee the meeting. It is important also for the teacher to see that the following guidelines are followed.

- Maintain a vigorous intellectual climate where all views are respected.
- Avoid the direct evaluation of each other's opinions.
- See that issues are thoroughly explored.
- Respect the authority of the board.

Phase V: Clarification and Consensus

During this phase, students spend two days clarifying and arriving at a consensus on the issue. The first day is spent with the students still divided into the respective sides of the issue, the board, the newspaper crew, and the camera crew. During this time the students clarify their best arguments in support of the side of the issue they represented. The board will be responsible for clarifying why they rendered their decision. The newspaper crew and camera crew will work on preparing their respective reports.

On the second day, students separate into their original groups. The groups were originally constructed so that all perspectives of the issue would be represented. The purpose of these groups is to come to a consensus on the issue. The students should use all information available to them in drawing their conclusions. This would include information from the debate, the research done, other groups, the newspaper and camera crews' perspective, and the board's recommendations.

The students' cooperative effort should represent the opinions of all the students in the groups. Their goal is to write those arguments that justify the original group's position on the issue.

Phase VI: Application

The final phase of this model is the most important phase. It is in this phase that the students take what they have learned and apply it to their surroundings. Students must be able to see the value in the science they have learned and see that, with this knowledge, they can have an impact.

The first step of this process is for each student to propose an overall action plan with resolutions. Some of the ways students have applied what they have learned and became involved in community activities include:

- writing letters to city council, state representatives, state senators, governor, or mayor
- leading or participating in activities such as community cleanups, recycling activities, or petition drives
- attending city council meetings or local environmental meetings

Whatever actions students take should be assessed in light of their action-plan statements.

The key to this model of instruction is that students have opportunities to apply the investigation skills and action strategies to the community in which they live.

Teacher's Role

The teacher's role during this exercise is important. As the students are researching, discussing, and debating, the teacher should encourage the students to commit themselves to one side of the issue, but be supportive if they change their minds when confronted with new evidence, and encourage them to consider other points of view. At all times, the teacher should remain neutral on the issue, encourage differentiation of positions, and promote synthesis of the different positions presented to the class.

Summary

It is important to remember that STS issues are not things that a teacher can pull out of a book, they are not simply newspaper articles about issues in science, and they are not "discussing" an issue for ten minutes once a week. It is the integration of societal and technological issues that makes science content much more meaningful. The jurisprudential inquiry STS model can be used to accomplish that integration. Students must see the value of science. By using STS issues in this manner, students see how the issue impacts them and also how they impact the issue.

References

Hungerford, H. R., Litherland, R. A., Peyton, R. B., Ramsey, J. M., & Volk, T. L. (1988). *Investigating and evaluating environmental issues and actions: Skill development modules.* Champaign, IL: STIPES Publishing Company.

Johnson, R. T., Grooker, C., Stutzman, J., Hultman, D, & Johnson, D. W. (1985). The effects of controversy, concurrence seeking and individualistic learning on achievement and attitude change. *Journal of Research in Science Teaching, 22*(3), 197–205.

Joyce, G., & Weil, M. (1986). *Models of teaching.* Englewood Cliffs, NJ: Prentice-Hall, Inc.

Pedersen, J. E. (1990). *The effects of science, technology and societal issues, implemented as a cooperative controversy, on attitudes toward science, anxiety toward science, problem solving perceptions and achievements in secondary science.* Unpublished doctoral dissertation, University of Nebraska, Lincoln.

Slavin, R. E. (1989). Research on cooperative learning: Consensus and controversy. *Educational Leadership, 47*(4), 52–54.

10

STS: A Time for Caution

Morris H. Shamos
Professor Emeritus, New York University

The STS approach to science education, now entering its third decade, seeks to keep alive the hope that some degree of scientific literacy may yet be achieved in the general population merely by reorienting the focus of science education in our schools. Where in the past, preparation for responsible citizenship was often cited as a major rationale for requiring science of all students, STS formalizes the societal impact of science by incorporating it directly into the science curriculum. The question we face is whether the STS movement, which appears to have caught the imagination of at least part of the science education community, will be any more successful than past efforts to develop a meaningful—and durable—level of scientific literacy among our high school and college students. The prospects for this, while seemingly brighter on the surface, remain bleak for many of the same reasons that have long plagued the scientific literacy movement itself, namely, lack of a *clear-cut* definition of STS, including how and by whom it should be taught, and want of sufficient incentive on the part of students. More than this, however, STS suffers from a terminology that seems to promise more than it can deliver in the way of science understanding and has attracted a number of opportunistic, anti-technology fringe elements, both of which make it suspect in the eyes of many science educators. Conventional science education has not succeeded in persuading many students of the power of rational thought. Unless STS can do far better in this respect it too will have failed what is probably the major challenge of science education. There are good reasons for caution in looking to STS as a savior of either science education or of society, else it suffer the same fate as many other educational fads—a brief moment in the spotlight, followed by exile to the annals of educational history.

The Perceived Need for STS

First, it is instructive to examine the reasons why the science education community, and to some extent the scientific community itself, has become enamored of STS. The basic reason is that *conventional* science education does not achieve the goal of a fully literate public; it never has and many, including this writer, believe it never will. The usual argument is that the science we teach is not relevant to the students' everyday life, so that apart from being hard to learn—yes, make no mistake about it, science is difficult for the average student, despite all attempts to simplify it—there is no compelling reason for the general student to want to learn it.

Science is difficult for most students to master for at least two basic reasons. One is its cumulative nature, which makes it necessary to build our understanding of it like a tall edifice, layer by layer; it is this property, in fact, that most distinguishes science from other forms of intellectual activity. The other is its failure to accord with "common sense." While scientific inquiry generally begins with observations in the *real*, or everyday world, and in the end returns to that world in the form of technology, i.e., practical things, the steps in between, where the real *science* is done, is largely unfathomable to all but specialists. We have no common-sense counterparts for photons, genes, molecules, or black holes. When scientists talk about these phenomena they reason by means of models, abstractions (inventions, if you like) that agree with what is known about such phenomena—or more often, about their effects—but are not meant to be realistic images of the phenomena themselves.

Taken together, the cumulative nature of science and its reliance on descriptions that often defy common sense, make it necessary to devote extraordinary effort to the task of becoming scientifically literate. Most individuals, certainly the vast majority of students who do not plan to become scientists, appear to be unwilling to make this effort. Furthermore, there is no compelling incentive for non-science students to expend the effort required to become literate in science—and to seek to retain that literacy throughout their adult lives. Most students simply do not believe that being literate in science is essential to the "good life" in America, and contemporary society certainly bears them out. Indeed, the vast majority of our society obviously manages quite well in virtual ignorance of science. This is the crux of the matter; while enjoying the everyday comforts and benefits derived from science and technology, society has managed to insulate itself from any actual, or even perceived need to understand their origins (Shamos, 1988).

Hence, the basic premise of STS is that by making science relevant to the students' everyday lives we may cause them to take more interest in the subject and work harder to master it. Another argument in its favor is that by making science education *socially* relevant we may also be striking a blow for better citizenship. That is, by awakening in the students an awareness of societal issues that are said to be science-based, we may encourage them to take a greater interest both in the science *and* in the related social issues, to the effect that they should be able to play more effective roles as productive adult members of society. It all sounds highly worthwhile, but STS has some potentially fatal flaws, both conceptually and operationally, which if not guarded against may well defeat all its worthwhile objectives.

STS: An Identity Crisis

STS has a serious identity problem. It is not a discipline in its own right, but a multi-disciplinary research field that attracts scholars from a variety of disciplines, from the science and engineering professions to law, ethics, psychology, political science, philosophy, history, anthropology, sociology, and even the humanities—all drawn either by fundamental social concerns or by a professional interest in policy matters having to do with science and society. STS defies simple definition; in universities there are very few STS departments, mainly interdisciplinary "programs," with the usual problems of attracting academic and financial support to such non-mainstream activities. It is easy enough to define STS as a *scholarly* activity: namely, as "an attempt to understand the complicated two-way relationship between science and technology on the one hand and the rest of culture-society-politics on the other" (Keniston, 1989, p. 41). But such a definition sets the guidelines for a research activity, not for a high school science curriculum. STS still lacks a clearly-defined structure on which to build such a curriculum; nor is it apparent that it will be possible to establish such a structure in the foreseeable future, because of the conflicting views that surround the STS movement.

Thus, while STS has become a serious research field for many scholars from different disciplines seeking a better theoretical understanding of the dynamics of the science/society interface, where precise definition of the field is not so critical, efforts to bring STS into the classroom have been fragmented. Much has been written about the goals of STS education, and for the most part such goals seem commendable, but the question remains whether these objectives are really attainable or will STS turn out to be just an empty promise? Summed up briefly, the advocates of STS education assume that such education will better prepare students to live in an increasingly technological world by showing them the interconnections between science and technology on the one hand, and society on the other, in a more meaningful fashion than has proved possible in the past.

The big question, of course, is whether STS can take the place of conventional science for the general student. It must be admitted that STS offers one attraction not found in conventional science, namely, the opportunity for direct student involvement in issues that many consider to be science-related. One of the problems of science education is that at the student level there is little or no room for personal opinion—so students become passive participants in the learning process, asking questions but unable to contribute in a meaningful way to the science itself. The reason is that by the time science gets packaged into textbooks it has already attained consensus in the scientific community and any conceptual uncertainties or errors are likely to be so subtle as to fall outside the ability of students to suggest sensible alternatives. Science texts often contain errors, of course, because scientific theories are rarely complete, but almost never are the discrepancies of the sort that can stimulate meaningful classroom discussion. The result is that controversy, debate, and personal opinion—on which the keenest students seem to thrive—cannot play an active role in the *conventional* science curriculum, but can be a significant part of STS.

Some Concerns about the Effectiveness of STS

Unfortunately, STS has the potential for doing worse than conventional science courses by conveying a grossly misleading impression of science. First of all, it is a mistake to believe that STS can turn students on to science as such, for most societal issues that are said to be science-based are really based in technology. The list of societal issues that are truly *science-based* is very short indeed, encompassing mainly such questions as federal funding for research (e.g., space probes, the Supercollider, the Human Genome Project), or whether certain types of scientific research should be discouraged, or even prevented (e.g., animal experimentation, genetic engineering, human gene transplants). Hence, if any literacy is to be gained from STS, it is more likely to be some form of technological literacy rather than scientific literacy. Not that there is anything wrong with this; for if technological literacy can, in fact, result from STS education, plus at least an awareness of the partnership between science and technology, STS will have accomplished far more than all past attempts to provide students with some durable understanding of the overall scientific enterprise.

But I fear that STS may simply become a forum for social criticism of science and technology, which much of it already is. By its very nature, STS seems to attract certain fringe groups of technology critics, anti-scientists, modern-day Luddites, and those who see it as a convenient vehicle to lay many of the ills of modern civilization at the doorstep of science and technology. Should such groups be permitted to distort STS to their own design, or should STS become dominated by the social science community, (which, while obviously having an important role to play in the STS concept, nevertheless has a different agenda than the science education community) the STS movement, as a part of the school *science* curriculum, will eventually self-destruct.

Some thirty years ago C. P. Snow precipitated his well-known "two cultures" controversy in relation to the scientific and humanistic cultures. But now we also have a third culture, apparently growing in presence as well as in numbers, consisting of fringe elements that collectively may be termed "science counter-culturists" or even "irrationalists." Some are blatantly anti-science and anti-technology, others claim not to be anti-science but nevertheless are so by any rational standard, and then there is still another group which merely wants to remake science in its own image. The origins of the first two groups can be traced to real or imagined concerns about the effects of technology on the environment, or on the physical, economic, or psychological well-being of society. The third group, however, is motivated only partly by a desire for social reconstruction; most of all, in the guise of a human-centered natural philosophy, it seeks to overturn the very foundation of science, namely, respect for truth and rational thought. These counter-culturists, in fact, reject rationalism as the best way of dealing with the science-society interface, or even of trying to understand nature.

Science and technology have always had their share of critics, some serious-minded, others opportunistic, but these were minor annoyances compared to those now swarming about science (particularly about the STS movement) like honey bees about a new-found source of nectar. The reason is obvious; many look upon science, not as a force for progress, but as we have seen, a source of many of the ills of modern civilization; a convenient vehicle for criticism and confrontation. These critics are overwhelmed by the complexity of modern science, reject it and seek to adopt in its place various self-centered philosophies that appear to provide them with a gratifying "spiritual" awareness of the universe. It is little more than an escape from reality. Under the collective umbrella of the "New Age" movement, these doctrines range from the more profound efforts of Marilyn Ferguson to create a new social consciousness of the human potential (Ferguson, 1980), through the paranormal sleight-of-hand of crystal energy, mysticism, the absurd "psychic powers" of Uri Geller, and creative visualization, to the ridiculous "channeling" claims of the scientifically incompetent but otherwise accomplished actor, Shirley MacLaine. It might all be pretty harmless and merely entertaining to the readers of her (very successful) books were it not for the outright frauds and charlatans who use the channeling nonsense purveyed by MacLaine and her acolytes to prey on the gullible with extravagant pseudoscientific claims, thereby separating them from their savings—or perhaps worse. They are mentioned here not to recount their various forms of deception or outright larceny, which are thoroughly catalogued in the literature, but to point out that one of the many practical arguments in favor of improving the scientific literacy of all citizens is that it should help to minimize one's prospect of being victimized in this manner. However, if all that STS manages to improve is some form of social awareness it clearly cannot achieve this purpose.

The Anti-Technology Movement

This is the new wave of anti-technology, one that challenges the basic fabric of science and seeks to capture the minds of the scientifically illiterate. The fact that many of those who wish to counter the inroads of science and technology on modern life are basically illiterate in these enterprises is small consolation, for so too is most of society they seek to persuade. Should STS ever become dominated by such groups and individuals, whose notions of science echo those of Theodore Roszak (1973) and Paul Feyerabend (1978), who would destroy the practice of science as we know it, or of those like the political theorist, Langdon Winner (1977), and philosopher Joseph Turner (1990), who would "democratize" science and technology (but in whose image?), then STS as an educational movement is surely doomed, for the science and technology communities will then lose whatever interest they presently have in the subject. Debating the societal issues of science and technology, real though these may be, with self-styled social "thinkers" who are largely ignorant of these disciplines, is a clear waste of our time and energy. Indeed, the issues cannot even be fairly debated because of a non-level playing field. It is more than simply a battle of words between scientists and those social scientists, calling themselves "constructivists," who assert that, contrary to the scientists' view, nature cannot be studied objectively; rather, it is a sense that the constructivists are merely toying with science, ignoring what success its methods have produced and prepared to discard these methods in favor of unproven assumptions. Bruno Latour carries the relativist-constructivist position to the sublime by asserting that science consists mainly in the *power* of its proponents—that it matters little how shaky one's proof may be for a given statement about nature, as long as others can be made to believe it, by any possible means (Latour, 1987). And Steve Woolgar seeks to discredit science as a means of obtaining reliable information about natural phenomena, claiming that understanding nature (in the scientific sense) is not as important as devising alternate explanations for it that are more pleasing to the social scientist (Woolgar, 1988). This is characteristic of the "scientific theories" advanced by the constructivists, but is it not also the *modus operandi* of the con-man, the flimflam artist, and the scientific charlatan?

One group of self-styled Neo-Luddites, for example, takes off from the premise that all technologies are political and intrinsically harmful to mind or body; and actually favors dismantling certain ones, such as the nuclear, chemical, genetic engineering, television, electromagnetic, and computer technologies (Glendinning, 1990). It should be noted that the Neo-Luddite movement, while professing itself not to be anti-technology, seeks not only to justify nineteenth-century Luddism as responsible collective activism, but also rejects rationality as the cornerstone, not only of responsible behavior, but also of science and technology. To replace the technologies that the Neo-Luddites would demolish should be newly-created technologies that, in their words, "are of a scale and structure that make them understandable to the people who use them and are affected by them." Presumably, if society went back to the hand-tool days of centuries ago, well before the industrial revolution, the Neo-Luddites might be happier, but few others would. Think how degrading this rationale is to the society they seek to "protect." They seem to be saying, in effect, that since the general public does not understand modern technology, rather than seek to raise its level of understanding, we should lower the level of technology. This is an old tactic of those who find that the social sciences, having failed to attain the same precision and predictive status of the natural sciences, would shrink the latter to their own dimensions.

All this might easily be dismissed as the pure nonsense it is, were it not for the fact that to win converts the Neo-Luddites must capitalize on the very same public ignorance of technology that prompts it to propose such an absurd remedy. The appeal of the Neo-Luddite movement, as of all modern anti-science or anti-technology fringe movements, is to fear and emotion, not to the reasoned dialogue and debate that forms the cornerstone of science. Speculation, hearsay, anecdotal "evidence," half-truths, wishful thinking; these are the stock in trade of the Neo-Luddites and their supporters. They *capitalize* on doubt rather than seek to resolve it. Preying on fears of the unknown and ignoring risk-benefit assessments are standard practice of these modern-day Luddites, many of whom seem to view technology as a convenient vehicle to attack government, big business, and science itself. "The end justifies the means" appears to be their guiding principal. Against all such fuzzy reasoning and its affinity to uncritical thinking, scientists and science educators can appeal only to objectivity and respect for verifiable "truths." Unfortunately, as we all know, when reason conflicts with emotion, or even with what many would term "common sense," reason frequently loses out, making it easier for these fringe elements to strike responsive chords in the minds of many in contemporary society.

There are others that should be counted among the active anti-science groups focusing their attacks on science and technology, some because they are genuinely concerned over the adverse effects of specific technologies or for humane considerations, but others mainly for political or commercial reasons. Among the former we find the highly visible animal *rights* (as distinct from animal *welfare*) group, PETA (People for the Ethical Treatment of Animals), which, while effective in many of its efforts to improve the treatment of animals in scientific research, resorts to the same distortions and generalizations to prevent their use at all in research that are characteristic of the Neo-Luddites; even violence and terrorism are considered by the more activist members of this group to be justifiable means of achieving their goals. Jeremy Rifkin's Foundation on Economic Trends is a good example of an organization whose main purpose is political. Rifkin's philosophy seems to be, at the very least, to maintain the technological *status quo* and to sue in the courts to help achieve that end. He is a self-appointed "professional" guardian of people's rights, who seems to know the optimum issues to choose for maximum public relations effect, and knows too that the best way to get the publicity he needs to keep him in the public eye is to litigate. If there is any rationale that can be discerned in Rifkin's philosophy, it is simply that society is at the mercy of technology and hence any new technology should be looked upon with suspicion and cast aside if there is even the smallest risk attached to it. The problem is that the risks envisioned by Rifkin are generally based upon extrapolations from remotely related experiences, if not upon pure fantasy and speculation, rarely upon objective calculations, even in those cases where enough data are available on which to base reliable risk/benefit ratios. They confuse the possible with the probable. They take full advantage of the uncertainties in scientific knowledge, however small these may be in a particular instance, to argue that because the scientific community cannot *guarantee* the outcome of its endeavors, scientists should not be trusted to deal with the moral or ethical problems that may result from their work. The end also justifies the means, in their view, and the end they claim to seek is the control of science and technology by society; the same as the goal and practice of the Neo-Luddites and other social reformists.

There is perhaps one difference between Rifkin and most professed Neo-Luddites; where the latter would demolish existing technologies to suit their particular world-view, Rifkin seeks only to prevent or at least to delay new technologies (or new applications of known technologies) from coming on line, particularly in the field of biotechnology. But their scare tactics are the same: the more they can alarm the public the more support they are able to gain from it. And the formula seems to work; it works because democratic societies relish confrontational issues, especially when the other party to the encounter is big business, government, or specialist groups like lawyers, doctors, or scientists and engineers. College students are particularly attuned to such issues—it is far easier to get them interested in the context of technology than in the technology itself—and Rifkin takes full advantage of this through frequent appearances on college campuses. Using the courts to help achieve his ends also works to his advantage, at least up to a point; Rifkin's lawsuits have managed to delay for years some experiments in biotechnology, and were it not for the fact that he is able, through such legal actions, to publicize his social and philosophical concerns he would be just another voice in the crowded arena of professional activists and deliberate obstructionists. But the courts can be his ally only for a while; eventually, the lawsuits are resolved, usually on the side of reason rather than emotion, leaving behind only legal costs, frustrated scientists, and in the final analysis, possibly some cost in human life or suffering resulting from delays in conducting experimental trials of new developments in biotechnology. If ignorance is indeed bliss, Rifkin would keep society in a state of perpetual paradise.

These are but two examples of our failure to convince students (and the public generally) of the importance of reasoning with the mind instead of the heart, or even of showing them the power of rational thought as applied to science. Whatever efforts we make in our schools and colleges to develop in students John Dewey's exemplary "scientific habits of the mind," it is obvious that in the real world rational arguments fail to persuade much of society. Since Dewey's time it has been fashionable to point to science as the model of critical thought, but the anti-science and pseudoscience groups are aware that we have not succeeded in communicating this to students generally, which gives them free license to proclaim their aberrant views of science and technology and hopefully win over the students and the public to their dogma. So, do we give up on rationality and on our basic belief that science offers a means of studying nature *objectively*, both of which are rejected by these sociologists and fringe science groups, who would like nothing better than to insinuate their world view into, and gain control of, the STS movement. In a sharp rebuke to the professional irrationalists, the late philosopher, Charles Frankel (1973), analyzed their objectives:

> As a pragmatic matter, what irrationalism asks is that society invest less—or nothing at all—in maintaining the institutions, and the code of ethics and etiquette, which have proved necessary to support the emotion of reason . . . In brief, for the irrationalist, the universe is good; it is man, rational man, who has willfully made it evil, all by himself. Irrationalism, behind its long arguments and often impenetrable rhetoric, is an attempt to solve the ancient problem of Evil and to restate the ancient myth of the Fall. (p. 930)

And in pointing out how reasonable objections to some of the abuses of technology can breed unreasonable generalizations of the scientific enterprise, Frankel went on to say:

> The careful rational methods by which knowledge and technique have been advanced have only rarely been used to examine the purpose to which this knowledge and intelligence are harnessed. It is natural that science, in such a setting, should seem to be a Frankenstein to those who are threatened by it. (p. 931)

The irrationalists are not interested in science as such, but only in cutting it down to their own "size." The answer to this should be clear to all science educators: whatever the curriculum or style of teaching, respect for the rule of reason, for truth and for disciplined honesty must predominate, for these are the cornerstones of science, as they should be for all *responsible* behavior. If general education in science and technology is to have any meaning at all, at the very least it should help students to distinguish fact from fiction, science from pseudo-science, and rational arguments from irrational. For its survival STS must not become a platform for nonsense. Instead, the science class-room, and particularly that portion of it devoted to STS, should be the forum for debunking the attempts of such fringe elements to distort the public mind, first by exposing their tactics, and then by stressing over and over again the central role in science of *objective, reproducible* evidence.

References

Ferguson, M. (1980). *The aquarian conspiracy.* Los Angeles, CA: J. P. Tarcher, Inc.

Feyerabend, P. (1978). *Science in a free society.* London, England: New Left Books.

Frankel, C. (1973). The nature and sources of irrationalism. *Science, 180*, 927–931.

Glendinning, C. (1990). Notes toward a Neo-Luddite manifesto. *NASTS News, 3*(3), 6, 11.

Keniston, K. (1989, March). STS Symposium. (as reported by W. Lepkowski) *Chemical Engineering News*, p. 41.

Latour, B. (1987). *Science in action.* London, England: Milton Keynes, Open University Press.

Roszak, T. (1973). *Where the wasteland ends: Politics and transcendence in post-industrial society.* New York, NY: Doubleday Anchor Books.

Shamos, M. (1988). The lesson every child need not learn. *The Sciences, 28*(4), 14–20.

Turner, J. (1990). Democratizing science: A humble proposal. *Science, Technology & Human Values, 15*(3), 336–359.

Winner, L. (1977). *Autonomous technology.* Cambridge, MA: MIT Press.

Woolgar, S. (1988). *Science: The very idea.* London: Tavistock Publications

To be sure, STS can become an organizer for more than a science course or a series of science courses. When STS is the context for learning, the activities cross many traditional boundaries, including social studies, mathematics, technology, vocational subjects, language arts, and fine arts. STS provides more opportunities for learning because the whole world is a source for questions, a place to pursue answers, and a place to try correctives. STS can make school the microcosm of society that idealists have always proclaimed it to be. But our schools seem to be a long way from achieving this. Recent analyses (Goodlad, 1984) reveal that typical schools do not exemplify the dynamics of a real society at all.

In Part III, experts from social studies, mathematics, and technology provide insights to new directions, developments, and research in their disciplines. Obvious linkages and potential for collaborations exist. Part III also includes research and information about how students learn, which is vital as we analyze STS in a broader perspective.

Towards the end of this section, another important research topic is examined concerning school/community partnerships and how they improve the curriculum, enhance learning, and change the role of teachers. Throughout the process students are engaged in real life issues. They seek out information to use rather than memorizing it because teachers say they should. STS is seen as a way of generally improving schools and, specifically, student learning as well as a way of using material and human resources from the community at large.

Reference

Goodlad, J. I. (1984). *A place called school—Prospects for the future*. New York: McGraw Hill Book Company.

11

STS across the Curriculum: In Mathematics*

Thomas A. Romberg
University of Wisconsin

In March 1989, the *Curriculum and Evaluation Standards for School Mathematics* was released by the National Council of Teachers of Mathematics (NCTM, 1989). This document presents a vision of school mathematics that the authors argue is needed, makes sense, and is possible to realize. Whenever sweeping changes are called for in current practices, practitioners should be able to marshal evidence to support the recommendations. The purpose in this chapter is to present a summary of such evidence for reforming school mathematics. Similar evidence exists and is appropriate for school science. It is this same evidence that is used to advance the STS approach.

During the two years it took to prepare the *Standards* and review the literature, discussions were held with members of the Commission on Standards for School Mathematics and with members of the writing groups, and a library of materials was available to the writers; thus, scholarly evidence was considered in the preparation of the *Standards*. The primary sources of evidence are listed in the appendix of *Everbody Counts*, a document prepared by the Mathematical Sciences Education Board in 1989, that summarizes the need for reform. Other important syntheses of this scholarly evidence are: *Mathematics Counts* (Cockcroft, 1982) and "Problematic features of the school mathematics curriculum" (Romberg, 1992).

However, it should be understood that the *Standards* is not a research document; it is not a set of text materials to be followed by teachers in classrooms to improve test scores, nor is it a piecemeal set of recommendations to make current instruction in mathematics more efficient and effective. Rather, it was deliberately created to be a political document based on a consistent philosophical perspective about mathematics, about what it means to do mathematics, and about how one learns to do mathematics. It argues for systemic change in the way mathematics is viewed as a school subject. Thus, the evidence used in preparing the *Standards* is related to the need to change school mathematics and the nature of the suggested changes. The reader who is looking for research results about program effects, such as increased enrollments, improved test scores, and other specifics will be disappointed. Such evidence will be forthcoming when instructional programs are created to implement the vision in the *Standards*.

---

* A version of this article appeared in *School Science and Mathematics*, 1990, Volume 90, Issue 6, pp. 466–479.

The rest of this chapter will discuss two areas that provide support for the vision: (1) evidence of a need for change and (2) evidence that supports the direction of change.

Why Do We Need Change?

There is extensive evidence that the current system is not working well for most students or for the nation as a whole. Recently, the Mathematical Sciences Education Board (MSEB) produced two documents summarizing this evidence: *Everybody Counts* (1989) and *Reshaping School Mathematics* (1990). Without repeating their full arguments, let me highlight two sources of serious concern: student performance and the needs of business and industry.

The first evidence usually cited that the education system is in trouble is the bleak national performance data. For example, results from the National Assessment of Educational Progress (NAEP) in mathematics (Lindquist, 1989) show that although most students are reasonably proficient in computational skills, the majority do not understand many basic concepts and are unable to apply the skills they have learned in even simple problem-solving situations. Also, when compared with students in other industrialized nations, our students do not fare well (McKnight et al., 1987). We expect less of our students, they spend less time studying mathematics, and fewer are enrolled in advanced mathematics courses than are students in other countries (Travers & Westbury, 1989).

Further comparisons of our system with those in other industrialized nations reveal that teachers abroad are full-time employees; they are paid salaries equivalent to those for engineers; they are expected to teach fewer classes than in the United States; they have more help, more time for reflection and for interaction with others, and time to update and refresh their knowledge. In addition, parents are expected to help their own children. With this system, if students have difficulty, lack of effort or help is assumed to be the cause; in this country, poor student performance is usually attributed to lack of aptitude.

Turning to the performance and enrollment pictures, it appears bleak for women and most minorities. For example, on the average, black students complete approximately one year less of high school mathematics than their white classmates (Anick, Carpenter, & Smith, 1981). And beyond the classroom, women and most minorities are seriously underrepresented in scientific and technological careers; only 13 percent of this nation's scientists and engineers are women and only two percent are black (NSF, 1982).

This evidence cannot be ignored. By any criterion, typical U.S. students do not perform well; however, examining this evidence by itself may lead to inappropriate conclusions. Current, poor performance does not imply that there has been a decline in performance. In fact, American students have never scored well in NAEP tests (e.g., Carpenter, Reys, & Wilson, 1978), or compared favorably with students in most other countries (e.g., Husen, 1967). And contrary to a decline in performance, Beckmann (1970) presented evidence that students in 1965 were considerably more mathematically literate than a comparable group of students in 1950. Thus, it is naive to argue that educators should return to the practices of some romanticized past.

Other compelling support for change comes from business and industry. In fact, the *Standards* were produced in response to calls for reform in the teaching and learning of mathematics presented in *A Nation at Risk* (National Commission on Excellence in Education, 1983) and *Educating Americans for the 21st Century* (National Science Board Commission on Precollege Education in Mathematics, Science, and Technology, 1983). According to the arguments in these documents, schools were failing to educate students to be productive employees in the current workplace. Our current system of education is the product of an industrial era that has ended. The school mathematics curriculum still reflects the industrial needs of the 1920s, not those of the 1990s. The authors of the documents argue that to be economically competitive in the twenty-first century, all students will need to know more mathematics and a somewhat different mathematics than is currently taught in the programs of most U.S. schools.

The real cause underlying the need for change in school mathematics is the shift from an industrial to an information society (Zarinnia & Romberg, 1987). Several authors (Naisbitt, 1982; Shane & Tabler, 1981; Toffler, 1985; Yevennes, 1985) have described some of the attributes of the new age. It is based on a new technology that replaces the human and mechanical means of communication—the printed page—with electronic means by which information can be shared almost instantly with persons anywhere. Information is the new capital and the new raw material. Communication is the new means of production. One should recognize that the impact of technology is an economic reality, not merely an intellectual abstraction. Today, basic communication skills are more important than ever before, since they are both contributing to and necessitating a literacy-intensive society. Certainly it is no accident that "technology" is the connecting element of the STS approach. Advances in current technologies are recognized as the immediate value of science studies.

This shift has immediate consequences for schooling and in particular, for the teaching and learning of mathematics. The content and structure of the curriculum should not be focused on indoctrinating students with past values, but should be derived from visions of the future (Shane & Tabler, 1981). Students in schools today must prepare to be productive citizens in the twenty-first century. The culture in that era will, of necessity, be different from that of today. We must attempt to visualize some of the important features of that society if we are to prepare today's children adequately for that world.

Which Way Should We Go?

Being able to demonstrate that a genuine need exists is necessary to justify change, but good intentions do not guarantee good results. Satisfying the need will only occur if there are demonstrated connections between the need and the proposed curricular changes. After reviewing the history of how the current system of schooling has developed in the United States, it became apparent that what was needed was a fundamental restructuring of school mathematics. True also of school science, it is this challenge that STS addresses. As the authors of the *Standards* (NCTM, 1989) argue:

> In any field, when systems are not working, those involved in them must decide whether the problem is the result of a lapse in quality control, a design flaw, or a combination of the two. Quality-control solutions improve the efficiency and effectiveness of what is being done without disturbing its basic features. Design solutions fundamentally alter the organization of the systems themselves. Both of these solutions are applicable to the subject of school reform. Quality-control changes in education, for example, have included "recruiting better teachers and administrators, raising salaries, allocating resources more equitably, selecting better textbooks, adding (or deleting) content or course work, scheduling people and activities more efficiently, and introducing new versions of evaluation and training" (Cuban, 1988, p. 342). However, design changes in education "introduce new goals, structures, and roles that transform familiar ways of doing things into new ways of solving persistent problems . . ." (p. 342)

> . . . Given this distinction about strategies for change, it should be obvious that we see the *Standards* as an initial step in a design-change process (p. 251).

The underlying problem with the current system is that it is based on an industrial metaphor approach. Industrial metaphor schooling is analogous to an assembly line; students are the raw material input to the system; teachers are workers passing on a fixed body of mathematical knowledge by telling students what they must remember and do (mostly be proficient at carrying out algorithms); and the output of the system is judged by scores from tests. This approach is based on the need to efficiently prepare the majority of students to fit smoothly into a mass-production economy. To meet this need, knowledge is dealt with as an objective—learning as absorption, teaching as transmission and control. But today's information society demands something more. Our society now needs individuals who can continue to learn, adapt to changing circumstances, and produce new knowledge. Knowledge is seen as constructive, learning as occurring through active participation, and teaching as guiding.

The industrial metaphor has produced a coherent schooling system which needs to be replaced by an equally coherent but different system. The evidence which supports the direction of change advocated in the *Standards* comes from four areas.

1. Changes in mathematics
2. Changes in how one comes to know mathematics
3. Changes in classroom practices in the teaching of mathematics
4. Changes in how students and programs are assessed and evaluated

I will now examine each of these areas in more detail.

Changes in Mathematics

Mathematics in the current system is a fixed collection of concepts and skills to be taught and mastered in some strict order. The result is that the curriculum divides knowledge into subjects for study, such as arithmetic, algebra, and geometry. Furthermore, in each subject, knowledge is further broken down into clearly defined, independent, self-sustaining parts. There is a logical sequence of development in which each part builds on a preceding foundation, and if students acquire knowledge in this manner, they will be able to use and apply this knowledge as needed. This is where the NSTA Scope, Sequence, and Coordination project has started. The STS approach is being used as the instructional means of delivery.

Scheffler's (1975) denunciation of this traditional, mechanistic approach to basic skills and concepts illustrates the difficulties with the perspective.

> The oversimplified educational concept of a "subject" merges with the false public image of mathematics to form quite a misleading conception for the purposes of education: Since it is a subject, runs the myth, it must be homogeneous, and in what way homogeneous? Exact, mechanical, numerical, and precise—yielding for every question a decisive and unique answer in accordance with an effective routine. It is no wonder that this conception isolates mathematics from other subjects, since what is here described is not so much a form of thinking as a substitute for thinking. The process of calculation or computation only involves the deployment of a set routine with no room for ingenuity or flair, no place for guesswork or surprise, no chance for discovery, no need for the human being, in fact. (p. 184)

Westbury (1980) pointed to the fundamental problem: the difference between the intellectual structure in schools of the industrialized era of the past century and that needed for today's information society. Today the structure is an administrative framework for tasks, but administrative stability impedes intellectual change. What is now being argued is that this view of school mathematics fails to see mathematics as a growing, dynamic discipline.

In the past quarter of a century, significant changes have occurred in the nature of mathematics and in the way it is used. Not only has much new mathematics been discovered, but also the types and variety of applications have grown at an unprecedented rate. Most visible of the new applications, of course, has been the development of computers and the explosive growth of computer applications. Most of these computer applications have required the development of new mathematics in areas where applications of mathematics were not feasible before the advent of computers (Howson & Kahane, 1986). Less visible, but equally important, has been the enormous wealth of ideas generated in several main branches of mathematics linked by unifying concepts of widespread applicability (e.g., Board on Mathematical Sciences, 1986). Students must study the mathematics used in such applications in order to grasp the power of mathematics to solve real-world problems.

Computers and calculators have profoundly changed the world of mathematics. They have affected not only what mathematics concepts are important, but also how mathematics is done (Rheinboldt, 1985). It is now possible to execute almost all of the mathematical techniques taught from kindergarten through the first two years of college on hand-held calculators. This fact alone must have significant effects on the mathematics curriculum (Pea, 1987). Although most developments at the forefront of a discipline cannot generally be expected to have a major effect on the early years of education, the changes in mathematics brought about by computers and calculators are so profound as to require readjustment in the balance and approach to virtually every topic in school mathematics.

Based on these changes in mathematics, the *Standards* argues for a reduced emphasis on arithmetic computation, especially mastery of complex paper-and-pencil algorithms, and an increased emphasis on number sense and the appropriate use of operations, judging the reasonableness of results, and choosing appropriate procedures. Along with this is an emphasis on problem solving, including the use of word problems with a variety of structures, everyday problems, strategies for solving problems, and open-ended problems that take more than a few minutes to solve. Mathematical topics that are considered increasingly important, but are seriously underrepresented in current curricula, include geometry and measurement, probability and statistics, algebra, patterns, relationships, and functions.

Several recent documents support this direction of change in content emphasis: *Ordering the Universe: The Role of Mathematics* (Jaffee, 1984), "The Science of Patterns" (Steen, 1988), *Reshaping School Mathematics* (MSEB, 1990), *On the Shoulders of Giants* (MSEB, 1991), and *Problematic Features of the School Mathematics Curriculum* (Romberg, 1992). The primary fact that emerges is that the single greatest issue in improving school mathematics is to change the epistemology of mathematics in schools—the sense on the part of teachers and students of what the mathematical enterprise is all about. The notion that mathematics is a set of rules and formulas invented by experts, which everyone else is to memorize and use to obtain unique, correct answers, must be changed.

Changes in How One Comes to Know Mathematics

To some, knowing mathematics is to become proficient at arithmetic and algebraic calculations, which are learned by following given examples and repeated drills. Today, most agree that to be productive in the workplace and to be informed citizens in an information society requires more sophisticated mathematical knowledge.

Fortunately, there are some common assumptions, shared metaphors, and some findings about learning emerging in the shift in mainstream psychology in this country, from its associationist and behaviorist traditions to the study of cognition, that provide evidence about how one acquires knowledge (Calfee, 1981; Greeno, 1987; Putnam, Lampert, & Peterson, 1989; Resnick, 1987). Virtually all cognitive theorists share the fundamental assumption that an individual's knowledge structures and mental representations of the world play a central role in perceiving, comprehending, and acting. An individual's perception of the environment and his or her actions are mediated through cognitive structures that are actively developed and modified as a result of experiences. This mediation through cognitive structures provides a basic definition of knowledge in cognitive theories: Knowledge is the sum total of the cognitive structures of the individual knower. To know and understand mathematics from this perspective means one has acquired or constructed appropriate knowledge structures. From this basic view of knowledge, there has emerged a host of more specific views of what it means to know and understand mathematics, which Putnam, Lampert, and Peterson (1989) have summarized in terms of five themes.

- **Understanding as representation.** In particular, this refers to the view that understanding mathematics means having internalized powerful symbols and systems for representing mathematical ideas and being able to move fluently within and between them.
- **Understanding as knowledge structures.** A large portion of research in cognitive science has been directed at describing the knowledge, in the form of cognitive structures and processes, hypothesized to underlie competent performance on various mathematical tasks. This approach builds directly on the basic view that understanding exists in the capacity of an individual to construct or acquire appropriate knowledge structures.
- **Understanding as connections among types of knowledge.** Of particular interest are connections between conceptual and procedural knowledge and between knowledge of the formal, symbolic mathematics taught in school and the base of informal knowledge children develop in out-of-school settings.
- **Learning as the active construction of knowledge.** Researchers have highlighted the nature of the process by which knowledge structures have been constructed or acquired by individuals. From this perspective, learning mathematics with understanding means actively reorganizing one's cognitive structures and integrating new information with existing structures.
- **Understanding as situated cognition.** All knowledge is considered to be interactively situated in physical and social contexts.

These five themes were reflected in the NCTM (1989) *Standards* when the authors adopted "mathematical power" as the phrase most evocative of the quality of mathematical literacy sought for the entire population. Their perception of mathematical power regards individuals and societies as empowered by mathematics. Therefore, one needs to think about what it means to be mathematically powerful, both as individuals and as a society, and to consider ways of identifying mathematical power.

All societies create and use mathematics. Mathematical power for the individual means that each person has the experience and understanding to participate constructively in society. Over the ages, people have invented and used mathematics to count, measure, locate, design, play, conjecture, and explain. They have also examined its generalized abstractions and developed out of them further mathematics—whether explanations, designs, proofs, or new theorems—which may or may not have been practically applied (Bishop, 1988). They continue to do all of these, but in a rapidly increasing variety of contexts, in increasingly complex situations, and with shorter and shorter time spans for development.

The NCTM *Standards* argue that to be mathematically powerful in a mathematical and technical culture, students should develop the power to explore, conjecture, reason logically, and integrate a variety of mathematical methods effectively to solve problems. In becoming mathematical problem solvers, they need to value mathematics and to reason and use mathematics coherently to make sense of problematic situations in the world around them. Hence, the document advocates four standards that should be applied to all of the other standards: (1) mathematics as problem solving, (2) mathematics as reasoning, (3) mathematics as communication, and (4) mathematical connections.

Changes in Classroom Instruction

The profile of current mathematics instruction that emerges from a survey of practices has been described by Welch (1978) as follows:

> In all math classes I visited, the sequence of activities was the same. First, answers were given for the previous day's assignment. The more difficult problems were worked by the teacher or a student at the chalkboard. A brief explanation, sometimes none at all, was given of the new material, and problems were assigned for the next day. The remainder of the class was devoted to working on the homework while the teacher moved about the room answering questions. The most noticeable thing about math classes was the repetition of this routine. (p. 6)

The role of teachers in the traditional classroom is managerial or procedural in that "their job is to assign lessons to their classes of students, start and stop the lessons according to some schedule, explain the rules and procedures of each lesson, judge the action of the students during the lesson, and maintain order and control throughout" (Romberg, 1985, p. 5). Furthermore, the individual lessons are selected by teachers to cover an aspect of a concept or skill within a given time slot. In practice, however, teacher's decisions about what to select are often limited, in spite of apparent latitude to arrange schedules and select activities. In most schools, the mathematical concepts and skills to be taught are provided for teachers via a curriculum guide, a syllabus, or, most often, a textbook. Such materials rarely give teachers many alternatives. In this traditional classroom, the teacher's job is related neither to a specific conception of mathematical knowledge to be taught nor to an understanding of how learning occurs.

The argument in the *Standards* is that students are more likely to be powerful if they learn mathematics in the context of problematic situations. As students use this approach to mathematical content, they learn to formulate problems and develop and apply strategies to their solution, both within and outside mathematics. In a range of contexts, they verify and interpret results and generalize solutions to new problem situations. In so doing, they apply mathematical modeling and become confident in their ability to address real-world problem situations. As they reason through their problem situations, students develop the habit of making and evaluating conjectures and of constructing, following, and judging valid arguments. In the process, they deduce and induce, apply spatial, proportional, and graphic reasoning, construct proofs, and formulate counterexamples.

The problem situations referred to in the *Standards* are intended to be solvable by multiple approaches. Students need experience in a range of prototypical situations so that they can analyze their structure, finding essential features and ways that aspects are related. "Prototypical" is intended in two ways: prototypical in that the situation should be representative of the kind of cultural context that has traditionally given rise to mathematics (Freudenthal, 1983) and prototypical in the sense of the familiarity of the particular context to the student. In that context, students need to be able to pose a question, see the next question, evaluate a strategy, and construct and discuss alternative methods. Having done so, they need to examine assumptions and arguments and make efficient choices.

In summary, the nature of classroom instruction should move away from the model of teacher as teller and students as passive recipients of mathematical knowledge to an emphasis on learning mathematics through problem solving, discussion, and other practices consistent with the notion that students need to be actively involved. There are obvious parallels with these developments in mathematics to teaching science with the STS approach. These are indicated in nearly all other sections of this monograph.

Changes in Assessment

At present the nature, forms, purposes, and design of assessment are dominated by the prevailing industrial metaphor view that helps perpetuate it. In fact, the contemporary approach to testing is a conservative inhibitor to needed reform. McLean (1982) has stated that "achievement tests, as we have known them, are obsolete and teachers should discontinue their use as soon as possible" (p. 1). Hilton (1981) argued the issue even more strongly when he stated that current tests

> . . . force students to answer artificial questions under artificial circumstances; they impose severe and artificial time constraints; they encourage the false view that mathematics can be separated out into tiny watertight compartments; they teach the perverted doctrine that mathematical problems have a single right answer and that all other answers are equally wrong; they fail completely to take account of mathematical process, concentrating exclusively on the "answer." (p. 79)

Clearly, a most important challenge facing the reform movement is the development of appropriate evaluation strategies. Pressure for using current tests, especially at the elementary and secondary school levels, makes it difficult for curriculum reforms that do not produce test score gains to survive. Most current tests favor students who have acquired a considerable amount of factual knowledge and do little to assess either the coherence and utility of that knowledge or the students' ability to use it to solve problems (Romberg, Wilson, & Khaketla, 1990).

Conclusion

The current reform efforts in mathematics that are reflected in the *Standards* must encompass more than simple reactions to current weak-nesses. To remedy weaknesses, we cannot return to the same methods of curriculum development, classroom instruction, and pupil assessment that were used in the past. A coherent system of school mathematics needs to be developed based on complementary views about mathematics, about how one comes to know, about the nature of explorative instruction, and about the assessment of mathematical performance. The same is true for science and that is what the STS movement is about.

References

Anick, C. M., Carpenter, T. P., & Smith, C. (1981). Minorities and mathematics: Results from the National Assessment of Educational Progress. *Mathematics Teacher, 74*, 560–566.

Beckmann, M. W. (1970). Eighth-grade mathematical competence: 15 years ago and now. *Arithmetic Teacher, 17*(8), 334–335.

Bishop, A. J. (1988). *Mathematical enculturation: A cultural perspective on mathematics education.* Dordrecht, The Netherlands: Kluwer Academic Publishers.

Board on Mathematical Sciences. (1986). *Mathematical sciences: A unifying and dynamic resource.* Washington, DC: National Academy Press.

Calfee, R. (1981). Cognitive psychology and educational practice. In D. C. Berliner (Ed.), *Review of research in education* (pp. 3–74). Washington, DC: American Educational Research Association.

Carpenter, T. P., Reys, R. E., & Wilson, J. W. (1978). *Results from the first mathematics assessment of the National Assessment of Educational Progress*. Reston, VA: National Council of Teachers of Mathematics.

Cockcroft, W. H. (Chairman) (1982). *Mathematics counts*. London: Her Majesty's Stationery Office.

Cuban, L. (1988). A fundamental puzzle of school reform. *Phi Delta Kappa, 69*(5), 341–344.

Freudenthal, H. (1983). *Didactical phenomenology of mathematical structures*. Dordrecht, The Netherlands: D. Reidel.

Greeno, J. G. (1987). Mathematical cognition: Accomplishments and challenges in research. In T. A. Romberg and D. M. Stewart (Eds.), *The monitoring of school mathematics: Background papers, Vol. 2: Implications from psychology; outcomes of instruction* (pp. 3–26). Madison, WI: Wisconsin Center for Education Research.

Hilton, P. (1981). Avoiding math avoidance. In L. A. Steen (Ed.), *Mathematics tomorrow* (pp. 73–82). New York, NY: Springer-Verlag.

Howson G., & Kahane, J. P. (Eds.). (1986). *The influence of computers and informatics on mathematics and its teaching*. International Commission on Mathematical Instruction Study Series. Cambridge, MA: Cambridge University Press.

Husen, T. (Ed.). (1967). *International study of achievement in mathematics: A comparison of twelve countries* (Vol. 1). New York, NY: Wiley and Sons.

Jaffee, A. (1984). Appendix C. Ordering the universe: The role of mathematics. In National Research Council, The Commission on Physical Sciences, Mathematics, and Resources, *Renewing U.S. mathematics: Critical resource for the future. Report of the Ad Hoc Committee on Resources for the Mathematical Sciences* (pp. 117–162). Washington, DC: National Academy Press.

Lindquist, M. M. (Ed.). (1989). *Results from the fourth mathematics assessment of the National Assessment of Educational Progress*. Reston, VA: National Council of Teachers of Mathematics.

Mathematical Sciences Education Board. (1989). *Everybody counts: A report to the nation on the future of mathematics education*. Washington, DC: National Academy Press.

Mathematical Sciences Education Board. (1990). *Reshaping school mathematics: A philosophy and framework for curriculum*. Washington, DC: Author.

Mathematical Sciences Education Board. (1991). *On the shoulders of giants*. Washington, DC: Author.

McKnight, C. C., Crosswhite, F. J., Dossey, J. A., Kifer, E., Swafford, J. O., Travers, K. J., & Cooney, T. J. (1987). *The underachieving curriculum: Assessing U.S. school mathematics from an international perspective*. Champaign, IL: Stipes.

McLean, L. D. (1982). Achievement testing—Yes! Achievement tests—No. *E + M Newsletter, 30*, 1–2.

Naisbitt, J. (1982). *Megatrends: Ten new directions transforming our lives*. New York, NY: Warner Books.

National Commission on Excellence in Education. (1983). *A nation at risk: The imperative for educational reform*. Washington, DC: U.S. Government Printing Office.

National Council of Teachers of Mathematics. (1989). *Curriculum and evaluation standards for school mathematics*. Reston, VA: Author.

National Science Board Commission on Precollege Education in Mathematics, Science, and Technology. (1983). *Educating Americans for the 21st century: A plan of action for improving methematics, science, and technology education for all American elementary and secondary students so their achievement is the best in the world by 1995*. Washington, DC: National Science Foundation.

National Science Foundation. (1982). *Science indicators, 1982*. Washington, DC: U.S. Government Printing Office.

Pea, R. D. (1987). Cognitive technologies for mathematics education. In A. H. Schoenfeld (Ed.), *Cognitive science and mathematics education* (pp. 89–122). Hillsdale, NJ: Lawrence Erlbaum Associates.

Putnam, R. T., Lampert, M., & Peterson, P. L. (1989). *Alternative perspectives on knowing mathematics in elementary schools* (Series No. 11). East Lansing, MI: Michigan State University.

Resnick, L. B. (1987). *Education and learning to think.* Washington, DC: National Academy Press.

Rheinboldt, W. C. (1985). *Future directions in computational mathematics, algorithms, and scientific software.* Philadelphia, PA: Society for Industrial and Applied Mathematics.

Romberg, T. A. (Ed.). (1985). *Toward effective schooling: The IGE experience.* Lanham, MD: University Press of America.

Romberg, T. A. (1992). *Problematic features of the school mathematics curriculum.* In P. W. Jackson (Ed.), *Handbook of research on curriculum: A project of the American Educational Research Association.* New York, NY: MacMillan Publishing Company.

Romberg, T. A., Wilson, L., & Khaketla, M. (1990). *An examination of six standard mathematics tests for grade eight.* Madison, WI: National Center for Research in Mathematical Sciences Education.

Scheffler, I. (1975, October). Basic mathematical skills: Some philosophical and practical remarks. In *The NIE Conference on basic mathematical skills and learning. Volume I: Contributed position papers* (pp. 182–189), Euclid, OH. Los Alamitos, CA: SWRL Educational Research and Development.

Shane, H. I., & Tabler, M. B. (1981). *Educating for a new millennium: Views of 132 international scholars.* Bloomington, IN: Phi Delta Kappa Educational Foundation.

Steen, L. A. (1988). The science of patterns. *Science, 240,* 611–616.

Toffler, A. (1985). *The adaptive corporation.* New York, NY: McGraw Hill.

Travers, K. J., & Westbury, I. (Eds.). (1989). *The IEA study of mathematics I: Analysis of mathematics curricula.* Oxford, England: Pergamon Press.

Welch, W. (1978). Science education in Urbanville: A case study. In R. E. Stake & J. Easley (Eds.), *Case studies in science education* (pp. 5.1–5.33). Urbana, IL: Center for Instructional Research and Curriculum Evaluation, University of Illinois at Urbana-Champaign.

Westbury, I. (1980, January). Change and stability in the curriculum: An overview of the questions. In *Comparative studies of mathematics curricula: Change and stability, 1960–1980* (pp. 12–36). Proceedings of a conference jointly organized by the Institute for the Didactics of Mathematics (IDM) and the International Mathematics Committee of the Second International Mathematics Study of the International Association for the Evaluation of Educational Achievement (IEA). Bielefeld, Federal Republic of Germany: Institut fur Didaktik der Mathematik der Universitat Bielefeld.

Yevennes, M. (1985). The world political economy and the future of the US labor market. *World Futures, 21,* 147–157.

Zarinnia, E. A., & Romberg, T. A. (1987). A new world view and its impact on school mathematics. In T. A. Romberg & D. M. Stewart (Eds.), *The monitoring of school mathematics: Background papers, Volume 1: The monitoring project and mathematics curriculum* (pp. 21–62). Madison, WI: Wisconsin Center for Education Research.

STS in Social Studies— Research and Practice

Donald H. Bragaw
East Carolina University

The great educational reform waves of the past decade have not made great inroads in the field of social studies. Despite two or three major reports dealing with the topics of social studies and history in the last two years, the field remains as static as it ever was. A great deal of discussion and debate has taken place in academe, but there is little evidence of these new ideas being used in the classroom. If any change has occurred, it has tended to be a reinforcement of earlier configurations of social studies focused largely on increasing the amount of time for studying traditional history, with greater attention being paid to geography. The latter has been spurred on by huge financial commitments and publicity from the National Geographic Society in an effort to stimulate a renewed emphasis in that subject. National tests, of mixed validity, conducted by the National Assessment of Educational Progress have once again (as they do every five to ten years) shown students to be ignorant of history, geography, and civics. National surveys conducted by self-interested groups and independent agencies have all concluded there is an educational malaise in the area of social studies, for which little or no budgetary support for improvement is forthcoming from either government or private foundation sources (Bradley Commission on History in the Schools, 1989; NAEP, 1990; National Commission on Social Studies in the Schools, 1989).

It is in the global setting that social studies can play a significant role. As an effective, operating discipline concerned with the study of people in society (Bragaw & Hartoonian, 1988), (globally speaking) it calls for schools and colleges to reevaluate the unrealistic concentration of medieval discipline walls in the interests of human and Earth survival. Learning and instruction organized around the information and skills construct of STS is one way to link knowledge in a manner which will serve an "undisciplined" world (Goodlad, 1986–1987). This emphasis on citizenship/civic-responsibility calls for the refocusing of learning at all levels and in all subjects on public policy formation, implementation, and change. The two concentrations: (1) STS and (2) the willingness to take action through democratic means to control technology's power over both people and nature, are important elements of the preservation of humanity (Engle & Ochoa, 1988). Has social studies responded to that demand?

The research base for the existence of STS in social studies is extremely sparse and not very authoritative. It would be in order, however, to make some inferences about the presence of STS in social studies based on data about its presence in the teaching of science (Heilbron & Kevles, 1988). Because social studies, like science, is dominated by textbook teaching, it is fair to say that, given the cursory study done of social studies texts, little or nothing of significance is taught about STS in social studies instruction. Indeed, what does exist can be described as the "who" and "wow" school of textbook writing. The parade of names—Curie, Newton, Franklin, Einstein, and Salk—provides students with the notion that somehow and somewhere people do things that are called discoveries, and on the basis of the writer's say so, those discoveries are referred to as major. There is little or no discussion about the implications of those discoveries, or their potential effects upon social or economic policies of a nation or the world. The "wow" school of writing offers an exclamatory statement which the students are asked to accept at face value. The dropping of the atomic bomb, for example, falls in this category. The fact is stated, and the impact of its discovery and use goes unexamined in terms of its effect upon people or the world. In North American history texts, the bomb ends the war and saves large numbers of American lives, but barely deals with the thousands of Japanese lives that were lost in the holocausts of August 6 and 11, nor how the entire nature of foreign and domestic policy had now been changed by scientific break- throughs and a powerful, destructive technology (Bybee, 1990).

As for the number of social studies classes integrating STS, much less using it as their core, the statistics are numbing by their absence. Social studies teachers are not—by nature, implication, or direction—apt to include major elements of science or technology in their instruction. Hard-pressed to cover major substantive areas of history, geography, and civics, STS is not a prime subject for discussion—despite the overwhelming evidence that our society must come to grips with the forces of nature that threaten to engulf our economies and our survival. As Rodger Bybee, a leading STS proponent, has pointed out, without a commitment to deal directly with integrating STS into the classroom and obtaining the support needed to encourage it, STS will fade like so many other fads (Bybee, 1990). Structurally, schools and schedules are still not adaptable to change that would accommodate cross- discipline or interdisciplinary subjects (Jacobs, 1989). Education theoreticians and educational pragmatists have not yet met on the field of integrated knowledge. Our schools still resemble the monastic cells of the twelfth century in which the monk conveys the contents of the manuscript to yet another scroll.

STS: A New Role in Social Studies

Social studies is a field of study that is complicated by being a broad and interdisciplinary subject. History, geography, and something called "civics" have been the major emphases—but the social sciences and the humanities have added conceptual spice to the configuration of topics. Other topics such as law-related education, global education, career education, and a host of others have been infused, "unitized," or created as separate courses over the years, adding to the social studies confusion. For many teachers, adding another topic such as STS as yet another area of study might serve only to tip the balance from being sensible about what is possible for teachers to teach and students to learn. That is true, however, only if one accepts the fact that STS is just another discreet subject or topic that needs to be explored, studied, and tested. The only way in which STS can logically, and sensibly, be included is to realize that it is raising issues of life and death for not only people but for the Earth itself, which people should study, understand, and respond to as public issues of a critical dimension. None of the other subjects or topics can make a claim such as that. But even that rationale for the addition of STS has not yet reached the status of a critical imperative in the school curriculum.

But, in spite of a lack of research or change, there has been major activity concerning STS among major social studies organizations. The National Council for the Social Studies (NCSS), the major professional voice of the profession, has recently revised its guidelines on the teaching of science, technology, and society. The guidelines address the issues of public knowledge, responsibility, and public action (NCSS, 1990). The original guidelines, asserting that "both the scientific and social science community must share a responsibility for helping students understand the effects of science" (NCSS, 1982), emphasized process learning of how to help students choose and then investigate science-related social issues. In the tradition of the 1970s, problem-solving had become the focus while substance was relegated to the background.

In the new guidelines there is clearly a major shift in emphasis: teachers must become knowledgeable in both science and technology and their social ramifications. There is an urgency in the new guidelines not present in the first set: "As scientific knowledge has increased and technology has become more complex and pervasive, people have found that technology can bring major benefits as well as significant costs to society" (NCSS, 1990, p. 189). It is from this perspective that the new guidelines advocate a participatory, public-issues orientation.

In addition to the guidelines, NCSS has also devoted significant space in its publications to encourage STS issues and programs and provide instructional suggestions. Over thirty years ago, NCSS issued a yearbook entitled *Science and the Social Studies* (Cummings, 1957). While not recognized as one of the first "STS" publications, the book was a milestone in an attempt to emphasize the STS nature of the world and build bridges between science and social studies programs. William H. Cartwright, the president of NCSS at the time, wrote prophetically in his introduction to the volume:

> The yearbook does make it clear that the natural sciences and the social sciences are not independent of each other and that the progress of society is intimately bound up with both. Whatever the organization of the curriculum, the sciences and the social studies cannot be completely separated. The impact of science on society is a social phenomenon. The effects of scientific progress on technology, agriculture, health, and war are social. They must be reckoned within the social studies (Cummings, 1957, p. viii).

In 1978, a major bulletin (a modified yearbook) entitled *Science and Society: Knowing, Teaching, and Learning*, asked social studies teachers to become conscious of the societal implications of the problematic advances of science and the technology it spawned (Charles & Samples, 1978). The articles focused on scientific thinking and how that thinking could impact on the nature of the society we live in. The bulletin was fervently optimistic but also laid out the pitfalls of uncontrolled science as well. It encouraged teachers to see the connections between science and social studies. The incentive for this bulletin had come from a recently formed (1975) Science and Society Committee of NCSS, a committee whose formation illustrates how much importance this organization began to give to the discussion of the social implications of scientific advances and problems.

In 1989 the Council issued *From Information to Decision Making*, which deals with the impact computer technology can have on the decision-making process. The publication asserts that we must train children how to use that technology for the benefit of all (Laughlin, Hartoonian, & Sanders, 1989). Issues of the Council's major publication, *Social Education*, have consistently highlighted the STS theme. A major portion of the April/May 1990 issue was devoted to the relation of STS to social studies and specifically on ways in which creative social studies departments and innovative teachers could implement STS programs. Suggestions included infusing, extending present units, and creating special courses. A forceful argument was also presented for STS as a natural integrator for programs across discipline lines.

The Social Science Education Consortium (SSEC) in Boulder, Colorado, has a long tradition of initiating and participating in STS projects (Benne & Birnbaum, 1978; Patrick & Remy, 1985). A recent key effort has been a program to help state agencies promote STS programs within their states. The program consists of a framework, a set of practical STS strategies for science teachers and another one for social studies teachers (with interdisciplinary suggestions), and a workshop manual for supervisors to use in implementing the statewide effort. The major feature of the framework is its clear attempt to encourage interdisciplinary cooperation in the areas of science and social studies in several ways.

Another project of the SSEC still in the field testing and refining stages is a set of six computer-assisted, decision-making modules on STS subjects. The modules will concern toxic waste, pesticides, AIDS, garbage, electronic surveillance, and robotics in the workplace. SSEC is also working with the Biological Sciences and Curriculum Services Center to further refine a curriculum framework dealing specially with the biological aspects of STS issues. SSEC will continue to play a major role in promoting STS in the social studies and sciences curricula.

STS has also become prominent in the field of history. History Day in 1989, a national program to encourage research, study, and hands-on history at the elementary and secondary levels, concentrated on the topic "Science and Technology in History." A further indication of emerging interest in STS in the academic field of history is the publication of an entire issue devoted to STS topics in the *Magazine of History,* a magazine for history teachers published by the Organization of American Historians. This effort complements an emerging interest within the field of history in the history of science. Increasing numbers of sessions on the history of science are available at professional meetings, and programs such as the University of Florida's History of Science, Technology, and Medicine are receiving NEH and NSF funding. Although both the Bradley Commission on History in the Schools and the National Commission on Social Studies in the Schools recognized the significance of the technological advancements on historical development, neither report has shown evidence of any clear direction for schools to adopt STS topics or themes.

While research on STS and its potential application to social studies is relatively sparse (although significant), there is ample evidence of both materials and programs that either exist or are in production. STS materials for schools and teachers to use are available; it is the will and appropriate incentives to use them that are yet to come. With the global environmental crises coming increasingly to the attention of schools, STS may well come into its own as a very logical and practical way to deal with this new imperative.

References

Benne, K., & Birnbaum, M. (1978). *Teaching and learning about science and social policy.* Boulder, CO: The Social Science Consortium.

Bradley Commission on History in the Schools, The. (1989). *Building a history curriculum.* Washington, DC: Author.

Bragaw, D. H., & Hartoonian, H. M. (1988). Social studies: The study of people in society. In R. S. Brandt (Ed.), *The content of the curriculum* (pp. 9–29). Alexandria, VA: Association for Supervision and Curriculum Development.

Bybee, R. (1990). The Science-technology-society (STS) theme in science curriculum: Policies to practices. Manuscript submitted for publication.

Charles, C., & Samples, B. (Eds.). (1978). *Science and society: Knowing, teaching and learning.* Washington, DC: National Council for the Social Studies.

Cummings, H. H. (Ed.). (1957). *Science and the social studies.* Washington, DC: National Council for the Social Studies.

Engle, S. H., & Ochoa, A. S. (1988). *Education for democratic citizenship: Decision making in the social studies.* New York, NY: Teachers College Press.

Goodlad, J. I. (1986–1987). A new look at an old idea: Core curriculum. *Educational Leadership, 44*(4), 8–16.

Heilbron, J. L., & Kevles, D. J. (1988). Science and technology in U.S. history textbooks: What's there—and what ought to be there. *History Teacher, 21,* 425–438.

Jacobs, H. (1989). *Interdisciplinary curriculum.* Alexandria, VA: Association for Supervision and Curriculum Development.

Laughlin, M. A., Hartoonian, H. M., & Sanders, N. M. (Eds.). (1989). *From information to decision making: New challenges for effective citizenship.* Washington, DC: National Council for the Social Studies.

National Assessment of Educational Progress. (1990). *The U.S. history report card.* (Report No. 19–14–01) Washington, DC: U.S. Department of Education.

National Commission on Social Studies in the Schools. (1989). *Charting a course.* Washington, DC: Author.

National Council for the Social Studies. (1982). *Teaching science-related social issues.* (Position Statement) Washington, DC: Author.

National Council for the Social Studies. (1990). Teaching about science, technology and society in social studies education for citizenship in the 21st century. (Position Statement and Guidelines) *Social Education, 54*(4), 189–193.

Patrick, J. J., & Remy, R. (1985). *Connecting science, technology and society in the education of citizens.* Boulder, CO: The Social Science Consortium.

13

STS in Vocational Areas

Leno S. Pedrotti

Center for Occupational Research and Development

Today the advent of rapidly changing technologies, both at home and abroad, clearly signals the need for an educational system that combines the best in vocational and academic learning—that is, teaching academic science courses in a vocational setting. Such a strategy is generally referred to as applied science.

But there is a difference. The academic science courses referred to here are not the largely abstract, theoretical courses generally made available to the four-year-college-bound population. Rather, they are full-fledged academic science courses taught in such a way as to engage the "concrete" learner who is more likely to be in a technical program of study.

Who the Applied Science Courses Serve

The applied science courses target the average student in the middle quartiles of the average high school population. These general students—often referred to as the forgotten half—are not usually headed for four-year degree programs. They may go to work immediately after high school or pursue technical careers requiring two years or less of post-secondary education for which they need a strong background in science. However, educators have discovered that the needs of the forgotten half cannot be met by requiring them to earn more credit in traditional courses. Frequently, the only science courses available to them are those that prepare students for entrance into four-year degree programs. Thus, these students tend to avoid such courses, if possible.

Applied science is designed specifically for the way these average students learn. Their learning needs are best met by courses that emphasize the application of abstract concepts in the real world and involve them in hands-on learning. By being exposed to science in this manner, these students are much more likely to take traditional courses in the future (Carter & Atkinson, 1989; Gloeckner, 1990; and Owens, 1990).

For example, here is what science teacher Patsy Rivers—who teaches both *Principles of Technology* (applied science) and the regular physics course at Hickman County High School in Centerville, Tennessee—says (personal communication with Patsy Rivers, 9/92). As a result of taking *Principles of Technology* in the ninth, tenth, or eleventh grade, students who would not ordinarily elect physics as a science course are now doing so in increasing numbers. In the hands-on oriented, *Principles of Technology* course, they develop confidence and interest in science and choose physics in their senior year. During the 1989–90 and 1990–91 years, one-fourth of her physics class was made up of *Principle of Technology* completers. In the 1991–92 year, over half of the physics class (9 of 17) had taken *Principles of Technology* earlier.

The Need for Applied Science Courses

The importance of applied science courses in the careers of many students is apparent from projections of the U.S. Department of Commerce. Among the emerging technology groups projected to have a significant economic impact by the turn of the century, four are biology and chemistry related: biotechnology, medical technology, advanced materials, and thin-layer technologies. Infusion of these technologies into the work force requires technicians with a foundation in biology and/or chemistry.

Other examples of technologies relying on this foundation are nuclear power technology which depends upon chemical processes to concentrate isotopes, new lasers that require large crystals grown by chemical techniques, and interferon cancer therapy which is possible because of the development of recombinant DNA.

A foundation in physics has numerable applications as well. Technicians must understand the mechanical, fluid, electrical, thermal, and electronic principles on which modern equipment operates. Workers who understand the technical concepts and principles underlying modern technology will be able to work more effectively in areas such as automotive repair, equipment servicing, industrial plant maintenance, and telecommunications. As these and many other technical fields continue to develop into major industries, large numbers of workers who understand basic science concepts and processes will be needed. In addition, workers will be needed who can apply scientific knowledge in traditional occupational areas such as health care, agriculture, and home economics.

Accomplishments of the Applied Science Curriculum

Principles of Technology, the first of the applied science courses, was introduced in the fall of 1986. It is now being used by over 60,000 students in 49 states and two Canadian provinces. Publications such as *Science Books & Films* (American Association for the Advancement of Science) evaluated *Principles of Technology* with "good" to "excellent" ratings for accuracy, currency, organization and coherence, comprehensibility for certain groups of students, and for its treatment of science, technology, and society interrelationships.

In three independent studies, *Principles of Technology* has been shown to increase student knowledge of applied physics—as differentiated from conceptual physics—to a level comparable to the baccalaureate-bound students who take the traditional high school physics course (Baker, Wilmoth, & Lewis, 1992; Dugger, 1988; Roper, 1989). Again, the significant fact here is that the students who succeed in *Principles of Technology* are among the segment of the high school student population that does not normally study physics. It also is important to note that an increasing number of public and private universities recognize *Principles of Technology* as satisfying a laboratory science entrance requirement.

Applied Biology/Chemistry, the most recent of the applied science courses, is still under development. Pilot testing of the first-year materials began in the fall of 1990, with over 100 pilot sites among 34 states in operation. In addition to the state members of the consortium, seven corporations and businesses have offered their support in the development of hands-on laboratories to serve the *Applied Biology/Chemistry* curriculum. In the three sections that follow, the pedagogical content and delivery of *Principles of Technology* and *Appled Biology/Chemistry* are summarized.

Principles of Technology

Principles of Technology is based on a course entitled *Unified Technical Concepts* (UTC) *in Physics,* which was developed by the Center for Occupational Research and Development (CORD) for post-secondary technical training. The central idea of the UTC course is that a unifying approach to physics is beneficial in the study of the basic energy systems—mechanical, fluid, electrical, and thermal. Unification is developed by demonstrating that concepts such as force, work, rate, and resistance apply and operate analogously in each of the four energy forms.

This applied science course was developed through a cooperative effort of 45 state and provincial (Canada) education agencies in association with the Agency for Instructional Technology (AIT) and CORD. The education agencies provided over three million dollars for the creation of *Principles of Technology* and tested the curriculum in approximately two schools per state. Following the test phase, the same education agencies took a lead role in introducing and implementing broad use of the course within their service areas. There are now 49 states, two Canadian provinces, and five other countries in the *Principles of Technology* consortium.

Principles of Technology is a high-school course in applied physics for students pursuing technical careers. It is a two-year curriculum course covering fourteen units (see Table 1). The curriculum is designed to be taught either in comprehensive high schools or in vocational-technical centers to tenth- and eleventh-grade students who do not necessarily plan to enroll in four-year colleges and universities in engineering or science programs. However, field tests have indicated that the course can also be used successfully for vocational students in all fields and students in a college-bound track. In addition, organizations are considering the use of *Principles of Technology* to retrain technical workers for high-technology jobs. The course may also be appropriate for science remediation by students entering technical programs in community and technical colleges.

Table 1

Sequencing of *Principles of Technology* Units	
First Year	**Second Year**
Force	Momentum
Work	Waves
Rate	Energy Convertors
Resistance	Transducers
Energy	Radiation
Power	Optical Systems
Force Transformers	Time Constants

Principles of Technology is taught in seven units in the first year and seven in the second year. Each unit shows how an important concept in physics—such as force—can be analyzed and applied to equipment and devices in mechanical, fluid, electrical, and thermal energy systems.

The first six or seven units can be taught as a stand-alone course for students who need a one-year applied science course and require a background in the technical fundamentals. The second year of the course (units 8–14) is most useful to students who plan to continue their study and to work in advanced technology occupations.

Materials developed and tested for *Principles of Technology* include student texts, videocassettes, classroom demonstrations, mathematics labs, hands-on labs, and tests. A teacher's guide for each unit suggests presentation strategies, information about how to perform classroom demonstrations, and additional information for problem-solving labs.

Applied Biology/Chemistry

Applied Biology/Chemistry is an integrated set of competency-based materials that can be infused into existing courses or taught as a stand-alone course. This course presents biology and chemistry in the context of work, home, society, and the environment. The *Applied Biology/Chemistry* materials include twelve instructional units containing video segments, laboratory activities, student texts, teacher guides, and resource books.

Table 2

Learning Units for *Applied Biology/Chemistry*	
Natural Resources	Disease and Wellness
Water	Life Processes
Air and Other Gases	Synthetic Materials
Plant Growth and Reproduction	Waste and Waste Management
Continuity of Life	Microorganisms
Nutrition	Community of Life

Each of the twelve units in *Applied Biology/Chemistry* includes two to six instructional units. Each unit includes its own set of objectives and learning activities.

The units involve students in experiences related to occupations and other life situations. Students study subject matter in terms of the central themes of science. All student activities emphasize applications, connecting the more abstract work of scientific principles to that of concrete experience. Course content is conveyed through learning activities that lead to mastery of specific objectives. The activities also allow students to learn how the central themes of science are relevant to work and other real-world situations. Activities may also include text readings, lectures, demonstrations, video segments, hands-on laboratories, and field experiences.

Hands-on learning activities are heavily emphasized, constituting at least 40 percent of the courses. The learning goals of each unit of *Applied Biology/ Chemistry* place particular emphasis upon higher-order cognitive processes. Students are required to demonstrate the ability to use the principles of biology and chemistry in solving problems and making decisions.

Elements of the Applied Science Courses

Instructional materials in the applied science courses —*Principles of Technology* and *Applied Biology/Chemistry*—include a student text with lab activities, a video, a teacher's guide, a bank of test questions, and a resource guidebook.

The **Student Text** lists objectives, introduces the topic of study, provides explanations to guide discussion of the subject matter, and provides opportunities for hands-on learning experiences. About 40 to 50 percent of instructional time is spent in hands-on activities that allow students to have experience in laboratory and field situations similar to or related to those encountered at work, in the home, or in the community.

The **Video** for a specific unit may include an overview at the beginning and a summary at the end; sequences showing occupational applications of science concepts; demonstrations that are hazardous or expensive to set up; tutorial sequences on difficult-to-explain topics, graphics, diagrams, animation, and illustrations. The primary functions of the video are to motivate students, to present role models, and to introduce scenarios for group discussion and problem-solving.

The **Teacher's Guide** provides suggestions for effective use of the course materials and suggests ways of organizing laboratory activities and setting up demonstrations. Solutions to lab problems are furnished and study questions are explained.

A **Student Test Bank** contains test items and answers from which teachers may develop their own tests.

The (implementation) **Resource Book** and overview video introduces the course and materials to administrators, counselors, teachers, students, parents, and business and community leaders. This introduction is useful for training teachers and facilitating start-up, evaluation, and maintenance of the instructional system.

Applied Science Creates a Foundation for a Career in Science

It is important to note that while these applied science courses are designed for the non-baccalaureate-bound students, the curriculum is rigorous in its approach to science. Non-baccalaureate-bound students need to understand and use mathematical and scientific principles in their work and daily lives. They need good science, taught in understandable, practical ways. The applied science courses provide an excellent foundation for students who discover latent interests in science and who choose to continue their study by taking traditional science courses later in their careers. In fact, as mentioned earlier, evidence indicates that the applied science courses in use stimulate students to take additional courses in science.

Part of the success of applied science courses is that they often serve as stepping stones to careers in science. For example, *Applied Biology/Chemistry* can serve in technical programs that train paraprofessionals in emerging technologies such as biotechnology and advanced materials, or in more traditional areas such as health care, food services, food processing, and agriculture/aquaculture. Those students who may be interested in entering these careers often avoid the in-depth science courses in high school. But the applied science courses can provide these students the opportunity to obtain basic science competencies without jumping directly into a traditional science course.

Responses to the Applied Science Curriculum

Success of the applied science curriculum can be measured in several different ways. Since the initial use of *Principles of Technology* in August 1985, responses to the curriculum have come from all areas of the education field including administrators, teachers, parents, and students. Verbal, written, and statistical responses have underscored the effectiveness of *Principles of Technology* and *Applied Biology/Chemistry*.

In April 1989, survey instruments were disseminated to gather student, teacher, and administrator opinions regarding *Principles of Technology* (PT) I and II, implemented in Colorado during the 1989–90 school year. Survey results (Gloeckner, 1990) revealed that:

- 71 percent of the students earned an "A" or "B" in their first semester PT class
- 47 percent of the students who responded stated that they planned to enroll in a science course next year; 34 percent indicated that taking PT made them want to enroll in future science courses
- 80 percent of the students who responded agreed that PT classroom demonstrations clarified mathematics and physics concepts for them

- 67 percent of the students felt that PT instruction, as compared to other traditional science courses, better prepared them for a technical career

Aside from research data, *Principles of Technology* has also helped students increase their enthusiasm and interest about school and science. The responses from many of the *Principles of Technology* teachers, students, and administrators in the field clearly indicate that applied science is a win/win experience for all involved.

Even though the *Applied Biology/Chemistry* curriculum is still under development, many of the teachers who are using the materials at the preliminary pilot-sites have made positive note of the results in their classrooms. A recent questionnaire for the first two units was sent to 55 teachers and 959 students. The teacher responses indicated that:

- 83 percent rated the format and organization of the text as "good" or "excellent"
- 81 percent said that the eighth-grade reading level was accurate
- 86 percent stated that the Teacher's Guide provided "enough" or "more than enough" information to help teach the units
- 83 percent said the level of instruction was appropriate for most of the students in the class
- 79 percent said that the students seemed to enjoy the units (Owens, 1990)

Summary

An understanding of scientific concepts is critical to productive living and working in a technological society. The theory-oriented courses currently dominant in secondary schools meet the needs of many college-bound students but are not adequate for those students who learn best through materials taught in the context of major life issues and materials that provide hands-on learning opportunities. Admittedly, a large number of college-bound students might learn best this way as well. The applied science materials are designed to prepare general students for technical jobs, to help them deal successfully with technological change, and to increase their readiness for future education or training.

References

Baker, R. A., Wilmoth, J. N., and Lewis, B. (1992). *Factors affecting student achievement in a high school Principles of Technology course: A state case study.* Auburn, AL: Auburn University, Center for Vocational and Adult Education.

Carter, L. and Atkinson, J. (1989, March 19–24). *How will tomorrow's leaders learn technology today?* Paper presented at the 51st Annual Conference, International Technology Education Association, Dallas, Texas.

Dugger, J. (1988). [Comparative study of principles of technology]. Ames, IA: Iowa State University, unpublished raw data.

Gloeckner, G. (1990). Oral communication, June 1990. (Based on state-wide survey in Colorado carried out by Professor Gloeckner, Colorado State University, Fort Collins, CO.)

Owens, T. R. (1990). *Applied biology/chemistry pilot test report.* (Published report). Portland, OR: Northwest Regional Educational Laboratory.

Roper, J. (1989). Technology creates a new physics student. *The Physics Teacher, 27*(1), 26–29.

Students and Learning: Student Conceptions of the Social Sciences and Social Institutions

Dennis W. Cheek
New York Science, Technology, and Society Education Project at the New York State Education Department

To have a comprehensive view of STS, one needs to consider the ways in which data and theories from the social sciences bear upon STS issues. Historic disciplines such as sociology, anthropology, psychology, economics, and political science all have the potential of informing citizen debate and decision-making on pressing STS issues, but no less important is the consideration of these areas by students confronting STS issues in the classroom (Cheek, 1992).

As has been seen in children's constructions in the world of science education, students' minds are clearly not blank slates upon which the teacher and the set curriculum write.

Need for a Constructivist Teaching Approach

Educational research, going as far back as the pioneer work of Stanley Hall (1883, 1891), has pointed out the need to consider the conceptions that students bring with them to the classroom. Every student brings a set of cultural baggage, perceptual lenses through which to see the world, deep-rooted philosophical and metaphysical beliefs, and social relationships both within and outside that particular class. All of these factors come into play when a student is asked to consider an STS issue or any other learning situation. A constructivist teaching approach, which reckons seriously with both the prescribed curriculum and the prescribed student and his or her existing views, is fundamental to good instruction and quality learning (Driver, 1988; Driver, Guesne, & Tiberghien, 1985).

Students' own views about social science disciplines and social institutions affect the manner, scope, and depth of insight into pressing STS issues. A student, for example, who believes that elected officials are not responsive to the wishes of their constituency is not likely to consider citizen involvement in the siting of a hazardous waste facility worthwhile. Students who believe that national and state laws are "handed down from on high" are not likely to involve themselves in either advocating new legislation or nonviolent noncompliance with existing laws (e.g., in the American civil rights movement).

While identification and understanding of the development of children's beliefs and perceptions of the social sciences and social institutions is a relatively new research area, there is sufficient data to warrant a discussion of its implications for STS education. The remainder of this analysis will consider salient research in the areas of politics, law, economics, inequality, and society at large.

Students' Views of Politics

Numerous theories over the past three decades have attempted to detail the process of political socialization (e.g., Hyman, 1959). Data for an exploration of political awareness was first collected by Fred Greenstein in 1965. Since then, increasingly sophisticated techniques resulted in an instrument to measure children's civic attitudes in different nations (Oppenheim & Torney, 1974). The 1980s saw an increased interest in the use of clinical interviews, supplemented by information collected by written instruments. Stevens (1982) reported on a study of British seven- to eleven-year-olds who were individually interviewed. The research team's interest focused on political awareness and, by inference, political socialization.

Seven-year-olds were found to have some political awareness and working vocabulary regarding politics. Their ideas were characterized by the researchers as "intuitive and symbolic" with ideas that were "discrete and unstructured" (Stevens, 1982, p. 149). Eight-year-olds showed more sophisticated understanding in terms of the vocabulary employed to describe political events and personages. Nine-year-olds were seen as reasonably balanced in their discussion of political events and the political process. This age group was the dividing line between reasoned discussion of politics and the more unstructured views of younger children.

Ten-year-olds were found to engage seriously in attempts to link their discussion with the political realities of the world rather than the idealistic speculation seen in nine-year-olds. Eleven-year-olds revealed far more sophisticated understanding, summarized by the researchers as follows:

> Further linguistic development gave an ease and confidence to discussion; competence in using political concepts extended to fluency of ideas. The ability to relate sets of ideas led to the linking of politics not only with roles, structures, and politics, but with topics such as conservation, women's rights, and an economic reorganization of the country. Cognitive contact has been made not only with the political world but with other questions that were understood to be open to analysis. (Stevens, 1982, p. 150)

A significant longitudinal study that helps illuminate the issue of political socialization is that of Moore, Lare, and Wagner (1985). The study was designed to look at American children's conceptions of politics from K–12 and beyond. Begun in 1973–74 with individual interviews, the 243 students from southern California were told they would be reinterviewed every four years until the year 2002 (Moore, 1987).

Specific theories of political socialization (e.g., Piaget & Bandura) were to be tested by the data collected. Finally, comparisons with earlier studies were planned to see if media-saturated political events (e.g., Watergate) influence political socialization change. Unfortunately at this point, full data summaries are only available for the first five years of this study (Moore, 1989; Moore, Lare, & Wagner, 1985). Some impressionistic results have been reported for data from fifth grade through high school (1979–86) but the coding and analyzing of data are still incomplete (Moore, 1987, 1989).

One finding was that Piaget's assertion that children cannot think about abstract matters before about fourth grade appeared to be in error. The data showed a correlation between increasing political understanding and more positive attitudes towards government, "although the most knowledgeable children are more likely than others to qualify their personal feelings" (Moore, Lare, & Wagner, 1985, p. 217). This was particularly true regarding the impact of their own actions on the political process. Overall, elementary-school-aged children believed they had a significant role influencing government and that government would respond to a need for assistance.

A large percentage of children interviewed believed that government officials do make mistakes on a regular basis. (It must be remembered that these interviews were conducted in the Watergate era.) Despite these feelings towards officials, nearly all students reported they would vote if given the opportunity and that they planned to vote when eligible.

Children's Conceptions of Law

Law appears to be the first area within politics that children understand (Moore, Lare, & Wagner, 1985). On the indices that the researchers used, children were one-half of a stage higher on the Law Understanding Index than on the Political Understanding Index. The authors noted that elementary children's understanding of the societal impact of law was along authoritarian lines (laws are automatically "right" and are "handed down from on high"). The researchers concluded that children hold a passive model of citizenship, with only five percent of the students interviewed advocating a role that went beyond merely voting in elections or an occasional letter about a particularly odious decision. There is also evidence that students in the latter half of the 1970s were less aware of politics than their grade counterparts in the early 1960s (Moore, 1987).

These results suggest that, unless existing student conceptions are challenged in an explicit manner, STS "action-taking" on an issue may be limited to that which occurs within the bounds of the class and not during the everyday life of the individual student. It points up the need for both continued research regarding student action-taking in STS education (see Chapter 23) and attention to the political and social dimensions of students' existing conceptions.

Children's Views of Economics

Major studies that address children's conceptions of economic principles include those of Berti and Bombi (1988), Furth (1980), and Schug (1991). Berti and Bombi interviewed 916 Italian children, ages three to fourteen, from middle class backgrounds. They found that young children did not have explanatory frameworks that resemble classical economic concepts. When asked why people work, responses focused on utilitarian considerations of personal need or the needs of significant others. For example, preschool children, when asked why bus drivers drive busses, reply "because the mummies have to go out" (Berti & Bombi, 1988, p. 159). Children in the upper cohort of the study reveal signs of an emerging understanding of monetary exchange, commodity production, supply and demand theory, and other impersonal characteristics that explain why people engage in work and how economic exchange systems function.

Even at age 14, some children within the group still cannot conceive of how wages are determined. They link the wages of a worker to the specific type of item produced in terms of the cost of the individual items. Workers who make smaller, less costly items, receive less money than those producing larger, individually more costly items.

Furth (1980) took a look at economic conceptions within the context of children's broader understandings of society. His sample of 195 children, ages five to eleven years, were selected from three primary schools in southern England. Overall, his findings reinforce those of Berti and Bombi.

Children's Conceptions of Society

Furth (1980) lays out four developmental stages children grow through on their way to adulthood.

    1. Personalistic elaborations and absence of interpretative system

2. Understanding of first-order societal functions
3. Part-systems in conflict
4. A concrete, systematic framework.

Children in Stage 1 exhibit marked confusion about the purpose and functions of money. Societal events and institutions are accepted as givens in a way which requires no explanations. All personal and societal events are framed within the contexts of a child's own psychological reaction to various events. During Stage 2, children envision a static social order and come to understand that money functions as a medium of exchange. At a rudimentary level they can distinguish societal roles from personal roles, but only for events close to their personal life experience.

By Stage 3, children have constructed a partial yet personal understanding of society, social institutions, and economics. The connections between various events and individuals within them can be identified and discussed in a limited way. Proffered explanations for social and personal events are often incomplete and contradictory, although the child is not generally aware of these features.

The final stage of Furth's system finds children able to think about and discuss interpersonal differences and how societal roles change according to context. The differences in actions and effects between personal and societal levels is recognized, and understandings about the history and symbolisms of cultures begin to emerge. Even at this point a child's understanding is idiosyncratic and "principally on an affective-emotional level."

A discussion of this elaborate theory is outside the scope of this paper. Only one-third of the twelve-year-olds in the study had reached Stage 4. Furth's (1980) two main conclusions need to be kept in mind when contemplating STS education for students: "(1) that children's thinking about societal events is different from, not simply a knowing less of, adult notions" and "(2) that it is also original and not merely a copy of adult models" (p. 297).

Children's Views of Societal Inequality

Many major STS issues involve the unequal distribution of the world's resources and the need for fairness in an unjust world. Children's conceptions of social inequality are better known than their views about politics, law, economics, and societal institutions. This area of research has blossomed due to its value in understanding race relations.

A major volume by Leahy (1983) surveys this extensive body of literature. His summary conclusions regarding present research in equity theory are worth noting.

> . . . the research in equity theory does not necessarily address the question of what criteria children and adolescents do use in deciding on unequal distributions. Second, young children may advocate unequal distributions before changing to equality norms. Third, some inequalities or rights are viewed at an early age as unjustifiable regardless of laws allowing for inequalities. Fourth, with increasing age adolescents are more likely than children to believe that inequalities may be redressed by changes in social structure (e.g., government or the economy). Finally, models of cultural transmission emphasizing social learning or inequalities are limited in that they do not account for qualitative age changes in conceptions of inequality nor do they account for a conception that may be antagonistic to the values of the dominant culture. (Leahy, 1983, p. 318)

Torney-Purta (1983), within the same volume, attempts to derive principles to explain how adolescents formulate ways to remedy social injustice both through personal action and changing the policies of social institutions. First, she notes that the normal psychological changes that occur as a person grows play a key role. Even fairly young children, for example, are good at perceiving instances of social injustice, threats to human rights, and assaults on human dignity. Second, cognitive ability is a factor in explaining individual responses. Third, a person's attempt to preserve a basic egocentrism by attempts to maintain his or her own reception of equal treatment and other "good" outcomes is readily apparent. Fourth, civil and political rights are generally perceived as more important than economic or social rights. Fifth, laws and policy are seen by adolescents and younger children as a means to protect themselves "from the chaos they believe is the basic state of society" (Torney-Purta, 1983, p. 306).

Conclusions

We are still woefully ignorant about student conceptions of the social sciences and social institutions. The information we do have suggests that children's and adolescents' views of our social institutions and life in a democracy are very different from that of adults. Engagement of students in the social dimensions of STS issues taps students' existing beliefs, naive conceptions, misconceptions, and attitudes. Science educators would do well to spend time not only finding out the nature of these conceptions but working collaboratively with social studies educators within their schools to actively address these existing understandings.

References

Berti, A. E., & Bombi, A. S. (1988). *The child's construction of economics.* New York, NY: Cambridge University Press.

Cheek, D. W. (1992). *Thinking constructively about science, technology, and society education.* Albany, NY: State University of New York Press.

Driver, R. (1988). Restructuring the science curriculum: Some implications of studies on learning for curriculum development. In D. Layton (Ed.), *Innovations in science and technology education* (Vol. II) (pp. 59–84). Paris, France: UNESCO.

Driver, R., Guesne, E., & Tiberghien, A. (Eds.). (1985). *Children's ideas in science.* Philadelphia, PA: Open University Press.

Greenstein, F. (1965). *Children and politics.* New Haven, CT: Yale University Press.

Furth, H. G. (1980). *The world of grown-ups: Children's conceptions of society.* New York, NY: Elsevier Publishers.

Hall, G. S. (1883). The contents of children's minds. *Princeton Review, 11,* 249–272.

Hall, G. S. (1891). The contents of children's minds on entering school. *The Pedagogical Seminary, 1,* 139–143.

Hyman, M. (1959). *Political socialization.* New York, NY: The Free Press

Leahy, R. L. (1983). The child's construction of social inequality: Conclusions. In R. L. Leahy (Ed.), *The child's construction of social inequality* (pp. 311–328). New York, NY: Academic Press.

Moore, S. W. (1987, April). *Piaget and Bandura: The need for a unified theory of learning.* Paper presented to the Society for Research in Child Development. Baltimore, MD.

Moore, S. W. (1989). The need for a unified theory of political learning: Lessons from a longitudinal project. *Human Development, 32,* 5–13.

Moore, S. W., Lare, J., & Wagner, K. A. (1985). *The child's political world—A longitudinal perspective.* New York, NY: Praeger Publishers.

Oppenheim, A. N. & Torney, J. (1974). *The measurement of children's civic attitudes in different nations.* New York: John Wiley & Sons.

Schug, M. C. (1991). The development of students' economic thought: Implications for instruction. In W. B. Walstead and J. C. Sloper (Eds.), *Effective economic education in the schools.* (pp. 137–152). Washington, DC: National Education Association.

Stevens, O. (1982). *Children talking politics—Political learning in childhood.* Oxford, England: Martin Robertson.

Torney-Purta, J. (1983). The development of views about the role of social institutions in redressing inequality and promoting human rights. In R. L. Leahy (Ed.), *The child's construction of social inequality* (pp. 289–310). New York, NY: Academic Press.

15

A Constructivist View of Learning: Children's Conceptions and the Nature of Science

Rosalind Driver and John Leach
University of Leeds, England

Over the last 15 years a substantial research program has been carried out around the world into children's conceptions about various natural phenomena. This research has been informed by a range of constructivist perspectives on learning. These perspectives share a view of learning which portrays learners as actively involved in the process of building their knowledge about the world around them through physical experiences and social interactions. The sense that a learner makes of any new situation depends not only on characteristics of that situation but on the knowledge and attitudes the learner brings to it. It is, therefore, important to know about learners' likely conceptual starting points as these influence how learning experiences will be interpreted (Driver, 1990).

Students' initial conceptions are not the only influence on learning science, however. They approach learning situations with particular attitudes to science and particular views of the nature of science itself. Children may have a range of ideas about the purposes of scientific activity which differ from their teachers' ideas. In addition, students may see scientific theories (and, indeed, their own theories) as unproblematic descriptions of reality. Theory and evidence are therefore not differentiated in the student's reasoning: descriptions and explanations are seen as the same thing (Kuhn, Amsel, O'Loughlin, 1988; Nadeau & Desautels, 1984).

The science curriculum has traditionally focused on teaching the technical content of science (and particularly science concepts) in order to maintain a supply of future scientists. The STS teaching agenda broadens this aim to include producing a scientifically literate public (Ziman, 1980). Public participation in and a sense of ownership of the purposes and directions of science and technology is a commonly stated policy objective in democratic societies (Royal Society, 1985; AAAS, 1989). Miller (1983) has argued that scientific literacy should be evaluated in terms of an individual's ability to read about, comprehend, and express an opinion on scientific matters as opposed to knowledge of the technical aspects of science alone. There is an important argument that, to improve scientific literacy, an emphasis needs to be placed on the methods of scientific enquiry and the nature of scientific knowledge (Millar & Wynne, 1988; Collins & Shapin 1984). This argument suggests that a view of scientific knowledge as conjectural, and moreover as being validated through social as well as empirical processes, would put individuals in a better position to make informed judgments about the validity of claims made about socioscientific and technological issues. Many such decisions require individuals to make judgments about the validity and reliability of scientific data and the way in which abstract, formal theories can be applied to concrete, complex situations.

In this paper we will illustrate how children can come to have more sophisticated views of the nature of their own theories through teaching that is informed by a constructivist view of learning. This meta-understanding of their own theories can be used to illustrate the nature of scientific theories as both theoretical and conjectural in status. Teaching can then be designed to offer learners a more informed view of the complexities involved with drawing on theoretical knowledge in decision-making about particular socioscientific issues.

Children's Knowledge Schemes

There is now extensive literature documenting the ideas children have about the natural world (Driver, Guesne, & Tiberghien, 1985; Gentner & Stevens, 1983; Osborne & Freyberg, 1985) and the way these develop through childhood (Carey, 1985; Strauss & Stavy, 1982). Work in this field reveals that when they begin science lessons, students already have knowledge schemes which they draw on in a learning situation. What students learn from lesson activities, whether these involve talk, written text, or practical work, depends not only on the nature of the tasks set, but on the knowledge schemes that students bring to these tasks (Driver & Bell, 1986). Learning thus involves an interaction between students' mental schemes and the experiences they have. The experience may fit with students' expectations, in which case little change is required in the students' schemes. On the other hand, the experience may be novel and students may change or adapt their knowledge schemes as a result. This process of using and testing current ideas in new situations requires active involvement of students in drawing on their present schemes, relating them to new tasks, and perhaps reorganizing them. In this way, learning science is seen to entail the progressive development and restructuring of learners' knowledge schemes.

One perspective on the process of knowledge construction, that of radical constructivism, portrays the learner as building knowledge through the personal interplay of experiences with their knowledge schemes. Central to this perspective is the notion of "fit."

> What determines the value of the conceptual structures is their experimental adequacy, their goodness of fit with experience, their viability as means for solving problems, among which is, of course, the never-ending problem of consistent organisation that we call understanding . . . Facts are made by us and our way of experiencing. (von Glasersfeld, 1983, p.51)

The epistemological implication of this view of knowledge as being constructed is that to know something does not involve the correspondence of conceptual schemes to what they represent "out there"; learners have no direct access to the "real world." The emphasis in learning is not on the correspondence with an external authority, but the construction by the learner of schemes that are coherent and useful to them. This view of knowledge "has serious consequences for our conceptualization of teaching and learning . . . it will shift the emphasis from the student's 'correct' replication of what the teacher does, to the student's successful organization of his or her own experiences" (von Glasersfeld, ibid.).

Social Factors in Learning

Learning about the world does not, however, take place in a social vacuum. Children have available to them, through language and culture, ways of thinking and imaging. Phrases such as "shut the door and keep the cold out" or "dew is falling" provide, through metaphor, ways of representing aspects of the physical world. This dynamic relationship between children's personal knowledge schemes and the schemes available through the culture has been commented on and explored by science educators (Sutton, 1980), psychologists, and anthropologists (Rogoff & Lave, 1984). Drawing on the work of Schutz and Luckmann, Solomon (1987) argued that "objects of common sense" only exist through social communication, whereby ideas are exchanged, explored, and reinforced.

> In what Schutz and Luckmann refer to as 'life world knowing' the essential criterion is no longer the internal logic of the explanation but that it should be recognized and shared with others. We take it for granted that those who are close to us see the world as we do, but through social exchanges, we seek always to have this reconfirmed. This continual reaffirmation of social notions makes them very durable and resistant to change. (p. 67)

Thus, whether an individual's ideas are affirmed and shared by others in classroom exchanges has a part in shaping the knowledge construction process.

Science as Socially Constructed

So far we have sketched how a constructivist perspective portrays the development of children's knowledge about the natural world. However, the knowledge drawn on within the scientific community and by other interested members of the public is also personally and socially constructed. Scientific ideas and theories not only result from the attempts of individuals and small groups to explain phenomena but also pass through a complex process involving communication and checking through major social institutions of science before being validated by the scientific community. This social dimension to the construction of scientific knowledge has resulted in the scientific community sharing a view of the world involving concepts, models, conventions, and procedures. This world is inhabited by entities such as atoms, electrons, ions, fields and fluxes, genes, and chromosomes; it is organized by ideas such as evolution and procedures of measurement and experimentation. These ideas, which are constructed and transmitted through the culture and social institutions of science, will not be discovered by individuals through their own empirical inquiry; learning science involves being initiated into the culture of science.

There is an important point at issue here for science education. If knowledge construction is seen solely as a personal process, then this is similar to what has traditionally been identified as discovery learning. If, however, students are to be given access to the knowledge systems of science, the process of knowledge construction must go beyond personal, empirical inquiry. Students need to be given access not only to physical experiences but also to the concepts and models of conventional science. The challenge lies in helping students to construct these models for themselves, to appreciate their domains of applicability and, within such domains, to be able to use them.

Developing a curriculum in science that encompasses this perspective needs to acknowledge that science is about more than experiences of the natural world. It encompasses the theories and models that have been constructed and the ways in which these are checked and evaluated as coherent and useful. Perhaps most significantly, from a constructivist perspective, these theories are seen not as absolute, but as provisional and fallible. Moreover, making and testing theories is a dynamic human enterprise which takes place within the socially defined community and institutions of science. Here students' experiences of developing and reconstructing their own conceptions in science may perhaps be drawn on to help them understand and appreciate the ways scientific ideas change and develop. Again, these ideas are central to an STS approach as defined by NSTA.

If the aim of STS teaching is to develop scientifically literate students who are able to read about, comprehend, and express an opinion about scientific issues (Miller, 1983), it will be necessary for such teaching to examine the processes by which knowledge becomes public knowledge in scientific communities. In any research discipline there are informal norms for appraising empirical research; in some cases these are formalized and may relate to assessing the reliability and validity of data on the basis of research methods used. Millar (1992) has argued that teaching should place greater emphasis on the 'craft' involved in collecting reliable data and interpreting it, in order for students to be able to interpret media reports which include scientific information.

As well as understanding some of the institutional norms for assessing the reliability and validity of knowledge claims, Wynne (1990) has argued that an understanding of the institutional embedding and control of science is vital for individuals to be able to comprehend socioscientific issues and reach a viewpoint. Duschl (1990) has argued that it is important that teaching allow students to study a range of socioscientific contexts in depth so that they appreciate the different status of theories in the scientific community (i.e., that some theories are more controversial than others). An added advantage to this approach is that students can come to appreciate that a number of factors other than theoretical knowledge influence decision-making in socioscientific contexts.

Implications for Teaching, Learning, and the Curriculum

Viewing the curriculum as a body of knowledge or skills to be transmitted is clearly naive. If we recognize that individuals construct their own knowledge as a result of interaction between their current conceptions and ongoing physical and social experiences, then it is perhaps more helpful to view the curriculum as a series of learning tasks and strategies. Posner (1982) considers the central conception that underlies the view of curriculum to be that of "tasks." However, he points out that "if we want to understand a student's experience, the process of learning, and the reasons why some learning outcomes are occurring and not others, we must understand the tasks in which students are engaging and not just the tasks the teachers think they are 'giving' to students" (p. 343).

The aim in curriculum development is then to create a classroom environment that "provides the social setting for mutual support of knowledge construction" (Bereiter, 1985). Such an environment encompasses not only the learning tasks as set, but the learning tasks as interpreted by the students. It also includes the social organization and modes of interaction between the students themselves and between teacher and students.

There are various features that characterize teaching and the learning environment from a constructivist perspective.

- Learners are not viewed as passive but are seen as purposive and ultimately responsible for their own learning. They bring their prior conceptions to learning situations.
- Learning is considered to involve an active process on the part of the learner. It involves the construction of meaning and often takes place through interpersonal negotiation.
- Knowledge is not "out there" but is personally and socially constructed; its status is problematic. It may be evaluated by the individual in terms of the extent to which it "fits" with his or her experience, is coherent with other aspects of the individual's knowledge, and is consistent with the knowledge schemes within particular social groups.
- Teachers also bring their prior conceptions to learning situations, not only in terms of their subject knowledge but also their views of teaching

and learning. These can influence their way of interacting with students in classrooms.

- Teaching is not the transmission of knowledge but involves the organization of the situations in the classroom and the design of tasks in a way that enables students to make sense of the "ways of seeing" of the scientific community.
- The curriculum is not that which is to be learned, but a program of learning tasks, materials, resources, and discourse from which students construct their knowledge.

This perspective also has implications for the way curricula are developed. A "planning by objectives" model of curriculum development is clearly inappropriate, as it fails to take account of the purposes and meanings constructed by the various participants. Instead, the progressive development of a curriculum may require a reflexive process in which feedback from all the participants, including researchers, teachers, and students, can provide information on how each are interpreting and carrying out a series of tasks. These can then be adapted to improve the extent to which learning is promoted.

Implications for Teaching

Accepting a constructivist perspective on learning has implications for planning schemes of work within science curricula, and for approaches to teaching (pedagogy).

How might the features outlined in the previous sections be embodied in actual science classrooms? What might schemes of teaching that reflect these features be like and how might they be implemented? What might be the outcomes of such a way of teaching? How might teachers and students respond? Here we outline how a particular project, the Children's Learning in Science (CLIS) Project, has explored these issues over recent years. The project has the aim of devising, testing, and evaluating teaching sequences in selected science topics, which were informed by a constuctivist perspective on learning.

Since teachers are involved in such a fundamental way in the successful implementation of a curriculum, the directors of this project state that the research and development of constructivist approaches to science teaching should be a collaborative exercise between teachers and researchers. Malcolm Skilbeck made the point succinctly when he said "the best place for designing the curriculum is where learners and teachers meet."

Teams of teachers, each with a researcher, collaborated in designing, testing, and evaluating, in an iterative way, teaching schemes in three topics: (1) energy, (2) the structure of matter, and (3) plant nutrition (CLIS, 1987). In addition to teaching students about scientific concepts in each area, the schemes allowed students to develop an awareness of their own theories as constructed entities. We suggest that this more informed view could be drawn on by teachers in STS topics, which require students to have a view of scientific theories as constructed and theoretical.

The following principles informed the way the schemes were developed (Driver & Oldham, 1986).

Features of the Classroom Environment

In designing the schemes, certain general features of the classroom environment were seen to be important to encourage students to restructure their ideas. These features included:

- ensuring the classroom environment is a supportive one where learners feel able to contribute their ideas

---

- using group work as a basis for the social organization of the classroom so as to give students opportunities to think through and exchange ideas with peers
- the teacher's role becoming a more diagnostic one with an emphasis on listening to students to understand their thinking and then intervening, when appropriate, with suggested ideas or experience to extend students' thinking

Phases in the Teaching

Each scheme had a number of phases. After a scene-setting orientation activity that gained the student's attention and interest in the topic, the first main activity used questions to elicit the ideas students already had about the topic. This elicitation phase was usually conducted first in small groups. After discussion and review in groups, each group was asked to represent their ideas on a poster or by other means and then present these to the class. Similarities and differences in students' prior ideas were identified and issues for further consideration were noted. The posters were displayed as a record during the rest of the unit of work and were amended later. It is not only teachers who need to be aware of students' prior concepts, it is important that students themselves make them explicit and clarify them. In the next phase, the restructuring phase, strategies developed in the trials were used to promote change in students' conceptions. This phase involved practical construction tasks, imaginative writing tasks, demonstrations, and more conventional textbook problems. At the end of the lesson sequence, students were given the opportunity to review the extent and ways in which their thinking had changed. The resulting published schemes (CLIS, 1987) included not only an outline of suggested activities but provided a map of the main trends in the kinds of ideas used by students in their classes and the routes they took in their thinking.

Strategies for Restructuring Students' Conceptions

A number of different teaching strategies have been used to encourage the construction of new concepts. The choice of strategy depends on the nature of the students' prior conceptions and the learning goals. It is not, therefore, appropriate to see these strategies as competing but rather as a range of strategies to be selected according to the criterion of "fitness of purpose"—which strategy is most likely to help learners to move towards explicit learning goals, given their existing conceptual understandings. The following are some of the strategies that have been used.

- **Broaden the range of application of a conception.** Students' prior conceptions may be a resource which can be extended. For example, for younger children energy is attributed to human energeticness and motion. By inviting children to consider what happens to their energy, the notion can be generalized to encompass the motion of inanimate objects leading on to an appreciation of energy being stored in springs, etc.
- **Differentiate a conception.** In many areas, students' conceptions can be global and ill-defined and particular experiences are necessary to help them differentiate their notions (for example, heat and temperature, force and energy, weight and pressure). In the area of energy, we found that students did not differentiate between the weight of an object and the energy transferred when the object is lifted. Due to this confusion, students would assert that an object gained weight on being lifted up, yet this was not supported by the evidence of spring balance readings. There was a need for a "something" that changed while "something else" remained constant (Brook, 1987).
- **Build experiential bridges to a new conception.** Research by Brown and Clement (1987) with college students has indicated the importance of

thought experiments in constructing conceptual bridges from ideas that students accept to new, possibly counter-intuitive, ideas. Our work has been with younger students, and perhaps not surprisingly, we find it can be important for such bridges to be constructed through practical experiences. A prior conception about energy which is widely held is that energy can disappear. In the case of a hot cup of tea in a room, students assert that the tea cools down and the heat energy disappears. To encourage the construction of the notion that energy does not disappear, but that it goes somewhere, possibly "spreading out" so it is less detectable, classes conducted a series of experiments in which a hot cup of water was allowed to cool in outer containers of cold water of progressively larger volumes. The temperature of the water in the inner and outer containers was recorded and plotted at regular intervals of time. After inspecting the resulting graphs, students were then asked to think about what happens when the outer container is the room itself. Having done the activity and plotted the graphs, students were able to construct in their imagination the notion of heat being "spread out" in the room.

- **Unpack a conceptual problem.** In some cases a conceptual problem occurs that cannot be solved directly but that requires a deeper problem to be addressed. A clear example of this occurs in the teaching of the kinetic-molecular theory of gases where children will accept the existence of particles but have difficulty with the concept of intrinsic motion. The prior conception to be dealt with here is the well-known conception of "motion requiring a force." An analysis of learning problems of this kind could give some guidance to the sequencing of topics in curricula as a whole.

- **Import a different model or analogy.** In lessons on the structure of matter, students were asked to examine the properties of a range of substances and to describe and explain them. The observation that a gas is "squashy" elicited ideas among many students that gases are not continuous stuff but made of particles with spaces between them. (An alternative model involving "squashy molecules" has also been proposed and defended.) Simple experiences with objects in one domain are being drawn on to account for behavior in another domain. It is probable that early experiences provide children with a series of schemes which are important for them to draw on by analogy in later science teaching.

- **Progressively shape a conception.** In teaching the particle theory of matter, we found the initial idea that matter is particulate rather than continuous was rapidly adopted by 12-year-old students. The properties of those particles and the way their behavior accounts for various macro-scopic properties have to be treated progressively as students come to explore the range and limitations of their theories. In adopting a model, students need opportunities to test it out, to see where it fails in order to adapt it. In applying a scientific theory, students may use only some aspects of it in ways that conform to scientific ideas with other aspects differing from the scientific view. For example, in applying a particle model of gases, students tend to adopt the idea that the speed of the particles increases as the temperature increases. However they also include other features in the model, for example the notions that particles are "squashy," expand on heating, or that there is air between particles are commonly used (Scott, 1987).

- **Construct an alternative conception.** In some cases, students' prior ideas are incommensurate with the scientific conceptions, and attempting to shape their notions into the scientific ideas only leads to problems. In a case of this kind we have acknowledged students' prior ideas and discussed them, helping students to see the limitations and problems with their current conceptions. We have then indicated that scientists have a different view and an alternative model is presented. Students have the opportunity later to evaluate the scientific model in relation to their prior ideas.

In this task of designing, testing, and evaluating teaching sequences which are better attuned to students' understanding, it has been necessary to consider the nature of students' conceptions and how they differ from the learning goals in order to identify appropriate pedagogical strategies. Strategies for promoting conceptual change need to be investigated in the context of particular domains of knowledge. General prescriptions of the conceptual change process by itself are not enough; information about the nature of the conceptual change to be promoted is necessary in designing instructional sequences.

Constructivist Approaches and Teaching the Nature of Science

As we indicated at the beginning of this paper, one of the goals of STS teaching is to give students a better insight into the status and limitations of scientific models and the ways in which reliable knowledge is developed within the scientific community. Clearly, in order to do this, reference needs to be made to historical and sociological accounts of scientists' work. In addition, however, it may be helpful for students to develop an understanding of some of the epistemological issues as they relate to their own learning in science.

Science lessons conducted from a constructivist perspective can provide important illustrations for students about the nature of science and scientific knowledge. The classroom atmosphere provides an opportunity for these matters to be discussed explicitly. The following are examples.

- When students make and record observations of the same event, all students may not focus on the same features. In some cases they may "see" the event differently. This may be evidence of the way students' prior ideas influence their observations and can be used to illustrate the "theory-laden" nature of scientific observations.
- When students have collected evidence and are asked to suggest models or "rules" to explain it, groups of students in a class may offer different models. How you decide which model is "best" raises a range of issues about the relation of models to evidence and the role of experimentation as a means of making decisions between competing models.
- Where students' ideas are rooted in extensive prior experiences, for example, in the area of mechanics, they may not change their conceptions easily. Even if they acknowledge a new idea, they may be unwilling to believe it (a situation also paralleled in science). What are the reasons for this "inertia" in people's models of the world? An exploration with students of their reasoning and feelings when their ideas are confronted may give them insight into the disputes and changes that have taken place within the scientific community.

References

American Association for the Advancement of Science (1989) *Science for all Americans.* Washington, DC: Author.

Bereiter, C. (1985). Toward a solution of the learning paradox. *Review of Educational Research, 55*(2), 201–226.

Brook, A. (1987). Designing experiences to take account of the development of children's ideas: An example from the teaching and learning of energy. In J. Novak (Ed.), *Proceedings of the second international seminar: Misconceptions and educational strategies in science and mathematics* (Vol. 2) (pp. 49–64). Ithaca, NY: Cornell University.

Brown, D. E., & Clement, J. (1987, April). *Overcoming misconceptions in mechanics: A comparison of two example-based teaching strategies.* Paper presented at the Annual Meeting of the American Educational Research Association, Washington, DC.

Carey, S. (1985). *Conceptual change in childhood.* Cambridge, MA: Massachusetts Institute of Technology Press.

Children's Learning In Science (CLIS). (1987). *CLIS in the classroom: Approaches to teaching.* Leeds, England: Centre for Studies in Science and Mathematics Education, University of Leeds.

Collins, H. M., & Shapin, S. (1984). Uncovering the nature of science. *The Times Higher Education Supplement,* 27 June 1984, p. 13.

Driver, R. (1990). The construction of scientific knowledge in school classrooms. In R. Millar (Ed.), *Doing science: Image of science in science education.* London, England: Palmer Press.

Driver, R., & Bell, B. (1986). Students' thinking and the learning of science: A constructivist view. *School Science Review, 67*(240), 443–456.

Driver, R., Guesne, E., & Tiberghien, A. (Eds.). (1985). *Children's ideas in science.* Philadelphia, PA: Open University Press.

Driver, R., & Oldham, V. (1986). A constructivist approach to curriculum development in science. *Studies in Science Education, 13,* 105–122.

Duschl, R. A. (1990). *Restructuring science education: The importance of theories and their development.* Columbia, NY: Teachers College Press, Columbia University.

Gentner, D., & Stevens, A. (Eds.). (1983). *Mental models.* Hillsdale, NJ: Lawrence Erlbaum.

Kuhn, D., Amsel, E., & O'Loughlin, M. (1988). *The development of scientific thinking skills.* San Diego, CA: Academic Press.

Millar, R. (1992). Science education and public understanding of science. In R. Hull (Ed.). *ASE Science Teachers' Handbook.* 2nd edition. Hatfield, England: Association for Science Education.

Millar, R., & Wynne, B. (1988). Public understanding of science: From contents to processes. *International Journal of Science Education, 10*(4), 388–398.

Miller, J. (1983). Scientific literacy: A conceptual and empirical review. *Daedalus, 112*(2), 29–48.

Nadeau, R., & Desautels, J. (1984). *Epistemology and the teaching of science.* Ottawa, Canada: Science Council of Canada.

Osborne R., & Freyberg P. (Eds.). (1985). *Learning in science: The implications of children's science.* London, England: Heinemann.

Posner, G. (1982). A cognitive science conception of curriculum and instruction. *Journal of Curriculum Studies, 14*(4), 343–351.

Rogoff, B., & Lave, J. (Eds.). (1984). *Everyday cognition: Its development in social context.* Cambridge, MA: Harvard University Press.

Royal Society (1985). *The public understanding of science.* London, England: The Royal Society.

Scott, P. (1987, July). *The process of conceptual change in science: A case study of the development of a secondary pupil's ideas relating to matter.* Paper presented at the Secondary International Seminar: Misconceptions and Educational Strategies in Science and Mathematics, Cornell University, Ithaca, New York.

Solomon, J. (1987). Social influences on the construction of pupils' understanding of science. *Studies in Science Education, 14*, 63–82.

Strauss, S., & Stavy, R. (Eds.). (1982). *U-shaped behavioral growth*. New York, NY: Academic Press.

Sutton, C. R. (1980). The learner's prior knowledge: A critical review of techniques for probing its organization. *European Journal of Science Education, 2*(2), 107–129.

von Glasersfeld, E. (1983). Learning as a constructive activity. In J. C. Bergeram and N. Herscovics (Eds.), *Proceedings of the fifth annual meeting of PME-NA* (pp. 41–69). Montreal, Canada.

Wynne, B. (1990, April 13). The blind and the blissful. *The Guardian*, p. 28.

Ziman, J. (1980): *Teaching and learning about science and society*. Cambridge, England: Cambridge University Press.

16

Coordination of STS and Community Goals

Frederick A. Staley
Arizona State University

FIf STS is to make a significant impact on students' learning, it may be of utmost importance for schools to find ways to coordinate their efforts with resources in the community. Attempts to involve the community in the schooling process have a long tradition in American education. The purposeful interaction of parents and the private sector with schools only blossomed in the late 1980s as public interest in school reform greatly increased. It was in the early 1980s that the many national reports and national, state, and local task forces served during what the National Alliance of Business (1989c) referred to as the Problem Identification phase of educational reform. It was during this phase that the seeds of STS were planted and business and parent involvement in schools was just beginning to increase.

Calls for educational reform so evident in the 1980s were not only calls for the reform of schooling but also calls for greater involvement of the community in the reform process. The mid-1980s represented the Initial Actions phase of school reform (National Alliance of Business, 1989c) where new state legislation and new programs to address problems in American education resulted in an increase in business/parent involvement in the schools. This included involvement in adopt-a-school, tutoring, and mentoring programs, as well as public demands for increased standardized testing and graduation requirements. The creation and growth of a broad range of STS programs at all levels of education flourished during this same period.

The latest phase of school reform, referred to as "Restructuring" by the National Alliance of Business (1989c) and others, is characterized by collaborative efforts of schools, community members, and community-based organizations; innovative initiatives in local systems; school-based management; curriculum changes; greater emphasis on accountability; and by requirements for substantial business involvement. A visible ingredient in these efforts is the recognition that STS can bring relevancy and meaningfulness back into the school's curriculum through the study of science and technology-oriented topics, issues, and problems which are of concern to the local school and community (Staley, 1987).

While many are claiming the benefits of STS as part of the school's curriculum, little research has been conducted to indicate how STS might also serve as a link with the community and with community efforts at school reform. The rest of this chapter will examine the research base for determining how best to coordinate school and community for educational reform, starting with a rationale for combining school and community resources. Then I will review research and reports that have begun to provide an empirical base for deciding how best to proceed with school-community STS collaboration, and finally, the implications for STS.

Rationale for Considering the Whole Community in STS

Many of the individuals and groups studying the problems of American education suggested the need for reform was a result of dramatic changes in our society, our economy, and changes in the political, economic, and environmental conditions in the world (Carruthers, 1990).

As for involving the community in the education process, support was offered by Goodlad (1984) and Brandwein (1981) who suggested that if real educational reform was to occur, all those involved in the educational community must be involved. Besides the school and the new involvement of businesses, the family and community members in charge of places where students go outside of school for recreation, social interaction, education, and employment must also become involved in the educational process. To this point, Boyer (1989) reported that most teachers were concerned about the growing gap between the home, the school, and the community and he warned, "In the next phases of school renewal, partnerships between the family and school must be strengthened, communities must confront the growing needs of students, and all of us must listen to the voices of the teachers" (p. 75).

Others have suggested that another reason for school-community collaboration was that many in the community were scientifically and technologically illiterate and that such collaborations could enhance the education of community members as well as the education of students (Brinkerhoff, 1986; Miller, 1983).

"American industry," says Hubbard (1989/1990), "recognizes that its future depends on a technically educated population and is willing to invest in education to insure that future" (p. 2). Furthermore, as Henderson (1987) concluded after studying the effects of parent involvement on students' learning, schools that have close connections with their communities produce students who out-perform those from schools that are isolated from their communities.

STS is not just a new approach to science education; it is also a response to the calls from the community for reform of education in general and for allowing the community to collaborate with schools in the reform process. Thus, the rationale provided for involving the community in the school reform process is also the rationale for the coordination of STS and community goals.

Research Base for Coordinating School-Community Efforts

While there are many interesting suggestions about why schools might coordinate with their communities, there are still many unanswered questions about who should be involved and how this should be accomplished. Unfortunately, there has been little research on specific STS school-community collaboration activities.

Most prior work on the topic of school-community collaboration of any kind has been more prescriptive and logical than descriptive and empirical in nature. Many of the recommendations for establishing school-community collaborations are offered with little data to back them up. One major attempt, however, to add to the data base on STS school-community collaboration was begun by Staley (1986) as part of a National Science Foundation grant in the Phoenix, Arizona, area. While attempting to reform the science curriculum among participating K–8 schools using collaborations among schools, parents, and business/industry, the three-year project yielded valuable information. The research agenda of this project was to determine those factors that contributed to or inhibited a school and community's ability to bring about substantial STS curricular reform through the cooperative efforts of all those involved. Twenty-five school-communities representing seven school districts in the west valley of Phoenix, 32 teachers trained as STS resource teachers, 16 rookie STS teachers, 37 business/industry/informal education and government institutions, and 63 employees from these institutions participated in this project. The school-communities included three lower economic, minority, urban/suburban communities; six lower economic, minority, rural/suburban communities; and 16 middle-class, predominately Anglo, urban/suburban communities. Results of this project are distributed at appropriate points throughout the following sections.

In this review, three categories of research are reported: (1) research related to the nature of collaboration, (2) research related to participants' perceptions in the collaborative process about goals and roles, and (3) research describing factors that appear to contribute to successful school-community collaboration.

The Nature of Collaboration

How Are Businesses Involved with Schools? Several attempts have been made to classify the levels of partnership involvement among schools and businesses. The National Alliance of Business in its *The Fourth R: Workforce Readiness* (1987), for example, has identified five levels of private sector partnerships with educational systems:

> Level One—policy making
> Level Two—partners in systemic education improvement
> Level Three—partners in management
> Level Four—partners in teacher training and development
> Level Five—partners in the classroom

This report indicated that as you go from level one to level five, there is decreasing impact on school reform, but there is also an increasing commitment required from all parties.

Based on his review of school-business collaborations, Staley (1990b) identified three levels of business involvement with schools:

> Level One—money/equipment from business/industry
> Level Two—people exchanges
> Level Three—idea exchanges

He further indicated that level three leads to the truest form of collaboration.

Collaborations have also been classified by their focus. Smith (1989) identified three types: (1) systemic partnerships that focus on effecting broad-scale changes in education, (2) single-purpose projects aimed typically at improving workplace skills and employability, and (3) adopt-a-school projects which pair individual businesses and schools to provide a broad range of benefits to schools.

How Are Parents Involved in Their Children's Schools? As part of more than a decade of research on teacher/parent practices in family-school connections, Epstein identified five types of parent involvement. These were:

1. parents fulfilling their basic obligations as parents (i.e., helping with homework)
2. communications from school to home

3. parent involvement at school (volunteers)
4. parent involvement in learning activities at home
5. parent involvement in governance and advocacy (in Brandt, 1989).

Henderson (1987) classified the types of parent involvement activities differently. She distinguished two types: (1) parent activity designed to improve the overall school program (i.e., volunteer work, involvement in school governance, or service in parent-teacher organization) and (2) parent activity aimed directly at assisting one's own child (i.e., attending parent-teacher conferences, helping with assignments, or attending school events).

Collaboratives among schools, businesses, and parents can comprise entire educational systems or single schools. Individual organizations or coalitions can represent the community side of the collaboration. Umbrella science and technology organizations such as those found in cities such as Atlanta, Boston, and Philadelphia and states such as Arizona, Colorado, Iowa, and Texas have also been developed to advocate, initiate, coordinate, direct, and evaluate collaboratives in science and STS education (Triangle Coalition, 1986).

School-Community Members' Perceptions on Collaboration

Business and Education: Coming Together. In years past, differences in perceptions of business and education existed along with a reluctance to collaborate (Levine, 1986).

> Representatives of business and the public schools, although recognizing the need for greater collaboration, are wary of one another. Business people are concerned about the quality of public schools but are reluctant to enter the arena of public education. They feel they have little expertise to offer, and they would rather not get involved in controversial issues. Educators, too, are ambivalent. Remembering business's earlier efforts to impose the factory model on the school, they are suspicious of the motives of the business community. On the other hand, they know public schools need a strong, concerned advocacy group. (p. 47)

Recently, however, the beliefs of many business and education leaders towards one another and towards education have begun to merge. Weisman, for example, reported that "within the past decade the two sectors have come to realize they need each other more than ever. Industry depends on the schools to provide a capable workforce in an era of intense international competition, they point out, while the schools have increasingly turned to the business community for monetary and professional help with the education reform movement" (Weisman, 1990, p. 11).

When asked why they chose to participate in an STS curriculum reform project, Staley (1990a) discovered that business/industry personnel viewed the potential to make an impact on curriculum as important. The group of more than 65 business/industry volunteers in the project also appreciated the opportunity to be of service to a school-community and the chance to accomplish something worthwhile. The business/industry volunteers in this project appeared to be motivated by rewards which were intrinsic in helping the school-community, rather than rewards which were extrinsic in advancing their status or careers.

But what are the educational goals upon which business and education agree? In the Staley project (1990a) the top four of nine broad emphases were ranked in identical order for both groups: (1) increased emphasis on thinking skills, (2) basic skills, (3) science and technology, and (4) study of the future. The ranking of thinking skills as a clear, number one choice was supported by the National Institute of Education (1983) who suggested that, while there may be conflicting interests in corporate involvement with public schools, business and education both have a common concern for developing the problem-solving skills of students.

These conclusions suggest that today, contrary to popular opinion, both educators and members of the business community appear to have similar ideas about the emphasis that should be placed on curricular reform efforts. Furthermore, the convergence of views about the importance of goals such as the development of higher-level thinking and citizenship participation skills provide further support and justification for STS which has these same goals. Finally, it appears that businesses and schools are beginning to view themselves as capable of collaboration in efforts to improve the quality of our public schools.

There are others, however, who suggest there is still a ways to go before unanimity of perception and goals for restructuring can be claimed. For example, Smith said after researching many school-business cooperatives, "There is little agreement on the specific aims school/business partnership should seek to attain. Broadly, everyone agrees on the need for improved educational performance and a better 'product' from the schools. Although some take this to signal the need for systemic change, a far more common interpretation of the call is for general 'school improvement,' a far weaker expression under which many quite small and limited partnerships can, and do, claim success" (Smith, 1989, pp. 64–65).

The Evolving Role of Business in Education Reform. A review of literature on roles business has played reveals an evolution in these roles which somewhat parallels the changes in perception of goals as noted above. To date, the course of business involvement with education has been primarily through the first and second level activities as described earlier by Staley (1990b). Only recently has business begun to engage in long-term efforts and decision-making of the type referred to earlier as level three involvement by Staley.

The National Alliance of Business (1989c) suggested that the evolution of business involvement was from activities like adopt-a-school or tutoring programs, which got businesses involved and made them "feel good," to attending school board meetings, visiting schools to see how education operates, and studying education issues. As business representatives became acquainted and more comfortable with schools and their environment, they were able to provide more assistance, involvement, and eventually become part of the policy-making process.

While the literature indicates that businesses and schools have begun to collaborate on school reform, Smith suggested that "School/business collaborations have thus far been augmentations of, rather than alternatives to, what is already in place. Too many programs are one-time, short-term, and serve limited numbers of schools and youth, hardly equal to the long-term, complex and pervasive problems schools and the educational system face" (Smith, 1989, p. 65). He continued, "Most of the accomplishments of the collaboratives . . . emanated from the business side, in the form of jobs, staff, monetary, and other resources. The schools have been for the most part recipients; their role has been largely passive, producing few tangible steps of their own" (pp. 65–66).

What Roles Should Parents Play. What is more clearly recognized from research is the effect parent participation in the schooling process has on student achievement. At the high school level, Steinberg (1989) suggested that the family is the most important, non-institutional influence on student performance in school.

"As education has become more institutionalized and specialized," Johnston (1990, p. 9) suggested, "the participation of the family in the education of their children has been eroded." STS as a vehicle for involving parents is one way to overcome this erosion. The issues and problems that are the focus of STS are examined in the classroom and then can lead to the home and community for further study and action.

In addition, some schools are beginning to develop curricula for parents on how to work with their children in specific curricular areas. Things like *Family Math* developed at the Lawrence Hall of Science, University of California, and *Family Science* developed at Portland State University may soon lead to Family STS in the United States. Ogawa (1989) has already designed a family-based STS program in Japan. Such efforts would serve to enhance the literacy of parents and other youth leaders along with their students.

An analysis of 49 of the most important studies on home-school participation identified the significant impact parents play in their children's schooling. Not only is the family the primary educational environment, but it can have strong effects from early childhood on through high school. Furthermore, children from low-income and minority families have the most to gain when schools involve parents (Henderson, 1987). Finally, Henderson admonishes that "We cannot look at the school and the home in isolation from one another; we must see how they interconnect with each other and with the world at large" (Henderson, 1987, p. 9f).

Factors Important to Successful Collaboration

Suggestions about factors that appear to contribute to or inhibit success in school-community collaboration come from a wide variety of sources. What follows is an attempt to identify those factors for which there is both descriptive-empirical as well as prescriptive-common sense support in the literature. The focus is on the collaboration of businesses/industry or parents with schools.

At the beginning of his STS project, Staley (1990a) found an interesting difference in perception between the 25 school principals who volunteered to participate and the 41 principals who chose not to have their schools participate in the project. These differences indicated that the principals' perceptions about basic skill instruction was one important variable in the potential for success in school-community collaboration. Those who volunteered tended to view basic skills as a "means" to achieving other goals such as problem-solving, decision-making, and citizenship participation—goals of STS instruction. Non-volunteering principals tended to view basic skills as the "ends" or main focus of instruction, and approaches like STS might detract from this emphasis. If this is the case, it could have direct bearing on the outcome of future collaborative STS projects involving schools and the community.

Many of the studies and reports of school-community collaboration describe multiple factors or combinations of factors that appear to contribute to successful collaboration. Staley's project (1990a) revealed that the more successful collaborations, as judged by their achievement of project objectives, were affected by factors such as the following: (1) teachers' perceptions of changes in their own teaching style, (2) teachers' perceptions of the balance in the use of the five STS Teaching Components (STS Content, Personal Use, Societal Impact, Historical Development, and Thinking Skills) in their teaching (see Mitman, Marchran, & Mergendoller, 1987), (3) teachers' perceptions of the support for the project provided by their principal, and (4) teachers' perceptions of the support for the project provided by business/ industry.

Analysis of the literature on school-community collaborations suggested that no suitable paradigm or model has emerged to guide and encourage the field. Several single factors that appeared to contribute to successful collabo-ration have been identified, however. Those factors which that identified by three or more sources in this review and those based on results of empirical research, program evaluation, or program descriptions relating to one or more collaborative projects were used to create the list which follows. These factors appeared to increase the likelihood, though by no means the certainty, of successful school-community collaboration.

- Evidence of a long-term and broad-based commitment of all parties to coordination. In addition, there was strong support from the top levels of the school and business structures for the collaboration (Ascher, 1989; Clark, 1984; Committee for Economic Development, 1985; Jensen, 1985; Levine, 1983; National Alliance of Business, 1989b, 1989c; Smith, 1989).

- Goals, objectives, periodic assessment, and monitoring systems clearly identified at the outset and modified as necessary (Ascher, 1989; Clark, 1984; Committee for Economic Development, 1985; Hord, 1986; Jensen, 1985; Jung, 1984; Massachusetts State Department of Education, 1988; MacDowell, 1989; National Alliance of Business, 1989b, 1989c; Scharf, 1986; Smith, 1989).

- Strengths and concerns shared and needs matched with available resources (Committee for Economic Development, 1985; Hill, 1989; Jensen, 1985; National Alliance of Business, 1989c; Scharf, 1986; Sockel & McClain, 1978)

- Frequent planning and the establishment of a mechanism of communication between parties (Jensen, 1985; National Alliance of Business, 1989b; Sockel & McClain, 1978).

- Innovative and risk-taking behaviors on the part of collaborative members (Clark, 1984; National Alliance of Business, 1989a; Scharf, 1986).

- The orchestration of an outside agent or change manager who helps to facilitate successful collaborative planning, implementation, and assessment. An institutional structure such as a private industry council or a chamber of commerce, for example, proved useful in coordinating local business commitment and helped ensure continued involvement (Ad Hoc Committee on Education, 1988; The Conference Board, 1988; MacDowell, 1989; National Alliance of Business, 1989b, 1989c; Smith, 1989).

- Involvement of business in school governance along with joint action and decision-making by members of the collaboration (Ad Hoc Committee on Education, 1988; Ascher, 1989; Committee for Economic Development, 1985; Decker & Decker, 1988; Levine & Trachtman, 1988; National Alliance of Business, 1989b, 1989c).

- All partnership members understand the needs, concerns, and constraints of the other members and then create a shared vision of desired changes (Cirone, 1989; Decker & Decker, 1988; MacDowell, 1989; National Alliance of Business, 1989b, 1989c; Smith, 1989).

- Trust established among members which leads to building bridges between institutional cultures (Ascher, 1989; Clark, 1984; National Alliance of Business, 1989b, 1989c; Smith, 1989; Sockel & McClain, 1978; Zuga, 1989).

A final suggestion that had direct relevance for STS was that the focus for business/industry involvement should be on that part of the curriculum that makes sense to the company. MacDowell suggested starting with curriculum reform instead of general school reform. "Concentrate on specific curriculum subjects in which they have expertise and interest and in which the results are measurable. If these curriculum reforms work, the partners can use them later as a lever to address structural reform" (MacDowell, 1989, p. 11). These thoughts were supported by Fraser (1986) who suggested that success of magnet programs depended heavily on the partnership between the school and the businesses associated with the magnet specialty.

Smith's study of several school/business collaboratives revealed the difficulty of achieving true collaboration.

Knowledge about educational processes is asymmetrically distributed in most partnerships. Business people willingly involve themselves in specifying 'measurable' bottom-line objectives, but all too frequently have little sense of how schools can or will go about accomplishing them. The reluctance to get more deeply involved is understandable: business people are not educators, and do not wish to be. Yet so long as the business half of these partnerships remains at a distance from the educational process itself, substantive changes in the way education goes about its business are likely to be limited, and perhaps insignificant. (Smith, 1989, p. 66).

Parent Involvement

There is a growing body of literature on factors that appear to contribute to successful parent involvement in school programs. Of the characteristics examined including size of the family, the number of parents present, and the employment and economic status of the family, the characteristics that seemed to affect family involvement and school performance were family attitudes, behavior, and activity (Linney & Vernberg, 1983).

Contrary to popular belief in the early 1980s, all families regardless of socioeconomic status had similar preferences about the nature and the conduct of school communication (Lindle, 1989). Concurring, Epstein suggested that contrary to the assumption that lower economic families do not have the same goals for their children as middle class families, "Data from parents in the most economically depressed communities simply don't support that assumption. Parents say they want their children to succeed; they want to help them; and they need the school's and teacher's help to know what to do with their children at each grade level" (in Brandt, 1989, p. 27). "If schools don't work to involve parents, then parent education and family social class are very important for deciding who becomes involved. But if schools take parent involvement seriously and work to involve all parents, the social class and parents' level of education decrease or disappear as important factors" (in Brandt, 1989, p. 27).

Another factor apparently contributing to the successful involvement of parents of students most likely to drop out of school (at-risk students) is the ability of school personnel to build a trusting relationship with parents. Building trust is a crucial and difficult step because most parents of at-risk students did not themselves have positive educational experiences.

As for other factors affecting family participation, a long-term study by Williams and Chavkin (1989) with the Southwest Educational Development Laboratory from 1966–88 identified seven elements for successful parent involvement programs in their five-state region:

- written policies
- administrative support
- training
- partnership approach
- two-way communication
- networking
- evaluation

The researchers suggested that, while there is not one "perfect" parent involvement program, these seven elements might serve as a useful set of criteria for developing other parent involvement programs such as Family STS programs.

Implications for STS

As the NSTA suggests, "STS requires that we rethink, restructure, reorganize, rewrite, and revise current materials used to teach science" (NSTA, 1990, p. 250). To become a legitimate form of curriculum reform, however, STS must be shown to have a positive impact on student outcomes. But first, we must find ways for STS to be brought to and accepted by the schools. Since STS deals with local issues and problems, STS must be developed for and by the local school-community. While much of the research in school-community collaboration does not deal specifically with STS, the findings reported here have significant implications for STS and the role STS might play to garner the support of the community in the school reform process.

One implication from the research on school-community collaboration is that those involved in the development, implementation, and assessment of STS ought to find ways to bring about the support and involvement of the business and parent community in the process. The community can become involved in the identification of STS issues and problems, provide decision/policy-making advice and political and economic support for actions which can make STS a vital part of school-community education.

The second implication of this research is to use STS as a vehicle for using the educational resources of the home and community to investigate and take action on relevant STS issues and problems. Since teachers and textbooks cannot be expected to possess the latest information and resources dealing with the issues unique to their community, those individuals and groups in the community who have expertise and resources dealing with identified topics could be drawn upon for their help and guidance. Community businesses can become extensions of the school and provide valuable learning experiences that the school does not have the resources to provide. As a result, business employees also develop an appreciation for their role in helping students become responsible citizens.

Finally, effective school-business partnerships ought to enable students to apply newly acquired skills, gain an understanding of the responsibility of citizenship and make worthwhile contributions to society—the characteristics of a scientifically and technologically literate person as described by the NSTA.

Conclusion

While the factors and combination of factors necessary for effective school-community collaboration have yet to be firmly established, there are three general trends about school-community collaboration that have emerged that can be helpful in coordinating STS with community goals. First, school personnel and business/industry personnel are becoming more alike in their perceptions of what needs to be done and the roles each could play in restructuring education. Second, schools and businesses are beginning to view themselves as capable of collaborating to bring about school reform. Third, in concert with these first two trends, schools and businesses are beginning to move from programs like adopt-a-school and job and grant programs to true collaborations, called Level Three Involvement by Staley (1990b), in which all parties in positions of responsibility offer ideas and participate in the decision-making process at the school level.

It is also obvious that, with the right mix of factors as suggested in this review, school-community collaborations have potential to effect change. "The best [school-community collaboratives] . . . have thus far served . . . as catalysts for raising and discussing educational issues of importance and heightening awareness, particularly in the private sector, of the need for change and improvement. The key remaining problem is in finding tangible courses of action, the critical next step in the evolution of these partnerships" (Smith, 1989, p. 66). Therefore, instead of continuing to search for that single model or approach to STS curriculum reform that will work everywhere, school principals, school boards, legislators, government administrators, and business leaders must find ways to coordinate efforts to stimulate innovation and adaptation of programs to fit unique local needs and circumstances.

References

Ad Hoc Committee on Education. (1988). *The role of business in reform: Blueprint for action.* New York, NY: The Business Roundtable.

Ascher, C. (1989). *Urban school-community alliances, trends and issues.* New York, NY: No. 10 ERIC Clearinghouse on Urban Education.

Boyer, E. (1989). What teachers say about children in America. *Educational Leadership, 46*(8), 73–75.

Brandt, R. (1989). On parents and schools: A conversation with Joyce Epstein. *Educational Leadership, 47*(2), 24–27.

Brandwein, P. (1981). *Memorandum: On renewing schooling and education.* New York, NY: Harcourt Brace Jovanovich.

Brinkerhoff, R. (1986). *Values in school science: Some practical materials and suggestions.* Exeter, NH: Phillips Exeter Academy.

Carruthers, G. (1990). *Sharing responsibility for success.* Denver, CO: Education Commission of the States.

Cirone, W. (1989). Partnerships: The community education process in action. *Community Education Journal, 16*(2), 12–15.

Clark, R. (1984). *Factors influencing success in a school-university industry partnership for teacher education.* Amherst, MA: University of Massachusetts.

Committee for Economic Development. (1985). *Investing in our children: Business and the public schools.* New York, NY: Author.

Conference Board, The. (1988). *Beyond business/education partnerships: The business experience, Research report No. 918.* New York, NY: Author.

Decker, L., & Decker, V. (1988). *Home/school/community involvement.* Arlington, VA: American Association of School Administrators.

Fraser, L. (1986). Atlanta: Magnet schools discover the power of partnership. *ProEducation, 3*(3), 33–34.

Goodlad, J. I. (1984). *A place called school—Prospects for the future.* New York, NY: McGraw Hill Book Co.

Henderson, A. (1987). *The evidence continues to grow.* Columbia, MD: National Committee for Citizens in Education.

Hill, P. (1989). *Educational progress: Cities mobilize to improve their schools.* Santa Monica, CA: The Rand Corporation.

Hord, S. (1986). A synthesis of research on organizational collaboration. *Educational Leadership, 43*(5), 22–26.

Hubbard, J. (1989/1990). Building an alliance for science. *Science Interface, 2*(1), 2.

Jensen, M. (1985). *Salem program demonstrates five keys to a successful business-school partnership.* Eugene, OR: Oregon School Study Council.

Johnston, H. (1990). *The new American family and the school.* Columbus, OH: National Middle School Association.

Jung, S. (1984). *Evaluation's contribution to the success of a Silicon Valley school/industry partnership: The Peninsula Academies evaluation.* Paper presented at the Joint Annual Meeting of the Evaluation Network and Evaluation Research Society, San Francisco, CA.

Levine, M. (1983). *School reform: A role for the American business community.* Washington, DC: Committee for Economic Development.

Levine, M. (1986). Business and the public schools. *Educational Leadership, 43*(5), 47–49.

Levine, M., & Trachtman, R. (1988). *American business and the public school.* New York, NY: Teachers College Press.

Lindle, J. (1989). What do parents want from principals and teachers. *Educational Leadership, 47*(2), 12–14.

Lindquist, M. M. (Ed.). (1989). *Results from the fourth mathematics assessment of the National Assessment of Educational Progress.* Reston, VA: National Council of Teachers of Mathematics.

Linney, J., & Vernberg, E. (1983). Changing patterns of parental employment and family-school relationships. In C. D. Hayes and S. B. Kamerman (Eds.), *Children of working parents* (pp. 73–99). Washington, DC: National Academy Press.

MacDowell, M. (1989). Partnerships: Getting a return on the investment. *Educational Leadership, 47*(2), 15–17.

Massachusetts State Department of Education. (1988). *How are we doing? A brief guide to the evaluation of school-business partnerships.* Quincy, MA: Office of Community Education.

Miller, J. (1983). Scientific literacy: A conceptual and empirical review. *Daedalus, 112*(2), 29–48.

Mitman, A., Marchran, V., & Mergendoller, J. (1987). *The teaching of scientific literacy inservice program.* San Francisco, CA: Far West Laboratory for Educational Research and Development.

National Alliance of Business, Inc. (1987). *The fourth r: Workforce readiness: A guide to business-education partnerships.* Washington, DC: Author.

National Alliance of Business, Inc. (1989a). *A blueprint for business on restructuring education.* Washington, DC: Author.

National Alliance of Business, Inc. (1989b). *The compact project: School-business partnerships for improving education.* Washington, DC: Corporate Action Package and National Alliance of Business, Inc.

National Alliance of Business, Inc. (1989c, May). The disappearing quality of the U.S. workforce: What can we do to save it? *Time*, Special Advertising Section.

National Institute of Education. (1983). *Barriers to private sector public school collaboration.* Washington, DC: National Institute for Education and American Enterprise Institute for Public Policy Research.

National Science Teachers Association Board of Directors. (1990). Science/technology/society: A new effort for providing appropriate science for all. *Bulletin of Science, Technology and Society, 10* (5&6), 249–250.

Ogawa, M. (1989). Family-based STS education: A new approach. *Bulletin of Science, Technology and Society, 9*(4), 239–244.

Scharf, J. (1986). Thirty-eight partnership strategies: Industry and technical institute. *Canadian Vocational Journal, 22*(1), 6–9.

Smith, T. (1989). School/business partnerships: Summary of findings from two research projects. In R. Bossone and I. Pollshook (Eds.), *School/college/business partnerships: Proceedings of the Conference of the University/Urban Schools National Task Force* (pp. 63–67). Santa Barbara, CA: The Graduate School and University Center of The City University of New York

Sockel, R., & McClain, T. (1978). *School-business partnerships: A practitioner's guide.* Boston, MA: Massachusetts State Department of Education.

Staley, F. (1986). *A school-industry-community approach to the development of scientific and technological literacy among elementary school pupils.* (A proposal prepared for the National Science Foundation.) Tempe, AZ: Arizona State University.

Staley, F. (1987). Models and strategies for a school-industry-community approach to reforming the K–8 science curriculum with an STS emphasis. *Bulletin of Science, Technology and Society, 7*(5&6), 758–764.

Staley, F. (1990a). *Assessment of school-industry-business STS curriculum reform efforts.* (A final report to the National Science Foundation.) Tempe, AZ: Arizona State University.

Staley, F. (1990b, March). *Promoting school, community, and business partnerships for education in science, technology and society: Strategies and recommendations from Arizona.* Paper presented at the National Convention of the Association for Supervision and Curriculum Development, San Antonio, TX.

Steinberg, L. (1989). *Noninstitutional influences on high school achievement: Contribution of parents, peers, extracurricular activities and part time work.* Madison, WI: University of Wisconsin, Center on Effective Secondary Schools.

Triangle Coalition for Science and Technology Education. (1986). *How to form and operate a local alliance.* Washington, DC: National Science Teachers Association.

Weisman, J. (1990). Corporations back up calls for reform by lending their expertise to schools. *Education Week, 10*(11), 10–11.

Williams, D. & Chavkin, N. (1989). Essential elements of strong parent involvement programs. *Educational Leadership, 47*(2), 18–20.

Zuga, K. (1989). *Influences of the industrial culture on a partnership program, teachers, and curriculum.* Paper presented at the Annual Meeting of the American Educational Research Association, San Francisco, CA.

Expanding the Meaning of STS and the Movement across the Globe

Uri Zoller
Haifa University, Oranim, Israel

I

t is technology, more than any other force in modern society, that quickly and dramatically affects and disturbs the personal, social, economic, political, and physical aspects of human existence. This is due primarily to the direct impact of technology on values by virtue of its capacity for: (1) making possible what was not possible before; (2) creating new opportunities (and illusions); (3) offering new options to choose from; and (4) playing a major role in most of the crucial existence/survival issues faced by individual nations and the international community.

Most people all over the world strongly believe that technological development is the key to both a rise in their standard of living and an improvement in the quality of their lives. Moreover, no matter in what state of technological development a certain nation is, the basic aspirations and expectations people have are essentially the same as those that dominate the highly sophisticated and technologically developed modern Western societies. Thus the major problem facing our society today is the too-high human expectations from ever-accelerating technological development processes that cannot be met in our finite world with unevenly distributed resources.

The people-made technological world has created enormously complex problems in the socio-techno-enviro-political context which pose a tremendous challenge to humankind and its problem-solving and decision-making capabilities (Keiny & Zoller, 1991). Intelligent, rational, responsible, and feasible decisions in this context—for implementation and taking action accordingly—are vital for the very existence and survival of our democracies. Therefore, every citizen should hold a reflective and active attitude concerning the complex issues involved. This, in turn, requires the understanding of technology and its effects on the individual, society, and the environment. However, although science and technology are useful in establishing what can be technically done, alone or together, neither can tell us what *should* be done; the order of priorities and desired goals to be attained in the socio-technological context are matters of value judgment.

We seldom have a single, positive effect from a technologically-bound factor on society and/or the environment, but rather weighted effects of additive and antagonistic factors, the ultimate result(s) being cumulative and having long-range consequences. STS proponents worldwide have argued that the study and understanding of the interactions and relationships of science-

---

technology-environment-society (STES) should become an integral part of contemporary and future science education for all (Aikenhead, 1980; Bybee, 1987; Fensham, 1983; Solomon, 1988; Waks & Parkash, 1985; Yager, 1985; Zoller, 1987). The time has come for rational, intelligent decisions to be made and appropriate actions to be taken by all who should take an active and meaningful part in the democratic, decision-making process. Thus, in a world of unprecedented technological development and an information explosion, the crucial problems are not the technical aspects of handling and processing information, but rather the reasoned capabilities of being both selective in using the available information and critical in its interpretation as the basis for rational decisions to be made and acted upon. Human ability to make decisions concerning science/technology/environment/society-related issues is substantially dependent upon education, science education in particular. The above constitutes the deep-rooted rationale for STS education, the ultimate goal of which is the STS-literate citizen.

What comprises STS literacy? STS literacy is the combined capability of: (1) understanding, dealing with, and communicating about the interactions among science, technology, and society; (2) assessing technology; and (3) exercising meaningfully the rights and responsibilities of citizenship in democratic societies. Such capabilities of STS for the citizenry means science and technology for personal, societal, technological, and political purposes. STS literacy may be defined in terms of the capabilities needed to solve problems and make decisions (Zoller, 1987, 1990). These include:

1. recognizing that a problem exists and then examining it along with its implications
2. understanding the factual core of knowledge and concepts involved
3. appreciating the significance and meaning of alternative resolutions
4. proceeding through the process of solving a problem, not an exercise:
   - select the relevant data and information
   - analyze the data for its reasonableness, reliability, and validity
   - evaluate the dependability of information sources used and their degrees of bias
   - plan appropriate strategies for further dealing with the problem(s)
5. clarifying one's values and then applying a value judgment (and being prepared to defend it)
6. proceeding through the steps of making a decision:
   - make rational choices among available alternatives or generate new options
   - make a decision (or take a position)
7. acting according to the decision made
8. taking responsibility

Clearly, both problem-solving and decision-making in the context of STS education and the high levels of thinking and critical system thinking required on the part of both students and their teachers are different and much more demanding than the exercise-solving process in ordinary science teaching and education (Keiny & Zoller, 1991).

The short-term purpose of STS education worldwide is to achieve operational STS literacy in students through progressive stages of awareness, concern, concept acquisition and understanding, conceptual change, and action. To achieve this literacy requires appropriate STS-oriented modules, courses, and curricula implemented within contemporary and future science education at all levels.

The long-term objective is to empower every citizen to participate actively and responsibly in guiding technology so that its ultimate outcomes and long-term consequences (within the STS context) will be environmentally sound, developmentally sustainable, economically feasible, and socially satisfactory.

The above summarizes briefly what appears to be the agreed-upon intentions of STS education from both national and international perspectives. Major points of concern are: (1) how to translate the agreed-upon intentions and attainable STS literacy goals into teaching strategies, educational programs, courses, and curricula within formal education for all levels; (2) how to ensure that STS-oriented courses and curricula become an integral part of and have a recognized status within existing formal curricula; and (3) how to evaluate STS courses already implemented in terms of their goal attainment in general and student performance/achievement in particular.

A detailed description of all that was recently done regarding these three areas worldwide is beyond the scope of this chapter. But a brief account of the reality followed by what research says about this reality of the STS movement will constitute the essence of the next section.

Examples of the STS Movement Worldwide

Following a casual infusion of STS content into standard school science by loyal teacher enthusiasts in the late 1970s, a few STS-oriented curricular modules were developed and implemented such as those of the Science in the Social Context Project (SISCON) in the United Kingdom and a handful of courses like Physical Science—Society and Technology for year twelve students in Australia (Fensham, 1987).

The 1980s ushered in quite a number of STS-type curriculum projects worldwide such as Science in Society (Lewis, 1981), the PLON Project (Eijkelhof, Boeker, Raat, & Wihnbeed, 1981), Science in the Social Context (Solomon, 1983), and Innovations: The Social Consequences of Science and Technology (BSCS, 1984). A second generation of projects and courses followed. Notable among these are: the Wausau Modular Science/Technology/Society Project (Sampler, 1985); The O-level syllabus Science, Technology, and Society (Associated Lancashire School Examination Board, 1986); the Science and Technology 11 Course (Ministry of Education School Programs, 1986); the Science, Technology, Society DODDS Project (Rossier, 1986); the Israeli Environmental Education Project (Zoller, 1986–1987); the ChemCom Curriculum (Ware, Heikkinen, & Lippincot, 1987); the Ontario academic course Science in Society (Ministry of Education, Ontario, 1987); Science and Technology in Society (SATIS) (Association for Science Education, 1988); Science: A Way of Knowing (Aikenhead, 1989); and Science, Technology, and Society (Perrin, 1989).

All of these STS-based curriculum projects, modules, and courses present science and technology in their social context, interacting with one another and with society, and/or technology in its environmental and social context. They claim very similar objectives and raise similar issues concerning their development, implementation, impact, future prospects, and/or survival (Zoller, 1992).

In the United States, the STS scene has been typified by a wide spectrum of exemplary programs, mainly at the secondary school level, which were developed and implemented *locally* with various degrees of success. More recently, the impact of the STS movement on the reshaping of technology education nationwide is apparent (Savage, 1990). In contrast, outside the United States, the STS approach found its expression in three major STS-oriented facets—technology education, environmental education, and STS education proper—all of which, wherever applied, have been institutionalized, managed, directed, and controlled by the centralized educational authorities in some form or another of a mandatory *national* curriculum project.

The first facet, technology education, is currently the leading trend in Western Europe. Two noted examples are the introduction in 1982 of technology as a compulsory subject in all classes of the Swedish nine-year primary school (Riis, 1984), and the current practice in the United Kingdom where technology education has recently become recognized as a distinct area of education and is being developed and already introduced into the national curriculum as a mandatory component (McCormick, 1990).

The second facet, environmental education, notably as part of basic education at all school levels, is probably the leading STS-type curricular/ educational orientation in the third world countries and Eastern Europe (Connect, 1989). This has been due to the efforts and guidance of UNESCO.

The third facet, STS education proper, is dominant in several countries which have already implemented an STS science curriculum on a national scale. Three representative examples are the PLON Project in the Netherlands, the Science and Technology 11 Course initially implemented in 1986 in British Columbia, Canada (Curriculum Development Branch, B.C., 1986), and Science in Technological Society (MABAT in Hebrew) implemented in Israeli primary schools since 1987 (Ministry of Education, The Curriculum Branch, 1988). Most of the available STS-related research outside the United States is associated with the latter two.

In the PLON modular physics course the content serves as an organizer for the science content and topic sequence into the framework of which STS was purposely infused (Eijkelhof, Boeker, Raat, & Wihnbeed, 1981). The science content *per se* is selected from the physics discipline and students are assessed on their understanding of the STS content, but not nearly as extensively as they are on the pure science content (e.g., 20 percent vs. 80 percent) (Aikenhead, 1989).

The newly developed STS course entitled Science and Technology 11 (ST 11), was first implemented province-wide in British Columbia in the academic year 1986-87 with 6,700 grade 11 students enrolled (approximately 18 percent of the grade 11 students), jumping to 9,200 in the second year (Curriculum Development Branch, B.C., 1987; Williams, 1988).

The ST 11 is a full-year modular science course with required and optional modules, making an STS focus its central thrust. All but the first and last modules contain instructional materials for ten hours of classroom activity, plus additional hours of alternative and extension activities. The first and last modules provide 15 hours of directed activity. All teachers are expected to complete 60 hours of essential material from the required modules (e.g., Introduction to Science and Technology, The Computer in the Workplace, Telecommunication). The remaining 40 hours from the total 100 hours of the course can be selected by choosing any four of eleven optional modules (e.g., Health Technologies, Resource Management, Waste-Technology's By-product).

The modules are clustered using three organizers, Personal Connections, Local/Vocational Connections, and Global Connections, that provide students with the opportunities to develop an appreciation of the interactive nature of science, technology, and society; gain knowledge of technologies as application of science; and develop the ability to respond critically to technological issues. (The latter are the three superordinate goals of the ST 11 course.)

The Israeli STS curriculum MABAT is targeted to grades 1–6. Content organization is based on the disciplinary nature of natural science on the one hand and societal and value considerations, which take into account the learner needs, on the other hand (Ministry of Education, 1988). In grades one and two the teaching/learning is focussed on animals, plants, and non-living matter in natural and people-made environments, including the basic needs of people in their immediate environment. In grades three and four, an extension of the study of animals and plants is followed by that of the human being, emphasizing his or her uniqueness, the interactions/relationships with the world of matter and the exploitation of resources (e.g., water and energy) by means of technology. Involvement in relevant decision-making processes constitutes an integral part of this state of the program. In grades five and six the development of a holistic view of phenomena and processes and their interrelationships is the focus, based on the deepening of the knowledge and concepts acquired in previous classes. Active, responsible participation of people in their physical and social environments is further emphasized, based on information and communication skills. Both the potential and limitations of this involvement are critically examined. The objective of developing within pupils an overall view of the interactions among science, technology, and society and encouraging them to take an action accordingly is thus apparent.

The courses described above constitute merely a small part of the prolific outpouring of STS materials that we have witnessed in the last few years worldwide. The various locally developed courses make strong claims concerning their intended STS-oriented educational goals and, in most cases, are not followed by evaluation studies. Consequently, we are far from being able to use convincing empirical research to evaluate all these claims. However, some research seems to indicate that an all-purpose, formal science course does not cultivate the social or ethical skills that students are supposed to be developing in STS education. Indeed, the difficulty that students (and, in fact, all of us) have in applying decontextualized knowledge in everyday affective situations has been well documented (Solomon, 1987). Moreover, research shows that people strive to reach consensus, if necessary at the expense of consistency of formal logic, because they need social confirmation of their own formal world-picture if it is to have any validity for them. Students and adults perceive the media, particularly television, as their major source of STS-related information (Wiesenmayer, Murrin, & Tomera, 1984). This finding emphasizes the problematic nature of expecting the students' view of STS to be shifted in the "desired" direction through school-based science curricula.

Interpreting the Effects of STS Instruction

Interpretative Analysis. A thorough analysis was conducted of the Australian STS course Physical Science, Society, and Technology as a representative case study of an STS course (Fensham, 1987). Universities have not yet approved this subject to be included in the students' entrance scores. The researchers concluded that strong resistance to the course will emerge if non-traditional science topics are part of an STS course, the course competes in attractiveness with traditional science courses, claims to provide a sound basis of science learning in the university, includes a substantial portion of socio-politico-economical aspects, and seeks to compete with the traditional science courses for status.

A similar analysis of the development, implementation, and reception (by teachers) of the ST 11 course in British Columbia revealed that teachers (science and non-science) were not interested in promoting the course (Gaskell, 1987). This is consistent with the current situation in the United States where most of the resistance to STS is found among secondary teachers. The British Columbia study found that while the ST 11 course did not lure students from the traditional discipline-based science courses, it did lure them from other non-science courses. Teachers of these latter courses are consequently unsupportive of STS. Nor does STS gain support from senior secondary science teachers who take pride in, and gain status from, the standards they achieve in the university-oriented science courses they teach. The chief problem, however, is the ST 11 course's perceived lack of academic status. The conclusion is that the survival of the course may depend on creating more space in the system of graduation requirements, so that academically-oriented students can elect to take it (Gaskell, 1987).

Quantitative Research. As with any course of instruction, STS courses strive to attain certain goals. Whether or not some or all of these goals were attained was the focus of a large-scale study conducted in British Columbia that examined students' views/positions on STS-related issues after having had STS instruction (Zoller et al., 1990). This study, based on the Views on Science-Technology-Society (VOSTS) questionnaire (Aikenhead, 1987) and the prestated objectives of the ST 11 course, came to the following conclusions:

- A substantial change of the views/positions of senior high school students concerning the complex topic science, technology, and society in the "desired" direction correlates with the exposure of students to the ST 11 course.
- Some of the prespecified, superordinate goals of ST 11, which are typical for STS courses worldwide, were attained, though some of the related sub-goals were not achieved.
- Key outcomes of STS-oriented courses can be assessed in a simple, straightforward manner, and the resulting database useful as a basis for decision-making and future educational policy-making concerning STS courses and curricula.
- Student responses are (locally) contextually dependent (i.e., contingent on the particular context within which the issue was dealt with in class) and, with respect to some STS issues, gender dependent. Although not all the students (both non-ST 11 and ST 11) are clear about the different roles of science and technology in society, important goals of the ST 11 course were met by ST 11 students, many of whom were described by their teachers as "non-academics." Thus, STS graduates understand that ". . . society controls technological developments . . . [and] influences and responds to scientific activity," and recognize that ". . . decisions concerning scientific and technological issues are influenced by values" (Zoller et al., 1990, p. 31–32). However, understanding the difference between science and technology was not achieved.

In short, this research suggests that appropriate STS courses do work and some of their major goals are attainable.

In a complementary study, the beliefs and positions of grade eleven students who were enrolled in an STS course (and those who were not) as well as their respective STS and non-STS teachers were assessed on a provincial scale in British Columbia. The STS Beliefs and Positions Profiles (SBPP) of these target populations have been established and those of the STS students compared with those of their STS teachers and with non-STS students. Similarly the SBPPs of non-STS students and their teachers were compared (Zoller, Donn, Wild, & Beckett, 1991).

Significant differences between the SBPPs of STS students and teachers and STS and non-STS students were found on most of the issues assessed, except for the STS literacy category.

The results and the analysis of data suggest the following:

- STS *education* rather than STS preaching or indoctrination is the norm in STS course teaching.
- The goal of STS-literate students (and teachers, apparently) has not yet been achieved.
- STS students' long-term retention capability of the established and desired SBPPs is questionable because the differences between the SBPPs of STS and non-STS students decreased when their STS views were assessed again a year later.

These results suggest that more needs to be done. Appropriate teaching strategies should be implemented in both STS courses and teacher training programs if the goal of STS literacy is to be attained and the achievements of the STS courses are to be retained by "STS graduates" (Zoller et al., 1990).

Finally, recent studies of the effectiveness of pre-service STS-oriented university courses in Canada (Zoller, 1991), and inservice courses for elementary science teachers implementing the new STS-oriented MABAT curriculum in Israel (Ben-Chaim, Jaffe, & Zoller, 1993), revealed a couple of things. Prospective science teachers comprehend STS-oriented instructional models and gain in their higher-level cognitive learning, but attention to the implementation phase is required to close the gap between functional paradigms of prospective teachers and STS educators. They also revealed that an appropriately designed, inservice STS course for elementary science teachers does result in a shift of their STS views/positions in the "desired" direction. Indeed, as was also demonstrated in another study, elementary science teachers extended their repertoire of teaching strategies and felt more secure about the new pedagogy associated with STS teaching after being exposed to adequate inservice training (Riis, 1984).

Future Promises

The major problems of contemporary and future STS education were formulated at the outset of this chapter. All the science-related goals of education are expected to be achieved through STS. Therefore, winning the battle of science education for all through STS requires much more than conceptualization of the curriculum-teaching framework only in terms of what to teach (i.e., what material/content should be covered in class) or what to test (i.e., subject matter, facts, and disciplinary content). In view of the following, STS proponents should look for alternative models of teaching, teacher training, curriculum change implementation processes, learning, and assessment: the remaining resistance to the STS movement in various interested and/or involved groups; the acquired awareness, but not the necessary perception change (and/or new forms of conceptual framework) of STS on the part of teachers; the difficulties science teachers have in seeing how STS relates to their subject matter; and considering the lack of skills, experience, and confidence of teachers to teach STS.

Progress towards attaining the ultimate goal of "STS literacy for all" is imperative for ensuring the future, sustainable development (and survival) of our democratic society. The relevant data accumulated thus far in this respect are promising. Yet the future success of the STS movement on the international scale is not guaranteed.

Thus, it is very encouraging to find that appropriate STS courses do have an impact on both students and teachers, resulting in a meaningful change in their STS world outlook in the "desired" direction. Although these first steps towards STS literacy of both students and teachers has been taken, much has yet to be accomplished. New methodologies and strategies need to be developed and more purposeful actions taken in order to overcome such obstacles as the prevailing difficulty students and teachers alike have in distinguishing between science and technology and in understanding the complex science-technology-society interactions. We also want students, once they acquire STS literacy, to retain it beyond the time frame of the course and use it to overcome a tendency to comply with a socially accepted consensus that is inconsistent with their formal logic and critical thinking.

Finally, it should be recognized that drawing up good and promising proposals—like STS—for education and science education is not enough. The role of the interested groups that exist in support of, or opposition to, the STS reform in science education should be recognized and careful action should be taken. Most important, since both students and teachers are the products of a long tradition of teaching which is antagonistic, in many respects, to the STS approach, any change in favor of the latter is expected to be difficult, lengthy, and painful, and confront strong opposition from various directions. The successful implementation and future prospects of STS in science education are contingent on the direct, active participation of both students and teachers in the decision-making, development, and implementation processes involved in this reform effort.

References

Aikenhead, G. S. (1980). *Science in social issues: Implications for teaching.* Ottawa, Canada: Science Council of Canada.

Aikenhead, G. S. (1987). *Views on science-technology-society.* Saskatoon, Saskatchewan, Canada: University of Saskatchewan.

Aikenhead, G. S. (1989). Categories of STS instruction. *STS Research Network Missive, 3*(2), 20–23.

Associated Lancashire School Examination Board. (1986). *Science, technology and society: Syllabus for mature students.* United Kingdom: Northern Examining Association.

Association for Science Education. (1988). *Science and technology in society (SATIS).* Washington, DC: Office of High School Chemistry, American Chemical Society.

Ben-Chaim, D., Jaffe, N., & Zoller, U. (1993). Empowerment of Israeli elementary school teachers to implement an STS-oriented science curriculum reform. *School science and mathematics.* Manuscript accepted for publication.

Biological Sciences Curriculum Study. (1984). *Innovations: The social consequences of science and technology.* Dubuque, IA: Kendall/Hunt.

Bybee, R. W. (1987). Science education and the science-technology-society (STS) theme. *Science Education, 71*(5), 667–683.

Connect. (1989). *UNESCO-UNEP Environmental Education Newsletter, 15*(3).

Curriculum Development Branch, B.C. (1986). *Science and Technology 11 instructional resources manual.* British Columbia, Canada: Ministry of Education, Schools Department.

Curriculum Development Branch, B.C. (1987). *Science and Technology 11 survey results.* British Columbia, Canada: Ministry of Education, Schools Department.

Eijkelhof, H., Boeker, E., Raat, H., & Wihnbeed, H. (1981). *Physics in society.* Amsterdam, The Netherlands: Vu Boekhandle/Vitgeveri.

Fensham, P. J. (1983). A research base for new objectives of science teaching. *Science Education, 67*(1), 3–12.

Fensham, P. J. (1987). Physical science, society, and technology: A case study in the sociology of science. In K. Riquarts (Ed.), *Science and technology education and the quality of life, (Vol. 2), Proceedings of the 4th International IOSTE Symposium on World Trends in Science and Technology Education* (pp. 714–722). Kiel, Germany: Institute for Science Education.

Gaskell, P. J. (1987). *Science and technology in British Columbia: A course in search of a community.* Paper presented at the 4th International Symposium of World Trends in Science and Technology Education, Kiel, Germany.

Keiny, S., & Zoller, U. (Eds.). (1991). *Conceptual issues in environmental education.* New York, NY: Peter Lang Publisher, University Press.

Lewis, J. (1981). *Science and society.* London, England: Heinemann Educational Books, Ltd. and Association for Science Education.

McCormick, R. (1990). Technology and the national curriculum: The creation of 'a subject' by committee. *The Curriculum Journal, 1*(1), 39–51.

Ministry of Education, The Curriculum Branch. (1988). *Science in technological society.* (In Hebrew). Tel Aviv, Israel: Tel Aviv University, Israel Center for Science Education.

Ministry of Education, Ontario. (1987). *Science in society Ontario academic course (OAC).* (Curriculum Guide for Science; Intermediate and Senior Divisions) (Pre-edit draft). Ontario, British Columbia, Canada: Province of British Columbia, Curriculum Development Branch.

Ministry of Education School Programs. (1986). *Science and Technology 11.* (Curriculum Guide). Ontario, British Columbia, Canada: Province of British Columbia, Curriculum Development Branch.

Perrin, B. (1989). *Science, technology and society.* Milton, Queensland, Australia: Jacaranda Press.

Riis, U. (1984). *Technology and natural sciences in school and in society: Culture, education, and service training.* Paper presented at the 12th IPN Symposium, Kiel, Germany.

Rossier, K. (1986). *Science technology society. DODDS research and innovation project.* Germany: Department of Defense Dependents Schools.

Sampler (1985). *The Wausau modular-science/technology/society.* Wausau, WI: Modular-Science/Technology/Society, Inc.

Savage, E. N. (1990). *Determinants of advanced technological content in technology education curriculum.* Paper presented at the NATO Advanced Research Workshop, Eindhoven, The Netherlands.

Solomon, J. (1983). *Science in a social context (SisCon).* United Kingdom: Basil Blackwell and the Association for Science Education.

Solomon, J. (1987). Research on students' reactions to STS issues. In K. Riquarts (Ed.), *Science and technology education and the quality of life, (Vol. 2), Proceedings of the 4th International IOSTE Symposium on World Trends in Science and Technology Education* (pp. 623–625). Kiel, Germany: Institute for Science Education.

Solomon, J. (1988). Science, technology, and social courses: Tools for thinking about social issues. *International Journal of Science Education, 10*(4), 379–387.

Waks, L. J., & Parkash, M. S. (1985). STS education and its three step-sisters. *Bulletin of Science, Technology & Society, 5*(2), 105–116.

Ware, S. A., Heikkinen, H., & Lippincot, W. T. (1987). Industry and technology. The ChemCom philosophy and approach. A team report. In D. Waddington (Ed.), *The education of industry and technology: Vol. 3. Science and technology and future human needs.* Oxford, England: Pergamon Press for the International Council of Scientific Unions Press.

Wiesenmayer, R., Murrin, M., & Tomera, A. (1984). Environmental education related to issue awareness. In Iozzi (Ed.), *Monographs in Environmental Education.* ERIC.

Williams, D. J. R. (1988). *SCT 11. The British Columbia experiment.* Paper presented at the Greater Edmonton Teachers' Convention, Edmonton, Alberta, Canada.

Yager, R. E. (1985). An alternative view. *Journal of College Science Teaching, 14*(3), 223–224.

Zoller, U. (1986–1987). The Israeli Environmental Education Project: A new model for interdisciplinary student-oriented curriculum. *Journal of Environmental Education, 18*(2), 25–31.

Zoller, U. (1987). Problem-solving and decision-making in science-technology-environment-society (STES) education. In K. Riquarts (Ed.), *Science and technology education and the quality of life, (Vol. 2), Proceedings of the 4th International IOSTE Symposium on World Trends in Science and Technology Education* (pp. 562–569). Kiel, Germany: Institute for Science Education.

Zoller, U. (1990). Environmental education and the university. The 'problem solving-decision making act' within a critical system thinking framework. *Higher Education in Europe, 15*(4), 4–15.

Zoller, U. (1991). Teaching/learning styles, performance, and students' teaching evaluation in STES-focussed science teacher education. *Journal of Research in Science Teaching, 28*(7), 593–607.

Zoller, U. (1992). The technology/education interface: STES education for all. *Canadian Journal of Education, 17*(1), 86–91.

Zoller, U., Ebenezer, J., Morley, K., Paras, S., Sandberg, V., West, C., Wolthers, T., & Tan, S. H. (1990). Goal attainment in science-technology-society (STS) education and reality: The case of British Columbia. *Science Education, 74*(1), 19–36.

Zoller, U., Donn, S., Wild, R., & Beckett, P. (1991). Students' versus their teachers' beliefs and positions on science/technology/society (STS)-oriented issues. *International Journal of Science Teaching, 13*(1), 25–36.

Great Strides with STS in Britain

Anthea Maton
Education Connections

There has been a great deal of change in science education in the late 1980s and now the 90s, not just in the United States, but in many other countries too. There is great concern that, as our lives becomes more closely intertwined with technology, the general citizenry will be unable to function at full capacity. This is an interesting turn of events if you remember the 1960s and 70s, when the problems put forward often were concerned with use of the leisure time that technology was going to force on us.

Technology is an integral part of our lives, and must be an integral part of our education system. In order to gain maximum benefit from something, one should understand it. One of the questions that educators are grappling with currently, and the subject matter of this monograph, is reasonably new to me. Born in Great Britain, science, technology, and society were never completely separated in my mind, either as a student or as a physics teacher. Only after I had been teaching in the United States for two years did I realize that most teachers did not automatically draw from everyday life to illustrate each and every aspect of the science that they were teaching.

I started to look at this phenomenon more closely and have drawn some conclusions. Up to now it has been extremely difficult to give time to teaching anything more than science subject matter, and although most topics can be illustrated from "real life" rather than from accepted science illustrations, teachers have little time or motivation, or indeed encouragement, to stray far from the textbook. As anybody knows who has taught science courses in American schools, there is a rush from the first day to the last to try to cover the syllabus (textbook?), and there is precious little time to stop and smell the roses. Not only do the finer points of a subject have to be covered, but also the introduction and the "meat" of the subject too. This proves to be a herculean task for even the most able, experienced teacher. What is interesting is that the sciences are almost the only subjects to be treated this way, as one year courses. Languages have year 1, 2, 3, etc., and social studies are taught every year. You may say that science is taught every year, which in good educational systems it is. The problem lies in the fact that the science disciplines are separated year by year, so that any relevance, or crossover between the disciplines is difficult to see. Why then do we continue to think that a science subject is any different, and that we can teach it in one fell swoop?

These misgivings about the present system of the teaching of science are behind the Scope, Sequence, and Coordination of Secondary School Science (SS&C) project. This project is the brainchild of the National Science Teachers Association and through the generous support of the National Science

Foundation and the Department of Education, the structure of science education is taking a turn for the better.

The basis for SS&C is reasonably simple. Science should be viewed as one subject, and within this subject, special areas are recognized; those of biology, chemistry, Earth/space science, and physics. These areas must be seen as overlapping and as highly relevant to each other. To learn any one area isolated from another is to detract from a full understanding of that subject. If science is seen in this way, it is reasonable to say that "science" should be taught every year and that no one area should be separated completely from another. This approach is already in practice in England and Wales (Scotland has its own education system) under their new National Curriculum (DES and Welsh Office, 1989a, 1989b), having gotten rid of the discipline areas completely, talking only of different topics in science.

The history of science education in Great Britain is a checkered one. It is not relevant in this chapter to go into any extensive study of that history, but the interested reader may learn all that they please by reading *A History of Education in the Twentieth Century World* (Connell, 1980). A study of the last three decades is of greater interest, as it is here that the debate on the need for the teaching of relevant science comes to the forefront. The 1960s saw the birth of The Nuffield Science Teaching Project. This project was an attempt to let the student interact more closely with the science that they learned by significantly increasing the amount of practical experience that they had. It used the method of "guided discovery" and was popular with teachers and students alike. The drawbacks were twofold: the project relied heavily on specially built equipment and it was neither truly investigative nor very relevant to the student.

In the late 1970s, the Schools Council Integrated Science Project (SCISP) was begun. This project was a move to keep fourteen- to sixteen-year-olds interested in science. Students studied biology, chemistry, physics, and some Earth science and, although it proved elitist being designed for the top 20 percent of students, it did introduce "a genuine investigational approach to science because children were assessed on their abilities to hypothesize, design and plan investigations, carry them out, interpret their results, and present reports. In addition, it introduced many social issues into science lessons for the first time (officially) because once again, the examination required children to weigh evidence and present balanced arguments about the implications of science . . ." (Boyle, 1991).

The call for more relevant science courses increased and through the 80s, many programs came to the fore. The Association for Science Education (ASE) set up the SATIS project in 1984. The Association had previously published two courses for eleventh and twelfth grades, *Science and Society* and *SISCON in Schools*. Both of the courses looked at the interactions between science, technology, and society. An attempt was made to adapt them for use with younger students, but it wasn't successful. A working party was set up to look at the requirements of this younger age group, and from this grew *Science and Technology in Society* (ASE, 1986). This collection of the technology to be found in all aspects of modern life is used alongside science lessons as a resource, providing not only valuable "meat" but also suggestions for outside speaker categories and for field trips that would enhance the subject under scrutiny. At the same time that SATIS was being written and field-tested, the government, through the Department of Education and Science, put forward *5–16: A Statement of Policy*, and ASE published *Education Through Science*.

Others were also coming to the conclusion that societal issues and technology should be a part of students' education. Sue Dale Tunnicliffe warns that "problem solving alone is no good, it must be in the context of a real situation" (1989, p. 90).

With this strong STS atmosphere *in situ*, it is not surprising that in 1989 the Department of Education and Science introduced a national curriculum that has as two of its core subjects, Technology & Design and Science (DES and Welsh Office, 1989a, 1989b). With English, mathematics, and a foreign language, these are the only subjects that remain compulsory throughout a student's school career.

It is going to be extremely interesting to follow the progress of this new curriculum as we in the United States develop our future pathways in science education. Whatever shape our curricula take, it must be remembered that students are central to all our efforts, and that they will have to deal with this increasingly complex world long after we are departed.

References

Association for Science Education, The. (1986). *Science and technology in society.* Hatfield, England: Author.

Boyle, A. (1991, March). *The third millennium, a multicultural curriculum for science education.* Paper presented at the Annual Convention of the National Science Teachers Association, Houston, TX.

Connell, W. F. (1980). *A history of education in the twentieth century world.* New York, NY: Columbia University, Teachers College, Teachers College Press.

Department of Education and Science and the Welsh Office. (1989a). *Science in the national curriculum.* London, England: Her Majesty's Stationary Office.

Department of Education and Science and the Welsh Office. (1989b). *Technology and design in the national curriculum.* London, England: Her Majesty's Stationary Office.

Tunnicliffe, S. D. (1989). Challenge-based science, London Borough of Richmond, England, U.K. In B. N. Honeyman (Ed.), *Science education and the quality of life: Proceedings of the ICASE world conference: Conasta 37* (pp. 90–92). Canberra, Australia: Australian Science Teachers Association and International Council of Associations for Science Education.

Part IV
Results of STS Instruction

A form of research has defined STS. It was a synthesis effort outlined and described in Part I. Part II reported on various research efforts that established a need for more efforts and more significant moves to such instructional approaches. Part III reviewed STS efforts in related disciplines, from philosophical views, in communities beyond the school, and in the international arena. Part IV is basic to the title of the monograph. It is a review of research which has emerged in the United States during the past decade which elaborates specific results in terms of student learning after experiencing science with STS approaches.

Some of the following chapters illustrate the advantages of STS in terms of student motivation. There are also specific advantages for females and minorities when STS approaches are used. More positive attitudes are among the most striking advantages for STS. Finally, students display and use their learning in situations beyond the school and the classroom. All of these are areas where STS instruction is demonstrated as superior to more typical approaches to instruction.

19

An Issue as an Organizer: A Case Study

Lawrence R. Kellerman
Arizona State University

The Iowa Chautauqua Program boasts 50 lead teachers. These are teachers who have successfully implemented an STS curriculum in their K–12 classrooms and who have elected to participate in a two-week leadership conference at the University of Iowa. During this conference, these successful and enthusiastic STS teachers are immersed in the STS philosophy, by practicing STS strategies and planning workshops for new teachers who express interest in STS. Much time is also spent writing, forging ties with industry leaders, and practicing various assessment strategies.

This chapter profiles the philosophy and teaching strategies of a lead teacher in Iowa James Kollman, a chemistry teacher at Denison Community Schools in Denison, Iowa. Mr. Kollman has taught at Denison since 1987 and has taught fairly traditional chemistry sections including college-preparatory and practical chemistry sections.

Mr. Kollman became interested in STS and the Iowa Chautauqua Program in 1988. After participating in his initial STS/Chautauqua workshop, he chose two sections of practical chemistry for implementing STS modules. These students were unlikely to enter college and, if attending college, less likely to be science majors. Their future needs would not cause problems with a departure from the standard curriculum and the textbook.

Most STS modules begin with student curiosity. This means finding something the students identify as interesting—often an issue selected from a current event, from something encountered in the community, from a TV report, or from the newspaper. Much to Mr. Kollman's surprise, his practical chemistry students selected ozone depletion in the atmosphere as their problem and focus for study. Mr. Kollman initially felt that the students would be lucky to spend two weeks on the topic. But much to his surprise, ozone became the theme for the entire course. In the end he found that these least-successful chemistry students encountered a need (i.e., a reason) for considering and studying 85 percent of the material in the basic textbook. He reported being shocked that these students asked questions that arose from reports, interacted with experts, and found news articles on their own. The questions indicated a need for information that was readily available in the textbook.

- What is meant by a chemical reaction?
- What is pH?
- What is a solution?
- What is chemical bonding?

The textbook became the resource guide for the students. It was there to use when needed rather than because it contained the assignment. Kollman has provided an example of the contrast between his STS teaching and his former textbook teaching (see Figure 1).

Kollman (1990, personal communication) reported that the STS approach helped his students develop thinking skills.

> One of the greatest benefits of STS education is the ability to get students involved and interested in the subject matter. I give students complete ownership of the selection of the issues they want to investigate. We begin by looking through newspapers and magazines for articles that have something to do with science, or at least have a scientific component. The students then brainstorm pros and cons of each issue. Criteria used in selecting an issue include availability of resources, importance of the issue, ease in relating the issue to the classroom subject, and interest of the class in the issue. Using these criteria students are able to eliminate some issues as possibilities. AIDS has been a very popular issue; however, chemistry students find it difficult to relate AIDS to chemistry. Biology students see the AIDS issues as being a natural, and it has been used by my biology classes a number of times. Issues that have been identified by my students for research include: hazardous waste, ozone, chemical warfare, oil spills, recycling, pollution, poaching, animal rights, acid rain, abortion, steroids, alternative fuels, atmospheric chemistry, toxic waste, food chemistry, alcoholism, and nuclear waste.

While not all of these topics are issues a given class deals with, it is a list from which to start. Other topics are added to the list as they begin to appear in news stories. Students began to keep an eye on the news (both broadcast and print) to find new issues to use in class. They began to realize that there is a link between their science class and what is happening in the world around them.

Since the students select the issues themselves, they have a built-in interest. When the topic was ozone, students wrote to the company that manufactured the foam products used by the lunch program to find out if the foam contributed to the depletion of the ozone layer. They became interested in the manufacturing process of the foam and the chemical reactions involved. The gas laws had meaning to them because the gas laws related to their issue. Kollman had students produce video tapes showing how the issue had an effect on the community.

Another indication of how involved and interested students can get was demonstrated by a group of four boys who went out at 1:00 a.m. to collect water samples downstream from a local packing plant for their water quality study. When asked why they went out so late to collect their samples they said, "We didn't want them to see us because we want to ask them some questions and see if they're giving us the truth. Besides, it's more fun this way."

This statement says a lot about STS. First, it indicates that these students have developed the idea that information should be examined and not taken at face value. In other words, these students are demonstrating critical thinking. Secondly, they are having fun. If students enjoy what they are doing, they do a better job. Student comments like Tina Bissen's, "It started out as just a report, but then we really got into it," indicate students really get involved in their own learning by designing their own activities. This allows each student to approach the material in his or her own learning style and leads to greater student progress. In addition, the students experience less stress.

Upon completing their research, students decide what to do with their information. This stage of their project allows the students to do something with their information. It gives the students a chance to show off what they learn and gives them an outlet for their concerns. At the completion of the research portion of his study of ozone, Greg Gunderson said, "Some people hadn't even heard of the ozone layer. We wanted to make others more aware of what we found out." One action taken by this class was to set up displays

Figure 1

Comparison of Textbook and STS Approaches
Grade Level: High School Chemistry
Teaching Length: 25 Days

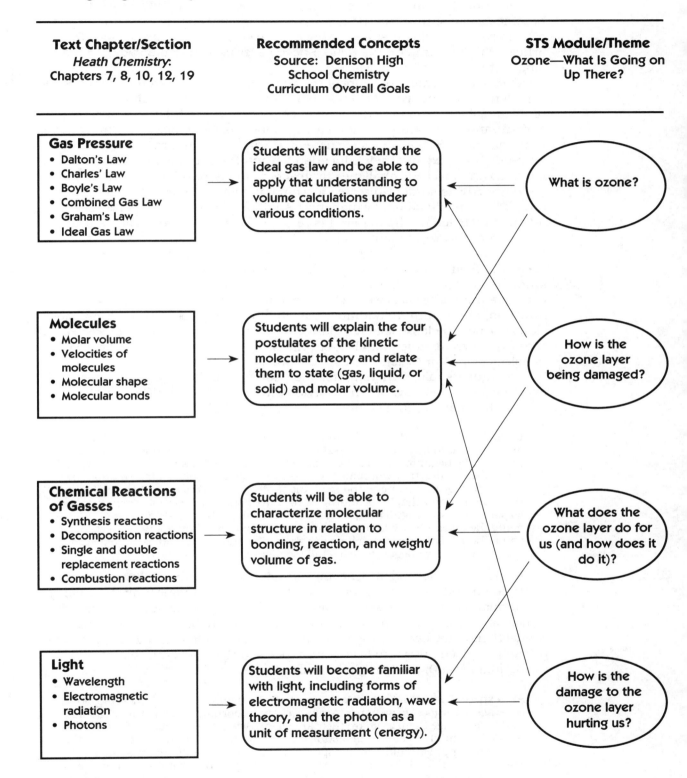

Text Chapter/Section	Recommended Concepts	STS Module/Theme
Heath Chemistry: Chapters 7, 8, 10, 12, 19	Source: Denison High School Chemistry Curriculum Overall Goals	Ozone—What Is Going on Up There?

Gas Pressure
- Dalton's Law
- Charles' Law
- Boyle's Law
- Combined Gas Law
- Graham's Law
- Ideal Gas Law

Students will understand the ideal gas law and be able to apply that understanding to volume calculations under various conditions.

What is ozone?

Molecules
- Molar volume
- Velocities of molecules
- Molecular shape
- Molecular bonds

Students will explain the four postulates of the kinetic molecular theory and relate them to state (gas, liquid, or solid) and molar volume.

How is the ozone layer being damaged?

Chemical Reactions of Gasses
- Synthesis reactions
- Decomposition reactions
- Single and double replacement reactions
- Combustion reactions

Students will be able to characterize molecular structure in relation to bonding, reaction, and weight/volume of gas.

What does the ozone layer do for us (and how does it do it)?

Light
- Wavelength
- Electromagnetic radiation
- Photons

Students will become familiar with light, including forms of electromagnetic radiation, wave theory, and the photon as a unit of measurement (energy).

How is the damage to the ozone layer hurting us?

showing products that were damaging to the ozone and alternative products that posed no threat to the ozone layer. Products for the display were donated by the local food store. The reason for the display was summed up by Kellie Tech who stated, "Maybe people will think next time they buy some of these products."

As students gain knowledge about an issue, they take it to heart. It becomes a cause they feel the need to do something about. "A year after the ozone project," Kollman states, "I have these students coming to me with new articles they've found on the topic. I have never had students show such a long-lasting interest in topics."

One of the greatest benefits of the STS approach to teaching science is the experience students gain in skills such as research, critical thinking, problem-solving, and integrating science concepts with their own experiences and situations. With an ever increasing emphasis being placed on higher-level thinking skills, STS is an excellent vehicle with which to provide opportunities for students to expand their education beyond the traditional classroom offerings and meet the challenge for teachers to address higher-level thinking.

Since STS is student-directed learning, it allows students to have input into their own educational experience. Additionally, since STS is issue-oriented instruction, the material is relevant to students and relieves some of the burn-out some students feel.

Students begin to make connections between the course work in science class and their other classes as well. In researching topics like deforestation, students are able to link their study of the biological issues present with concepts from other classes such as economics, math, social studies, nutrition, and health. In addition, they are frequently required to draw upon skills learned in classes such as language arts and math. To paraphrase a couple of current educational catch-phrases, what they are dealing with is "whole science," or "science across the curriculum."

As students take ownership for their education, they are able to design experiences in their own learning styles with as much complexity as they choose. Kollman (1990, personal communication) said,

> It has been my experience that students are not used to this type of freedom and are reluctant to take the reins, but as they discover that it is truly *their* research project they begin to expand their projects. My students have enjoyed educating the teacher. Often they will come to class excited about some new information they have found or that came in the mail and really seem to enjoy it when I tell them that I didn't know that bit of information. I have gone from being the 'expert' in my classroom answering all the questions (that I could) to having students say; 'We're doing the research. We know more about the topic than you do. Why do we need you in here?' This is a very telling question. The question is indicative of the fact the students have begun to learn independently.

Along with independent learning, students develop the ability to analyze information and use critical thinking. Students begin to question the validity of information and the possible biases of authors; they begin to explore side issues as they emerge, and students actually search for ways to make connections; they become their own teachers. As students progress with their research projects, they are becoming experts in their field of research.

Kollman (1990, personal communication) explains further.

> As "experts," students command attention. I attempt to get them some press coverage in the local newspaper to reinforce the importance of what they are doing. And I encourage them to share their knowledge with others. They have done this by teaching mini-lessons to elementary and middle school students, by setting up displays in public buildings, by sponsoring poster contests and displaying the posters in local businesses, and by asking the mayor to declare 'awareness days' city-wide to make the public more aware of the issues and facts they've uncovered. Students begin to feel like they are experts when they begin to share their information with an interested audience. It doesn't matter to them if the audience

is made up of students in an elementary school class, their families, or members of a local service organization. As long as someone is willing to listen, the student feels validated as an expert in his or her specific area of research.

Since formal education ends at some point in each student's life, isn't it important to provide them with the skills necessary for them to process information? Since students won't always have an expert or teacher available to help them understand the information they encounter, they must, at some point, develop the skills necessary to continue to learn on their own. In traditional classrooms, a wonderful job is done of breaking down information into small, digestible bits and telling the students what is important and what they will be tested over without ever explaining why something is important or why it rates being a test item. STS provides students with the opportunity to sift through information on their own and make their own decisions about what is important based upon their criteria. Beyond teaching information, STS teaches information management and how to analyze data critically; it allows for the connections to be made between bits of information. Information is transient; scientific information is subject to change and revision. The ability to work with information is crucial, and STS is probably the most effective way to teach students how to work with information.

Kollman (1990, personal communication) has provided assessment data that illustrate the advantages of his STS teaching over textbook teaching.

Figure 1

Comparison of Student Improvement in Five Assessment Areas

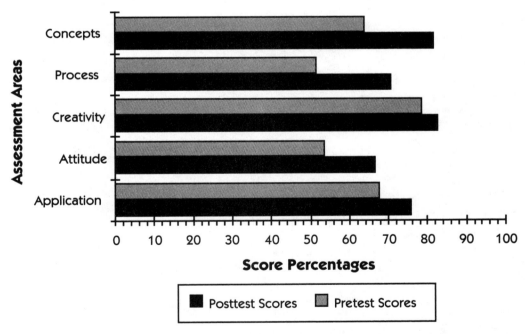

STS requires different teaching strategies. STS cannot exist if it is viewed as a new form of content. It is not primarily a new curriculum organized around different content. Instead STS provides a vehicle for assisting students to learn. This vehicle is largely one of different strategies for teachers to employ. Teachers rely on students as critical factors in the classroom plan and the learning environment. Without concern for new instructional techniques, STS initiatives are not likely to succeed.

20

Decision-Making: A Goal of STS

E. Joseph Piel
State University of New York at Stony Brook

So often science classes require students to merely regurgitate facts and non-facts, so much so that they become quite proficient at it. This regurgitation of facts becomes the sum and substance of their science education. The fact that they have learned little else in the process is a concern to all who are involved in the reform of science education.

The expectation is that if we can become involved in decision-making in problems we are interested in, we learn to enjoy decision-making and, in the process, also become adept at making decisions. This is an expectation that has not been adequately tested. There are a number of reasons for this lack of information on how well decision-making is learned and practiced. Is there more success in decision-making as a group process than as an individual exercise? Does decision-making under conditions of uncertainty differ substantially from decision-making when there is a certain answer? At present there do not seem to be any good instruments available to find the answers to these questions. In order to approach the answers, we need to look at decision-making situations and processes which are appropriate at the school level.

Decision-making situations are the heart of teaching and learning in the STS model, and there are many examples of decision-making systems. Each of them should include *modeling* of the situation, setting of *criteria*, examination of the *constraints*, and *optimization* among the various, often conflicting, components. What do we mean by these terms? The *model* is a mathematical, pictorial, or descriptive statement of the situation. The *criteria* are the goals we hope to reach through the decision-making process. The *constraints* are the many factors, such as people, laws, and technologies, that must be considered in the solution of the problem. And the *optimization* is the process we go through to come as close as possible to meeting the criteria (the optimum solution) in light of the various constraints. This is often referred to as the trade-off process.

A Model of the Decision-Making Process

People are more interested in making decisions about problems that make sense to them than abstract, textbook-type problems. This is where STS teaching has the overwhelming advantage over the "disciplines" as taught by most teachers.

Ask the following questions using a "real" situation or decision mentioned by students or found in the local news or from any other source.

Modeling:

• *Is there a problem mentioned or inferred in the situation?*

Problems come in all sizes; what is a problem to some is an answer to others. The answer to this question might require research into the science and technology of the situation. For example, the use of Styrofoam cups may or may not be considered a problem, based on the source of information which is available.

• *How did it become a problem?*

Here again, there is a need to look deeply into the situation and a possibility for some in-depth study of the history of science and technology. We must remember that for you, and certainly for me, the development of plastics from petroleum is a current event, but for the students it might well be history.

Criteria and Constraints:

• *What is the ideal solution and what are the factors that get in the way of reaching that solution?*

The *ideal* answer to the solid waste problem (criterion) is to have *no* waste product that is damaging to the environment. Ideal solutions are seldom attainable, however. The factors (constraints) that get in the way of meeting that criterion might be economic, political, technological, or scientific.

Optimization:

• *What are the alternatives from which a potential solution might come?*

Any potential solution to a problem in the STS area will fall into one or more of the following areas:

> Educational—behavior modification
> Legislative—a set of rules or laws
> Technological Fix—applying a technology

Constraints (again):

• *What are the ramifications of the application of any of the alternative solutions?*

Next, one should consider future ramifications of applying any of the suggested solutions to the problem. Often during the decision-making process, in devising and/or choosing an appropriate alternative, questions regarding the science or technology involved in the situation will arise. At this point the value of STS teaching is demonstrated. While the original problem might have been societal, the "decision-makers" need to (and want to) learn more about the science and technology involved in the situation.

The decision-making process is not confined to a single class period. It involves independent research, discussion with experts, discussion with parents at home, actual hands-on work in the laboratory (which might be in the science lab, in the parking lot, or in the student's basement) and discussions in class. While the use of this system can be applied to individual decision-making situations, STS situations, for the most part, require group decisions.

Application of the Above Decision-Making Model in the Classroom

As an example of how an STS situation is taught in the classroom, we will consider the pros and cons of a solid waste incinerator. This was the chosen topic at Ocean Township High School, Oakhurst, New Jersey, in classes taught by Ron Truex. There were 129 students in five STS classes.

The classes went through the decision-making process regarding the disposal of solid waste in their town. The approach to the decision was: Is it a problem? How did it become a problem? What are some alternatives? and What effect will the alternatives have on the community? Based on their study of the situation, the students came to the conclusion that an incinerator in their town was not the answer.

In the process of coming to that decision they had expert lectures by visiting proponents and opponents of the incinerator as well as concerned parents and community officials. They also studied the science behind the disposal of solid waste. If this had been the end of their involvement with the situation, we might never know what effect, if any, there was in learning decision-making skills and processes. This, however, was not the end of the story. As a result of their confidence in having studied the problem completely and applying appropriate decision-making processes, the students took their decision to public meetings regarding the siting of the incinerator. Their arguments were well-documented and were received appropriately along with those of experts who also testified.

It may well take years and more study by experts before there is enough information to determine if the decision that the students suggested would have been a good one, had it been accepted. But that is beside the point. The question is, did they actually develop the skills appropriate to informed decision-making? At this time the only evidence we have is that most of them think they did.

The class also studied a number of other situations such as nuclear energy, birth control, smoking and health, and drugs. At the end of the semester the students were asked if the course helped to develop skills for decision-making. Of the 129 students who were involved, 91 said that the course had helped develop their decision-making skills. But of the 91 who said "yes" to the question, only nine came close to describing any of the skills they had developed. These examples included: "I learned to look at all sides of a controversial question," "I am more aware because I actually know what I am talking about and learning about," "I was once totally against incineration, now I am not sure," and "I learned the importance of watching how things change before making a decision."

There are no good instruments available at this time to measure either group or personal decision-making under conditions of uncertainty. We can measure the difference between the decisions reached by the novice vs. the expert in areas where there is a certain and accepted answer to the problem being decided. All we need to do is to check the answer of the novice and the expert against the "right" answer.

Testing this type of decision-making, where following a set of logical steps results in the "right" solution, tests *knowledge of the process*, but not the actual application of the decision-making process. Students may know something about making decisions, yet not be good decision makers. Even essay questions on decision-making are difficult to write and even more difficult to analyze as proof that the person has mastered the skill of decision-making.

A typical essay-type question asked in a decision-making course is: If you were organizing a Delphic study to determine the feasibility of siting a plastics recycling plant in your county, whom would you invite to participate? In order to answer the question, the student needs to know what a Delphic study is, how it operates, and what is involved in the recycling of plastics. The final measure of what the student would do with the final results, which is the primary purpose of the study in the first place, cannot be determined unless the study is carried out and a decision is made and the effect of that decision is measured over time. Expertise in decision-making is difficult to measure even when dealing with trained professionals. Experts are found on opposite sides of many of the major questions of the day whether it be in decision-making or in predicting the future. One of the real concerns of the STS decision-maker is "How can I predict what effect my decision will make on society in the future?"

In Johnson (1988) there is a quote of Armstrong (1978) which seems to sum up the situation regarding expertise in predicting the ultimate results of a decision. "People are willing to pay heavily for expert advice about the future . . . The evidence is that this money is poorly spent. Expertise beyond a minimal level in the subject area is of almost no value . . . The implication is obvious and clear cut: Do not hire the best expert you can—or even close to the best. Hire the cheapest."

While all this might be true, and even a bit discouraging, that should not preclude us from attempting to teach decision-making. Actually, it should point out the necessity for making all people aware of the need to understand the process and to have experience in applying a decision-making process to their individual problems. And they should also examine the decision-making process followed by the experts as they publish their decisions.

Model of a Classroom-Tested Decision-Making Process

There are models of decision-making activities that are both enjoyable and effective in the classroom. They all include ways of determining the seriousness of the problem and systems for solving it, but few provide an effective way of examining the potential effects of the implementation of the solution.

An effective way of considering the future ramifications of a decision is the *Futures Wheel*. This description of the *Futures Wheel* is adapted from "Curriculum Grades 4–8" published in 1985 by the Acid Rain Foundation.

Following a thorough examination of a problem and the need for action, divide the class into groups of four or five and have each group come up with an "appropriate" alternative solution. Provide each group with a large sheet of newsprint, and then have them follow the steps below.

1. Have the recorder in each group draw a circle in the center of the sheet and write a few words describing the "solution."
2. In each group the students suggest things that might result from that solution. Each of the new events are written in circles connected by single lines to the original statement. These are *first order connections* to the alternative solution.
3. Now, ask the same question, "What might happen as a result of this event taking place?" Connect these *second order* events by a double line to the first order event.
4. On a scale of minus ten to plus ten, rate the possible societal effects of the second order events. Add up all the plus and minus values to decide how the original solution affects society as a whole.
5. It is now time to check against the probability of each of the secondary events taking place as a result of the primary event.
6. If the class does not understand that events have a probability of happening in a range from 0 to 1, this would be a good time to develop that concept.
7. Once the group understands the basic concept, rate the *probability* of each second order event occurring. This often requires further study of the problem and the science and technology involved.
8. Next multiply that *probability* by the *value assigned* to the event and compare the new summation with the results of the first assessment.
9. If the total score is a plus number, this indicates the alternative solution will have a positive effect on society as a whole and should be adopted. If it is negative, that is an indication that another alternative should be tested.
10. If all alternatives are negative, it is time to test the original situation using the *Futures Wheel* to determine if it is best to leave the situation alone, or to apply the least negative of the alternatives.

Figure 1

Sample Futures Wheel
(Decision to increase funding for solar research)

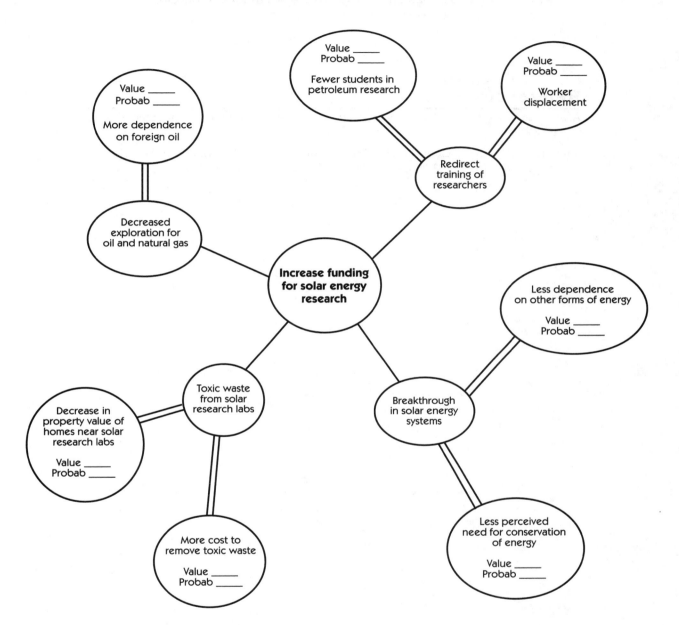

During this activity there will be many arguments as to the validity of connecting any one of the resulting events to the previous event and many more regarding the numerical value and the probability of the event occurring as a result of the first order event, or even of the first order event happening. Where is the scientific evidence that leads you to that conclusion? What is the history behind your opinion? These are the teachable moments which STS instruction provides.

There is no published evaluation of the effectiveness of this system of decision-making, or any other system. Anecdotal reports from teachers who have used the "Is It a Problem" system developed by the developers of *The Man Made World* in secondary schools and colleges, or the *Futures Wheel*

System in both middle school and high school, indicate that they are effective in getting group involvement in the process.

An important piece of needed research is devising an evaluation system which will measure the decision-making ability of students. When that is developed, it would be useful to apply that system to groups of students who use the *Futures Wheel System* or any other system for the development of decision-making under conditions of uncertainty.

References

Armstrong, J. S. (1978). *Long range forecasting: From crystal ball to computer*. New York, NY: Wiley

Johnson, E. J. (1988). Chapter I. In M. T. H. Chi, R. Glaser, & M. J. Fair (Eds.), *The nature of expertise* (p. 25). Hillsdale, NJ: Lawrence Erlbaum Associates.

21

Gender Differences in the Science Classroom: STS Bridging the Gap

Susan M. Blunck, Caroline S. Giles, and Julia M. McArthur
University of Iowa

Are we holding on to hope that somehow we can help students change to accommodate school science programs? If females and males differ in their way of knowing, why haven't schools developed appropriate teaching strategies that are more responsive to these differences? What types of transformations are needed in science education to help us bridge the gap in terms of gender issues? The focus of this chapter is on gender issues and the effects of inclusionary approaches to science teaching, specifically Science, Technology, Society (STS) techniques. Research is beginning to emerge that shows STS and other problem-centered practices to be more inclusionary and to stand out as powerful alternatives for making science more meaningful for all students.

"Ugly Duckling" Effect

Science education has long been plagued by what can be coined the "ugly duckling effect," an effect which a great number of students, especially females, are suffering from in science education. In the story "The Ugly Duckling," the young ducklings wouldn't accept the orphaned young swan because it was too different and too ugly. These differences blinded the ducks to the possibilities and potential for the cygnet. A similar scenario can be described for many female science students. Many females (and some males as well) have been thought of as being so different from the stereotypical science student of the traditional science classroom that their potentials in science have been overlooked.

But today schools are striving more than ever to create educational programs that are non-sexist and multi-cultural in their orientation (Oakes, 1990). The concern is for building science programs that will more effectively meet the needs of all students (NSTA, 1990). Equity in science education implies fairness in the distribution of services, equal access to programs, and the inclusion of non-discriminatory teaching practices in science. Since the advent of Title IX in 1972, segregation in our schools on the basis of gender has become a legal as well as a moral issue. Even though efforts spearheaded through Title IX have tried to provide for equal access to science courses and extracurricular activities related to science, research shows that students are treated differently based on a number of student attributes and traits, including gender (Good & Brophy, 1987). *How Schools Shortchange Girls*, a

---

1991 report by the American Association for University Women, points out many ways that girls are shortchanged in science and mathematics education (AAUW, 1992). For many educators, the hope is that female students will eventually change to accommodate the way that science is traditionally taught. Educators often do not consider that perhaps the problem is not with the individuals but stems from the way science is being taught in our schools. The question may not be so much, What is the matter with our students? but rather, How do we incorporate what we know about the development of male and female learners and then move towards more productive and inclusionary science practices and pedagogy? Without this consideration, females are often set off to the side in science and dismissed as not good enough, just as the ugly duckling was, because they have different needs, experiences, and beliefs. In many situations, blame and shame are cast upon the students if they do not succeed in science or choose not to participate (Kelly, 1987). As a result, most females move away from science and achieve success in other areas.

Explanations for the Effect

Much research and discussion has focused on this "ugly duckling effect" in science education, primarily characterizing the learners and defining the problem. Researchers have looked for, among other things, psychological and developmental explanations to describe differences between male and female learners (Kelly, 1987). A number of factors, including societal and parental pressures and childhood experiences, affect students' attitudes towards science (Kahle & Lakes, 1983). Female students have been shown to exhibit less positive attitudes towards science than their male counterparts (Skolnick, Langbort, & Day, 1982). They tend to view science as masculine and impersonal (Keller, 1982). Males tend to be more confident in their abilities when it comes to science (Kelly, 1987). As for the actual classroom performance, research has consistently shown that females do not perform as well as males in science classes. Many females view science classes as difficult (Kahle, 1983). And for females between the ages of nine and fourteen, interest in science and achievement levels decline (Hardin & Dede, 1978; National Assessment of Educational Progress, 1978, 1988). This type of research has provided useful information for science educators in terms of identifying differences.

It can be argued that this type of research only tends to reinforce the differences and perhaps even widen the gap between male and female science students (AAUW, 1991). Many attempts to deal with this effect have failed because they have been focused on the "problem" population and do not deal with the effect within the context of the regular classroom. The remedies have often taken the form of pull-out curricula, or fragmented curricula, which involved add-on components that failed to blend with other dimensions of the curriculum (Wilbur, 1991). This lack of integration and coordination often portrays the experiences as corrective rather than nurturing, reinforcing the idea that the students can be fixed to fit the mold.

Eliminating the Effect

Research is beginning to emerge that holds promise for a brighter future for females with respect to science education. Approaches to science instruction and curriculum design are being examined and new models based on the needs, experiences, and beliefs of the learner are beginning to emerge. The central tenets of the majority of problem-solving approaches are based on the principles of constructivism. At the center of a constructivist approach are the ideas that knowledge is not passively received but actively constructed by the learner and that cognition is adaptive, allowing for personalized organization of the experiential world (von Glasersfeld, 1988). The majority of students today would not fall into this category of a "constructed-learner" (Belenkey, Clinchy, Goldberger, & Tarule, 1986).

It is important that a vision emerges for ways science could be taught that would bring female and male students together as a community of learners. The research tides seem to be shifting towards the sociological and structural questions in hopes of uncovering evidence and explanations that will provide for more inclusive constructs and validate a broader spectrum of the population. Our goals for the 1990s and beyond should not be centered on replacing a womanless curriculum with a manless curriculum, but rather to transform the curriculum to include everyone (NSTA, 1990). The hope should not be for gender-free science but for gender-balanced science. "Only when the curriculum reflects the diversity of experiences, roles and achievements present in our population will it begin to prepare students for the diversity of the world. Transforming the curriculum is one important step towards increasing that diversity and connecting students to the curriculum" (Rosser, 1990, p. 18). Connecting students to the curriculum and allowing them to construct their own understandings based on personal experiences is critical in creating meaningful science experiences for students whether they be male or female.

The problem-centered curriculum stands out as a powerful alternative for making science more meaningful for all students (NSTA, 1990). The types of problem-centered approaches characterized in this discussion are those that ensure science and technology are considered in a social context, with the assessment of their benefits for the environment and human beings being central to the approach. Rosser states that adopting this perspective "may be the most important change that can be made for all people, both male and female" (Rosser, 1990). These problem-centered approaches have been given many different labels. Perhaps the most commonly used labels have been Science, Technology, Society (STS), issue-oriented, project-oriented, and problem-centered. For this reason it is difficult to relate one specific approach to gender or, for that matter, anything else. But for this discussion, the characteristics of the instruction are more important than the labels. Many gender issues that arise in today's science classroom result from the exclusionary pedagogical techniques that are still in place in traditional science programs (Belenkey, Clinchy, Goldberger, & Tarule, 1986). We need to be looking for approaches that are inclusive and have a normalizing effect on the differences between male and female learners. Our challenge is to develop approaches that integrate a number of essential, inclusive elements into the approach.

Perhaps one of the most important characteristics of an inclusionary approach to science teaching is the idea of connections. In the book *Women's Ways of Knowing*, the authors attempt to describe how women are taught and the way they learn science (Belenkey, Clinchy, Goldberger, & Tarule, 1986). Reactions to this book were interesting. Many women felt that the description and research set forth in the book matched their experiences perfectly. The interesting thing was that many men felt that the book accurately described their experiences and wondered why the book had the title it did. The authors also examined the work of successful women scientists. They found that the majority of these scientists "viewed all knowledge as contextual, experienced themselves as the creators of knowledge, and valued both subjective and objective strategies for knowing" (Belenkey, Clinchy, Goldberger, & Tarule, 1986). Most of these women were classified as "constructed-knowers." Research and work accomplished by these women emphasized connecting in some way. Connections between science and human beings were a very important concern. These connections could serve as the link to attract more women, people of color, and those white males not now attracted to science when science is taught in a traditional manner (Rosser, 1990). Students in the traditional science classroom have very few opportunities to personalize their learning by making connections with experiences from the real world. This notion of a "connected curriculum" should serve to connect students to

- themselves—by providing an environment for them to build positive feelings towards science-related personal attributes and skills
- science—by encouraging them to develop a personal interest stemming from their questions and experiences
- each other—by helping them establish relationships based on an appreciation of people's strengths and weaknesses
- the teacher—by creating a relationship built on providing personal support and mutual respect
- the real world—by encouraging them to get involved outside the classroom

These connections provide females and other students with an opportunity to see themselves reflected in the day-to-day experiences in the classroom. Emily Style (1988) believed that there must be many windows for students to look out onto the experiences of others and mirrors that reflect the personal realities of students. In a connected approach to science teaching there should also be opportunities for students to explore the real world and apply what they know to make stronger connections in their own minds. The concept of connectedness is central to many problem-solving approaches, including STS.

In addition to the concept of connectedness, Wilbur (1991) identified six other attributes of a "gender fair" approach to science teaching.

- A "gender fair" approach acknowledges and affirms variation.
- It should be inclusive, viewing differences within and among groups of people in a positive light. Students should see themselves reflected in the approach and identify positively with personal messages they uncover.
- It should be accurate, helping students uncover information and ideas that are verifiable and capable of withstanding critical analysis.
- It should be affirmative, emphasizing the value of individuals and groups.
- It should be representative, presenting multiple perspectives of an issue.
- It should be integrated, weaving together the interests, needs, and experiences of both males and females.

When these elements are in place, assessments have shown that student attitude becomes more positive for middle school and high school students, especially female students (NAEP 1978, 1988).

And how is student attitude affected by STS instruction? The Iowa Chautauqua Program, an inservice program for STS teachers K–12, has been looking at just this question. The Iowa definition of STS has considered and incorporated the inclusive characteristics presented in this discussion. Some interesting changes in student attitude have been discovered. These attitude changes reflect more positive perceptions about science in general and specific teacher characteristics. But perhaps most important, the gap between female and male learners has narrowed.

Not until recently has evidence started to emerge on the differential gender effects of inclusionary approaches. Blunck and Ajam (1991) looked at the gender-related differences in students' attitudes towards science, science classes, and science teachers. The experimental design involved using a pretest/posttest measure of treatment and control groups. Using data collected by 20 Iowa STS teachers, the study found that female students enjoyed their STS science classes more than males. Before STS instruction, females exhibited more negative attitudes towards science. After their STS experiences, the attitudes of females shifted significantly. Female students also exhibited more positive attitudes towards their science teacher.

Perhaps the most exciting finding from this study is that STS instruction seems to be narrowing the gap that usually exists between female and male learners. Certainly the hope with an inclusive approach such as STS is that attitudes will change positively, but there should also be a hope that the gap will narrow. This study represents only the tip of the iceberg but does serve as an example of what can happen when inclusive constructs are incorporated into teaching practices. Figures 1 and 2 reveal changes in student attitude related to students' perceptions of science and their science teacher. Data reflect the percentages of students (male and female) responding on the pre- and posttests. The differences are significant at the <0.05 level.

Figure I

Questions where STS has shown a differential effect on gender-related differences in students' attitudes favoring females

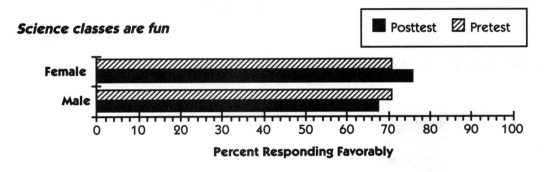

Science classes are fun

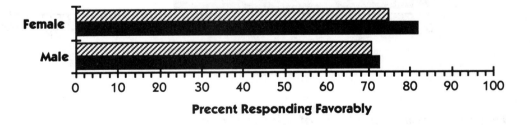

Teacher likes us to ask questions

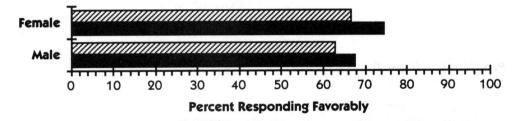

Teacher likes science

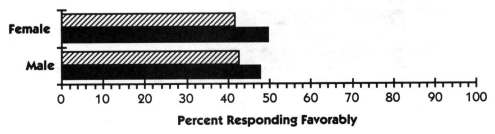

Teacher encourages creativity

Figure 2

Areas of students' attitudes towards science where STS has shown a normalizing effect favoring females

Science classes are exciting

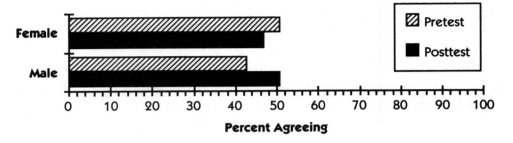

Science classes are difficult

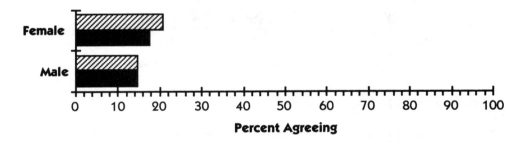

Problem solving is fun

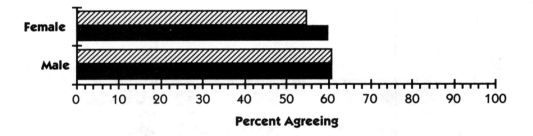

I wish there were more kinds of science classes

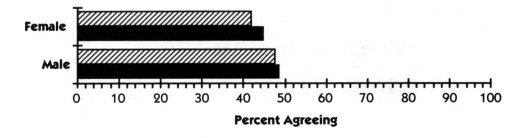

Most recently Mackinnu (1991) has investigated the differential gender effects of STS instruction compared to a textbook approach. Over 700 students and fifteen teachers were involved in this study. The experimental design involved using a pre- and posttest scheme with treatment and control groups. Before instruction, females showed more negative attitudes towards science than their male counterparts. But after instruction, those female students in STS classes showed more improvement in their attitudes than those taught by a comparable textbook approach. "This means that STS instruction does minimize the gap between male and female attitudes towards science for the teachers involved in this study" (Mackinnu, 1991, p. 118). Comparison of the t-tests on pretest and posttest scores showed a decrease in the number of classes with significant differences between males and females.

The Transformation Process

Given the fact that the majority of researchers agree that school science programs must be transformed and restructured to better meet the needs of both male and female students, STS and other inclusionary approaches are emerging as viable alternatives to traditional science programs. The attempts to restructure school science programs must address gender-related issues. For too long, we have focused on creating interventions to "fix" students so they accommodate a traditional science classroom setting instead of recognizing the qualities and potentials of these non-stereotypical science students, much as the potentials of the ugly duckling were overlooked.

As the research on inclusionary practices continues to grow, the challenge becomes one of developing approaches that will allow individuals to see themselves reflected in their science experiences. STS is only one of many approaches that is focused on bridging the gender gap. The challenge for science educators who are involved in these efforts is to collect evidence on the gender effects of their instruction. Inservice programs should stimulate awareness and the development of innovative approaches to deal with the problem. Too often we are quick to dismiss the idea that gender issues still exist within our science classrooms. It is the sensitivity of the teacher to these issues in the science classroom that will, in the long run, make the biggest difference of all.

References

American Association for University Women. (1992). *How schools shortchange girls*. Washington, DC: American Association of University Women.

American Association for University Women. (1991). *Shortchanging girls: Shortchanging America*. Washington, DC: American Association of University Women.

Belenky, M. F., Clinchy, B. M., Goldberger, N. R., & Tarule, J. M. (1986). *Women's ways of knowing*. New York, NY: Basic Books.

Blunck, S. M., & Ajam, M. (1991). Gender-related differences in students' attitude with STS instruction. *Chautauqua Notes, 6*(2), 2–3.

Good, T. L., & Brophy J. E. (1987). *Looking in classrooms*. New York, NY: Harper and Row Publishers.

Hardin, J., & Dede, C. J. (1978). Discrimination against women in science education. *The Science Teacher, 40*, 18–21.

Kahle, J. (1983). *The disadvantaged majority: Science education for women*. Burlington, NC: Carolina Biological Supply Company. AETS Outstanding Paper for 1983.

Kahle, J. B., & Lakes, M. K. (1983). The myth of equality in science classrooms. *Journal of Research in Science Teaching, 20*, 131–140.

Keller, E. F. (1982, Spring). Feminism and science. *Signs, 7*(3), 589–602.

Kelly, A. (1987). *Science for Girls?* Philadelphia, PA: Open University Press.

Mackinnu (1991). *Comparison of learning outcomes between classes taught with a science-technology-society (STS) approach and a textbook oriented approach.* Unpublished doctoral dissertation, University of Iowa, Iowa City.

National Assessment of Educational Progress. (1978, 1988). *Science achievement in the schools* (Science Report No. 08–S–01). Denver, CO: Education Commission of the States.

National Science Teachers Association. (1990). Science/technology/society: A new effort for providing appropriate science for all. (The NSTA position statement.) *Bulletin of Science, Technology & Society, 10*(5&6), 249–250.

Oakes, J. (1990). *Multiplying inequalities: The effects of race, social class and tracking on opportunities to learn mathematics and science.* Santa Monica, CA: The RAND Corporation.

Rosser, S. V. (1990). *Female-friendly science: Applying women's studies methods and theories to attract students.* New York, NY: Pergamon Press.

Skolnick, J., Langbort, C., & Day, L. (1982). *How to encourage girls in math and science: Strategies for parents and educators.* Englewood Cliffs, NJ: Prentice-Hall.

Style, E. (1988). Curriculum as window and mirror. In *Listening for all voices: Gender balancing the school curriculum.* Summit, NJ: Oak Knoll School.

von Glasersfeld, E. (1988). *Cognition, construction of knowledge, and teaching.* Washington, DC: National Science Foundation.

Wilbur, G. (1991, August). *Gender-fair curriculum.* Research report prepared by Wellesley College Research on Women.

STS Education and the Affective Domain

William F. McComas
University of Southern California

I t is doubtful that anyone would seriously argue that all learning in school science classes can be assessed by the present regime of teacher-made tests and standardized examinations. But a review of school assessment practices would reveal few exceptions to the rule that school science evaluation is typically limited to the lower levels of the cognitive realm. While it would be comforting to find that present assessment schemes are sufficient, the total student learning experience simply cannot be assessed solely by measuring the amount of information a student has amassed, nor even by measuring the ability of a student to apply what has been learned. What students feel about what they are learning and the new perspectives of the discipline they develop through their study should be considered by those designing and implementing instructional programs. In recent years, a number of educators (McComas, 1989a, 1989b; Schibeci, 1981; Yager & McCormack, 1989) have renewed the argument that students' attitudes with respect to their school science experience should be assessed. But perhaps Schwab (1962) provided the best justification for such an examination with his suggestion that in order for students to maintain and support scientific inquiry *outside* of school, it is necessary that they develop favorable attitudes towards all aspects of science while *in* school.

One of the most serious issues associated with an examination of student attitude assessment is found in the conclusions reached by a number of investigators (Lawrenz, 1976; National Assessment of Educational Progress, 1978; Yager & Penick, 1986) who showed that student interest in science declined *following* their participation in science class. This assertion has been substantiated more recently by Mullis and Jenkins (1988) in their summary of the 1986 National Assessment of Educational Progress. They stated that "most students in the third, seventh, and eleventh grades appear to be unenthusiastic about the value and personal relevance of their science learning, and their attitudes seem to decline as they progress through school" (p. 132), and that "less than half of seventh graders—and even fewer eleventh graders—perceived science would help them to earn a living, be important to them in life, or be used in many ways during adulthood" (p. 126). The results of the most recent NAEP study in 1990 confirm this trend of increasing disinterest in science. Jones, Mullis, Raizen, Weiss, and Weston (1992) report that there is a steady increase in the proportion of students expressing a dislike for science. In the 1990 study, 80 percent of fourth graders stated that they liked science, but that proportion dropped to 68 percent for eighth graders and 65 percent for those in twelfth grade.

Finally, there is even more reason to be concerned when reviewing the findings of Simpson and Oliver (1990). From a longitudinal study of almost 5,000 students beginning in grades six through ten and extending past high school graduation, these researchers found that both attitudes and motivation to achieve in science declined among all students from the start to the end of each school year and also fell off from one year to the next. Together, all of these studies show that, generally, the longer students study science the less they like it. Needless to say, indicators such as these provided by Simpson and Oliver (1990) and by successive NAEP examinations are discouraging.

The study reported here provides some perspectives on students' attitudes with respect to their participation in an instructional focus on themes and issues central to STS. In addition, the STS orientation is coupled with a plan to take teachers out of the spotlight by making them facilitators of student learning. Students, for their part, are expected to take a greater than customary role in providing direction for classroom discussion by building on their questions and concerns. To these ends, a new attitude-assessment instrument specific to the student-based, STS teaching environment was required.

Methods and Instrumentation

Germann (1988), reviewing the literature with respect to science attitudes, has identified several distinct attitude types. He points out that there is one range of scientific attitudes that most appropriately would be classified as cognitive and another that is in the affective realm. Cognitive scientific attitudes include knowledge of the ways in which science operates and information regarding scientific approaches to securing evidence and solving problems; in short, "thinking as scientists do" (Germann, 1988, p.690). Another array of attitudes would best be classified in the affective domain. These attitudes include a measure of what a person feels about careers in science, the process and procedures of science, and what they think about the nature of science teachers and science instruction. Many of these affective domain attitude dimensions are addressed in an attitude-assessment instrument developed for use as part of a series of STS training workshops for inservice teachers developed at the Science Education Center at the University of Iowa.

The Iowa Attitude Assessment Inventory (McComas & Yager, 1988) was, in part, based on affective domain items drawn from the NAEP studies. Its central objective is to assess students' perceptions of their science classes, science teachers, and the value of science study. The instrument consists of 51 items, most phrased in the form of a question such as, "Does your teacher enjoy science?" The multiple choices of Yes, No, and I Don't Know are provided as possible responses for the majority of the items.

The approximately 150 teachers[1] who attended training workshops providing experience with the STS instructional philosophy were asked to administer the attitude measure to their students both before and after a four- to nine-week unit stressing the interface between science, technology, and society. In all, the opinions of 1,735 students who completed both the pre- and post-unit attitude assessment instrument are included in Table 1 as matched pairs. This attitude survey is one of the largest matched-pairs studies yet conducted to assess student perspectives regarding science, science education, and science teachers in the STS educational environment. The results were analyzed by applying the McNemar chi-square statistic to point out any significant changes from pre-measure to post-measure.

[1] Approximately 27 percent of the teachers had their primary assignment in grades K–4, 43 percent in grades 5–7, and 30 percent in grades 8–12.

Results

For the majority of items on the Iowa Attitude Assessment instrument, a significant difference was noted between pre- and post-assessment. All statistically significant results are detailed in Table 1. Data from a smaller, but similar, pilot study of students of participants in STS workshops during 1987–88 (McComas, 1989a) help to substantiate the findings detailed here. In most cases, the percent of affirmative responses to an item from the 1987–88 study matched those from the survey reported here. Even the changes from premeasure were similar in magnitude when the results of both studies are compared.

Table 1

Percent of all affirmative responses from students receiving STS instruction in grade levels 1 and 3–12 showing significant changes from pretest to posttest attitude assessment.
(Chi-squares are significant at the 0.05 level)

Opinions about Science and Technology

	Pretest	Posttest	Change	Chi-square
Science (knowledge) is useful . . .				
Outside of school.	58.8	63.2	+ 4.4	0.013
In the future.	61.2	58.8	- 2.4	0.013
It is important to plan experiments to test ideas.	74.8	72.7	- 2.1	0.003
Technology affects my daily living.	51.2	55.6	+ 4.4	0.002

Opinions about Science Classes and Studying Science

	Pretest	Posttest	Change	Chi-square
Science study is helpful . . .				
Generally.	59.2	63.4	+ 4.2	0.022
In future study.	67.0	64.2	- 2.6	0.001
In making choices.	47.0	48.2	+ 1.2	0.023
Science class is . . .				
Interesting.	75.4	75.4	+ 0.0	0.000
Exciting.	46.7	48.8	+ 1.1	0.046
Difficult.	18.7	16.9	- 1.8	0.030
Boring.	19.8	21.6	+ 1.8	0.009

Table 1 (continued)

Science class . . .

Gives assistance with knowledge of careers.	29.3	37.8	+ 8.5	0.000
Provides fun trying to solve problems.	57.9	59.7	+ 1.8	0.023
Provides information to help me solve science-related world problems.	50.6	55.0	+ 4.4	0.015

Opinions about Scientists

	Pretest	Posttest	Change	Chi-square
Being a scientist would . . .				
Be fun.	41.2	36.7	- 4.5	0.001
Make me feel important.	56.1	53.7	- 2.4	0.012

Opinions about Science Teachers

	Pretest	Posttest	Change	Chi-square
My science teacher . . .				
Always encourages me to express my own opinion.	25.4	31.7	+ 6.3	0.000
Always encourages me to think for myself.	49.0	54.6	+ 3.4	0.000
Always encourages me to be creative.	42.4	49.7	+ 7.3	0.000
Asks frequent questions.	62.4	68.2	+ 5.8	0.000
Likes me to ask questions.	65.4	72.0	+ 6.6	0.000
Lets me give my own answers.	77.1	81.8	+ 4.7	0.000
Really likes science.	73.0	78.0	+ 5.0	0.000
Admits to not knowing all the answers.	59.9	71.2	+11.3	0.000
Makes studying science exciting.	54.3	54.0	- 0.3	0.040

Opinions about Solving Real-World Problems

	Pretest	Posttest	Change	Chi-square
I can help solve the problem of . . .				
Pollution.	33.2	35.7	+ 2.5	0.037
Energy waste.	28.9	31.0	+ 2.1	0.000
Overpopulation.	15.7	18.5	+ 2.8	0.037

Discussion

Despite the fact that a causative effect of an STS instructional orientation cannot be assured because of the design of the study, there are numerous indications that exposure to an STS philosophy generally results in positive changes in students' feelings about their school science experience. Three of the questions targeted at attitudes regarding the practical applications of science increase from first evaluation to the second. Students indicate that science is useful in making choices, is useful generally, and useful outside of school.

An item category showing many significant changes from pretest to post-test is that of students' opinions about their science teacher. Over three-quarters of all the questions asked of students about their science teacher resulted in positive, significant changes. Their teacher encouraged them to give their own answers, express opinions, ask frequent questions, and be creative as well as to think for themselves more frequently. In addition, students thought that their teacher really liked science. None of this seems surprising when teachers are revitalized by refocusing their instruction on the students and considering what is of interest to them.

Interestingly, the greatest change across the unit of STS instruction was to the question about the teacher knowing all the answers. It is clear that STS teachers have successfully communicated the idea that they do not—and perhaps should not—know all the answers to student questions. Before the STS unit, 60 percent of the students surveyed thought their teachers generally admitted to *not* knowing all the answers. But after the issue-based module of instruction, 71 percent of students responded positively to this question; their teachers did not have all the answers. Among the possible explanations is that STS issues did, in fact, extend beyond the teachers' knowledge bases. Another possibility is that teachers felt that they no longer had to supply answers to all student questions or that they should not be the sole source of information for students. Either explanation is consistent with the goals inherent in an STS philosophy of instruction. This same item showed the greatest change even in the smaller 1988 study (McComas, 1989a). In that survey, the corresponding pre-and postmeasure numbers were 57 and 69 percent. When teachers adopt the philosophy that issues—not just correct answers—are the real concern, this is no surprise.

Students demonstrated increasingly more positive attitudes towards science class—finding it more interesting and exciting while less difficult—with exposure to an STS unit. The slight increase in the number of those finding science boring is curious, but of little concern since this proportion is quite small at both the pre- and posttest levels. Students also expressed the view that science class helps with knowledge of careers; this item showed a huge increase of over eight percentage points. Science class also seems to provide a measure of fun with problem-solving activities and provide an increased opportunity to see how technology affects daily living. The fact that students seemed to see science study as slightly less useful in future study after STS instruction than before is a puzzle. This may be due to a realization on the part of students that they are capable of addressing their own questions, and taking relevant personal action has created in these students a suspicion regarding the usefulness of the orientation of traditional science instruction.

For good reason, only rarely would most science teachers ask students about their ability to handle real-world problems. Much of what is discussed in typical science classes does not relate to such issues. But in this study, students were given the opportunity to comment on six real-world problems and their personal ability to address each issue. Generally, students report that they had increased ability to use information from science class to solve real-world problems. With respect to three specific problems (pollution, energy waste, and overpopulation) there was a significant increase across the STS instructional unit. Three others (hunger, disease, and natural resources) did not show significant change. While there is no definitive explanation, it may be that the field of science used as the basis of the STS units played a role. Teachers tended to engage students in physical science-type issues when first attempting an STS orientation. The three topics failing to show a positive statistical change are from the life sciences and perhaps were a bit more unfamiliar to students.

One of the most confusing revelations from the survey is in the area of student impressions about scientists. There was no change when reviewing responses to questions about scientists being rich, working hard, being bored, or feeling lonely, but the number of students reporting negative feelings about being a scientist increased with respect to two aspects. After exposure to STS, students felt that being a scientist would be less fun and would make them feel less important. These results are difficult to explain, but since the business of school science is not to train future scientists per se, such results are less troubling than they might be otherwise. What is a small concern is that students do not seem, generally, to have gained an appreciation of what it means to be a scientist. Perhaps this should be considered in the design of future STS training workshops.

Lastly, we return to the central area of concern with respect to attitudes, that of declining student interest in science over time. One of the most exciting results from this study and, because of the strong indications from the NAEP studies, one that may most securely be said to be caused by exposure to an STS teaching philosophy, is that of students' increased interest in science over time. Although the Iowa Attitude Inventory did not ask the NAEP question, "Do you like science," the instrument did include the items, "What is your favorite class?" and "Is science generally useful?" The results to these questions may be seen in Tables 2 and 3 as responses grouped in grade levels.

The proportion of students choosing science as their favorite subject is certainly not resoundingly positive, but when one considers that students could indicate any other subject including art, music, and gym as their top choice, the result is not particularly disheartening. What is encouraging in the results shown in Table 2 is that for each grade level more students chose science as their favorite subject after their exposure to an issue-based science class than before such an experience. Both Table 2 and 3 show similar trends.

Table 2

Percent of students identifying science as their favorite subject at various grade levels				
Level	Grades	Pretest	Posttest	Change*
Upper Elementary	4–5	14.4	15.3	+ 0.9
Middle School	6–8	13.4	17.6	+ 4.2
Secondary School	9–12	14.6	16.7	+ 2.1

* These values are derived from the total, grouped, unmatched sample of student responses and have not been subjected to a statistical check to determine if the differences seen are significant from pretest to posttest or from level to level.

Table 3

Percent of students agreeing that the science they are studying is generally useful				
Level	Grades	Pretest	Posttest	Change*
Upper Elementary	4–5	57.6	61.0	+ 3.4
Middle School	6–8	60.5	63.7	+ 3.2
Secondary School	9–12	59.5	63.2	+ 3.7

* These values are derived from the total, grouped, unmatched sample of all student responses and have not been subjected to a statistical check to determine if the difference seen is significant from pretest to posttest or from level to level.

These data indicate that students exposed to an STS philosophy like science more and find science more worthwhile at the conclusion of their study than they did at the beginning. This finding stands in direct opposition to the general trend noted with traditional science instruction and shown so clearly in the NAEP (1978) studies and in the research conducted by Simpson and Oliver (1990).

In conclusion, it is true that some of the questions posed of students did not demonstrate a significant increase across the science, technology, and society unit, and a very few items decreased—thus requiring some additional study—but overall student attitudes improved during the course of STS instruction. Students, in general, are increasingly more positive about issues regarding their science teacher, science itself, and science class when exposed to an STS orientation for their science instruction.

Postscript: Developing and Maintaining Positive Attitudes through STS

This chapter has provided a rationale for assessing and fostering attitudes in science classes and provides important clues that STS instruction plays a role in the development of appropriate and positive science attitudes. What is yet to be discussed is the nature of the specific actions that can facilitate the inclusion of an STS focus in school science programs. In short, the move towards an STS instructional orientation can be facilitated by considering the needs and concerns of students, administrators, teachers, and parents. This author would argue strongly that only by taking into account the feelings of these groups and applying a suitable model for institutional change can STS augment or supplant traditional science instructional practices.

McComas, Blunck, McArthur, and Brockmeyer (1991) discuss many of the issues inherent in a shift towards an STS orientation and the corresponding development of positive attitudes. In brief, teachers must be encouraged to begin eliciting questions from students, giving them a sense that their ideas and feelings are important. Students, for their part, should be expected to take an increased responsibility for what is discussed in class as they move forward and ultimately apply what they have learned by taking action outside of school. Administrators who wish to support STS must allow both teachers and students to break away from traditional instructional methods, and parents are advised to take an active role in their child's education by working with them to explore ideas of concern and backing the new STS focus for science education.

By encouraging students to ask and explore their own personally relevant questions, educators can stimulate the development of positive attitudes towards science and science classes while helping them to understand what scientists do. The formation and maintenance of positive and appropriate student attitudes with respect to science and science class is at the heart of STS education. The spotlight on assessment in the affective domain coupled with the movement of school science programs towards an issue-based and integrated focus will serve well to make science education programs more useful to the students today and to the nation tomorrow.

References

Germann, P. J. (1988). Development of the attitude toward science in school assessment and its use to investigate the relationship between science achievement and attitude toward science in school. *Journal of Research in Science Teaching, 25*(8), 689–703.

Jones, L. R., Mullis, I. V. S., Raizen, S. A., Weiss, I. R., & Weston, E. A. (Eds.). (1992). *The 1990 science report card: NAEP's assessment of fourth, eighth and twelfth graders.* Washington, DC: Education Information Branch of the Office of Education Research and Improvement.

Lawrenz, F. (1976). Student perception of classroom learning environments in biology, chemistry and physics courses. *Journal of Research in Science Teaching, 13*(4), 315–323.

McComas, W. F. (1989a, December). Changing student attitudes with S/T/S education. *Chautauqua Notes, 5*(1), 1–3. The Science Education Center of the University of Iowa.

McComas, W. F. (1989b). The issue of effective and valid student evaluation. *Education and Urban Society, 22*(1), 72–82.

McComas, W. F., & Yager, R. E. (1988). *The Iowa assessment package for evaluation in five domains of science education.* Iowa City, IA: University of Iowa, Science Education Center.

McComas, W. F., Blunck, S. M., McArthur, J. M., & Brockmeyer, M. A. (1991). Changing the focus: Fostering the development of science, technology and society programs in schools. In D. W. Cheek, (Ed.), *Broadening participation in science, technology and medicine: Proceedings of the sixth annual technological literacy conference, Washington, DC.* Bloomington, IN: ERIC Clearinghouse for Social Studies/Social Science Education, pp. 157–169. (ERIC Document Reproduction Service.)

Mullis, I. V., & Jenkins, L. B. (Eds.). (1988). *The science report card: Elements of risk and recovery.* Report Number 17–S–01. Princeton, NJ: Educational Testing Service.

National Assessment of Educational Progress. (1978, May). The third assessment of science 1976–77. Report Number 08–S–08, related exercise set. Denver, CO.

Simpson, R., & Oliver, J. S. (1990). A summary of major influences on attitude toward and achievement in science among adolescent students. *Science Education, 74*(1), 1–10.

Schibeci, R. A. (1981). Do teachers rate science attitude objectives as highly as cognitive objectives? *Journal of Research in Science Teaching, 18*(1), 69–72.

Schwab, J. J. (1962). *The teaching of science as inquiry.* In J. J. Schwab & P. F. Brandwein, (Eds.), *The teaching of science* (pp. 3–103). Cambridge, MA: Harvard University Press.

Yager, R. E., & McCormack, A. J. (1989). Assessing teaching/learning successes in multiple domains of science and science education. *Science Education, 73*(1), 45–58.

Yager, R. E., & Penick, J. E. (1986). Perceptions of four age groups toward science classes, teachers and the value of science. *Science Education, 70*(4), 355–363.

Increased Actions by Students

Peter A. Rubba and Randall L. Wiesenmayer
The Pennsylvania State University and West Virginia University

Science and technology are inexorably intertwined with modern society. Few aspects of modern life are free of the impact of science and technology. The constant interactions among science, technology, and society spawn issues on which human values, beliefs, and attitudes frequently dictate differing points of view. Acid rain, AIDS, deforestation, use of food additives, genetic engineering, global warming, and ozone depletion are among the myriad science and technology-related societal issues, STS issues for short, that are current threats.

What will it take to resolve these STS issues and others that will arise in the future? In the broadest sense it will take citizen involvement; more specifically, it will take citizens empowered with the knowledge, skills, and affective qualities needed to take responsible action on STS issues.

This social responsibility perspective (Waks & Prakash, 1985) on STS issues entered the school science education arena roughly two decades ago through environmental education (EE). Stapp et al. (1969) proposed that EE should focus on the development of a citizenry that is aware of and concerned about the environment and associated problems. Moreover, he proposed that EE should help citizens develop the ". . . knowledge, attitudes, motivations, commitment, and skills to work individually and collectively toward solutions of current problems and the prevention of new ones" (Stapp et al., 1969, pp. 31–36). Stapp's perspective set the tone for later efforts at defining the domain of EE and, more recently, the domain of STS education.

The 1975 Belgrade Charter (1976) set forth objectives for EE that focused on helping students resolve environmental problems. In 1977, representatives from 70 nations at the Tbilisi Intergovernmental Conference on Environmental Education (1978) composed a set of objectives for EE that addressed knowledge, attitudes, skills, and participation. Working mainly from the Tbilisi Declaration, Hungerford, Peyton, and Wilke (1980) proposed the "superordinate goal" for environmental education to be:

> . . . to aid citizens in becoming environmentally knowledgeable and, above all, skilled and dedicated citizens who are willing to work, individually and collectively, toward achieving and/or maintaining a dynamic equilibrium between quality of life and quality of the environment. (p. 43)

The three authors postulated in an accompanying goal structure that, to attain the superordinate goal, learners need to develop: (1) knowledge of foundational ecological concepts, (2) an awareness of prominent environmental issues and the belief that these can only be resolved via citizen action, (3) the ability to investigate issues from differing perspectives, to propose alternative solutions, and to evaluate these, and (4) the ability to take actions consistent with the investigation and evaluate the results.

Recommendations for STS Education

This same social responsibility perspective was embodied in the reports and position statements of the early 1980s that recommended the inclusion of STS in school science (Aaronian & Brinkerhoff, 1980; Harms & Yager, 1981; National Science Board, 1983; NSTA, 1982) and social studies (National Council for the Social Studies, 1983) in the United States. Recent revisions of the NSTA and NCSS guidelines maintain this emphasis. The NSTA position statement *Science/Technology/Society: A New Effort for Providing Appropriate Science for All* notes:

> The scientifically and technologically literate person . . . engages in responsible personal and civic actions [on STS issues] after weighing the possible consequences of alternative options . . . (NSTA, 1990, p. 250)

Teaching About Science and Society in Social Studies: Education for Citizenship in the 21st Century (NCSS, 1990, p. 192) notes that teachers should assist students to:

- identify present action plans that clearly illustrate the relation of science and technology to decisions about personal and social issues and problems
- prepare an action plan
- implement the plan
- evaluate the results of the course of action

The early research supporting action as a goal for incorporating STS into the school science curriculum also comes from EE. Sia (Sia, Hungerford, & Tomera, 1986) and Hines (Hines, Hungerford, & Tomera, 1987) each analyzed the substantial body of research on environmental citizenship behavior to identify the factors/variables that predicted action on societal issues. The two studies showed that citizens who act on environmental issues, (i.e., ecologically based STS issues) possess four characteristics: they (1) are aware of issues, (2) are knowledgeable about actions that might be taken to resolve the issues, (3) have the ability to carry out or take actions on issues, and (4) possess certain personality and attitude characteristics that dispose them to act.

Researchers who examined curricular implementation of the factors (Klingler, 1980; Ramsey & Hungerford, 1989; Ramsey, Hungerford, & Tomera, 1981; Simpson, 1990), found that middle/junior high school students take a greater number of actions on environmental issues when the instruction contained all four factors. Instruction limited to the delivery of science content or only to making students aware of prominent environmental issues and possible courses of action (the first two components identified by Sia and Hines) did not lead students to take action nearly as frequently.

These studies from environmental education suggest that if we are to help students become active citizens on STS issues, they must learn how to investigate issues and ways to take action, in addition to increasing their awareness and knowledge of STS issues. The same studies, along with recent ones in STS education by the first author (Rubba, 1989a, 1989b), also demonstrate the need for students to have an opportunity in the classroom to apply issue investigation skills and action strategies in resolving an issue. It would appear that when the four components identified by Sia and Hines come together in STS education, students should develop the capabilities to act on STS issues and the associated perception of efficacy that will dispose them to continue to take action.

A Goal Structure for STS Education

We (Rubba & Wiesenmayer, 1985, 1988; Rubba, 1987) presented a goal structure and 53 learner competencies for STS instruction, modeled after the work of Hungerford, Peyton, and Wilke (1980) and based on the research in environmental citizenship behavior. The goals and competencies propose that when STS is integrated into school science (or social studies) for the purpose of helping students develop the knowledge, skills, and willingness to take action on STS issues, four levels of STS instruction need to be included: (1) STS Foundations Level, (2) STS Issue Awareness Level, (3) STS Issue Investigation Level, and (4) STS Issue Action Skill Development Level.

STS Foundations Level instruction provides students with knowledge of concepts in the natural sciences and social sciences, and on the nature of science, technology, and society, to enable them to make informed decisions on STS issues. Broad natural science concepts that cut across the respective biological, Earth, and physical science disciplines, such as those presented by Showalter (1974) (e.g., change, field, interaction, model, and system), and ones specific to the STS issue, are candidates for study. Social science concepts from anthropology, economics, political action, psychology, and sociology (e.g., attitude, behavior, institution, culture, social structure, ethics, society resources) also need to be studied in order to help learners understand our social system and view themselves as members of society. In addition, students need to develop an understanding of the nature of science and technology (their similarities and differences) while becoming cognizant of the typical interactions that occur among science, technology, and society.

At the STS Issue Awareness Level, students learn how the interactions among science, technology, and society sometimes result in issues that can be resolved via a process that involves examining all sides of the issue and then taking action. A major emphasis at this level is to promote an understanding of how factors such as religion, politics, economics, and personal interests—related human values, beliefs, and ethics and alternate solutions for resolving issues—affect one's view of STS issues. Students should become aware of the complexity of STS issues facing humankind, the impact of these issues and possible alternative solutions, and the need for responsible individual and group actions to achieve resolution.

At the STS Issue Investigation Level, students develop the knowledge and skills necessary to investigate STS issues and evaluate possible solutions with regard to various value positions via STS education that has two components. The first encompasses training with problem investigation skills, e.g., identifying and stating problems, using secondary sources, collecting data via primary sources, interpreting data, and drawing conclusions. The second component comprises opportunities for students to apply these skills in investigating STS issues so they develop capability and confidence in using the skills towards the resolution of STS issues.

At the STS Issue Action Skill Development Level, STS education seeks to develop skills students can use, working individually or in groups, to take effective action on STS issues. It includes instructional activities designed to develop an understanding of five categories of actions, i.e., consumerism, legal action, persuasion, physical action, and political action. Students also have opportunities to apply these modes of action in resolving STS issues and evaluate the effectiveness of doing so.

STS Issue Investigation and Action Units

STS instruction designed around these four levels comprises a project approach consisting of four- to six-week units that can be integrated into science courses. We refer to these as STS Issue Investigation and Action units after Hungerford's reference. An STS Issue Investigation and Action unit typically begins with activities on the nature of science and technology and characteristic interactions among science, technology, and society. Next, critical STS issues are identified and analyzed to determine what makes them issues, what are the relevant science and social science concepts, and what are the prominent value positions of the issue. An understanding of certain of the identified science and social science concepts may need to be developed at this point. Text or video case studies of STS issue resolutions may be used to demonstrate that only through responsible citizenship action is there a possibility for STS issues to be resolved and that even one person can have an impact.

An STS issue that is relevant to the community and students is then identified by the class, or a number of such issues may be selected by groups within a class, under the teacher's guidance. The aspect of the issue to be studied is typically expressed as an STS focusing question in order to provide guidance during the investigation and action activities. Students learn various skills necessary to investigate an issue as they apply the skills to the STS focusing question. Using primary and secondary library sources, securing data and information from governmental and private agencies, collecting natural science data on-site, or using questionnaires and opinionnaires to survey members of the community are among these investigation skills. More traditional instructional activities typically are used to help students develop an understanding of issue-relevant science and social science concepts. The students analyze the information collected and propose alternative resolutions for the STS issue. The pros and cons of each resolution strategy are then weighed and students decide on a course(s) of action. Finally, students carry through with the action plans they developed as members of a group or individually and evaluate the effects of their actions.

The Test of an STS Unit

We tested an STS issue investigation and action unit on solid waste management (Wiesenmayer & Rubba, 1990). The unit was developed for the Altoona (Pennsylvania) School District by five of the district's junior high school science teachers under Wiesenmayer's leadership during a two-week summer workshop. The teachers selected the trash issue for its timely, local significance and its relevance to junior high school students. Altoona and surrounding communities faced the close of area landfills; they were in the initial stages of developing a regional plan for trash disposal. As for the students, the teachers thought this issue might enlighten them, as adolescents generally behave as though we live in a disposable world.

Among the twenty class periods dedicated to the STS unit, six were devoted to STS issue foundations and awareness, eight to issue investigation, and six to issue action, as defined in the STS goal structure (Rubba & Wiesenmayer, 1988). Instruction on natural science concepts and some social science concepts related to the issue of trash disposal was integrated into the unit. The unit was tested in ten of seventeen class sections of seventh-grade life science at the city's two junior high schools and taught by the teachers who developed it. The other seven classes, the control classes, studied the district's regular life science curriculum. Data were collected on three dependent variables, including students' STS content achievement, life science achievement, and actions taken on STS issues beyond the twenty-day instructional period.

The findings showed statistically significant pre- to posttest gains among the ten class sections that completed the STS unit on each of the three dependent variables. The seven class sections that followed the regular life science curriculum showed statistically significant gains only in life science achievement. In addition, posttest differences were statistically significant between the class sections that studied the STS unit and life science on STS content achievement and action taken on STS issues.

We concluded that the STS Issue Investigation and Action unit was effective in helping middle/junior high school students develop: (1) an understanding of the interrelationships among science, technology, and society, (2) the ability to take actions on STS issues, and (3) the affective qualities needed to take such actions. While the increase in scores on the instrument used to measure knowledge of life science concepts was not as large for the STS classes as for the regular life science classes, the statistically significant increase suggests that STS Issue Investigation and Action units can encourage meaningful science concept development to the degree they are built into the unit, particularly the issue foundations and investigations sections.

STS Issue Investigation and Action units of this type could be made a part of science courses over a number of years, starting at the middle/junior high school level through high school. In fact, making an STS Issue Investigation and Action unit a part of every middle/junior high school and high school science course would allow the STS issues examined to be pedagogically selected and sequenced. It also would allow fulfillment of the NSTA (1982) recommendations for the percentage of science instructional time to be dedicated to STS—15 and 20 percent at the middle/junior high school and high school levels, respectively.

Conclusion

STS Issue Investigation and Action instruction is an empirically established strategy that holds great power for helping students develop the abilities and willingness to take action on STS issues, capabilities that are critical for citizenship in a science and technology-based society. As science teachers contemplate questions associated with whether to and how to integrate STS into science instruction, it should be kept in mind, as Ramsey (1989) reminds us:

> ALL students . . . WILL BECOME CITIZENS. All students will be consumers of the products and services of science and technology. All will assume and be responsible for the benefits and the risks of scientific and technological knowledge, products, systems, and services. All will be decision-makers concerning matters of science and technology, either willfully via participation in democratic decision-making or apathetically via the lack of such participation. (p. 40)

References

Aaronian, R., & Brinkerhoff, R. F. (1980). *The Exeter conference on secondary school science education.* Exeter, NH: Philips Exeter Academy.

Belgrade Charter, The. (1976). Connect. *UNESCO-UNEP Environmental Education Newsletter, 1,* 1–2.

Harms, N. C., & Yager, R. E. (Eds.). (1981). *What research says to the science teacher Vol. 3.* Washington, DC: National Science Teachers Association.

Hines, J., Hungerford, H., & Tomera, A. (1987). Analysis and synthesis of research on responsible environmental behavior: A meta-analysis. *The Journal of Environmental Education, 18*(2), 1–8.

Hungerford, H. R., Peyton, R. B., & Wilke, R. J. (1980). Goals for curriculum development in environmental education. *The Journal of Environmental Education, 41*(1), 42–47.

Klingler, G. (1980). *The effect of an instructional sequence on the environmental action skills of a sample of southern Illinois eighth graders.* Unpublished masters thesis, Southern Illinois University, Carbondale, Illinois.

National Council for the Social Studies, Science, and Society Committee. (1983). Guidelines for teaching science-related societal issues. *Social Education, 47*(4), 258–261.

National Council for the Social Studies, Science, and Society Committee. (1990). Teaching about science, technology, and society in social studies: Education for citizenship in the 21st century. *Social Education, 54*(4), 189–193.

National Science Board Commission on Precollege Education in Mathematics, Science, and Technology. (1983). *Educating Americans for the 21st century: A plan of action for improving mathematics, science, and technology education for all American elementary and secondary students so their achievement is the best in the world by 1995.* Washington, DC: National Science Foundation.

National Science Teachers Association. (1982). *Science-Technology-Society: Science education for the 1980s.* (Position Paper.) Washington, DC: Author.

National Science Teachers Association. (1990). Science/Technology/Society: A new effort for providing appropriate science for all (The NSTA position statement). *Bulletin of Science, Technology and Society, 10*(5&6), 249–250.

Ramsey, J. (1989). A curriculum framework for community-based STS issue instruction. *Education and Urban Society, 22*(1), 40–53.

Ramsey, J., & Hungerford, H. (1989). The effects of issue investigation and action training on environmental behavior in seventh grade students. *The Journal of Environmental Education, 20*(4), 29–34.

Ramsey, J., Hungerford, H., & Tomera, A. (1981). The effects of environmental action and environmental case study instruction on the overt environmental behavior of eighth grade students. *The Journal of Environmental Education, 13*(1), 24–29.

Rubba, P. A. (1987). Recommended competencies for STS education in grades 7–12. *The High School Journal, 70*(3), 145–150.

Rubba, P. A. (1989a, March). *The effects of an STS teacher education unit on the STS content achievement and participation in actions on STS issues by preservice science teachers.* Paper presented at the 1989 Annual Meeting of the National Association for Research in Science Teaching, San Francisco, CA.

Rubba, P. A. (1989b). An investigation of the semantic meaning assigned to concepts affiliated with STS education and of STS instructional practices among a sample of exemplary science teachers. *Journal of Research in Science Teaching, 26*(8), 687–702.

Rubba, P. A., & Wiesenmayer, R. L. (1985). A goal structure for precollege STS education: A proposal based upon recent literature in environmental education. *Bulletin of Science, Technology and Society, 5*(6), 439–445.

Rubba, P. A., & Wiesenmayer, R. L. (1988). Goals and competencies for precollege S/T/S education: Recommendations based upon recent literature in environmental education. *The Journal of Environmental Education, 19*(4), 38–44.

Showalter, V. (1974). What is unified science education: Part 5: Program objectives and scientific literacy. *Prism II, 2*(3&4), entire issue.

Sia, A., Hungerford, H., & Tomera, A. (1986). Selected predictors of responsible environmental behavior: An analysis. *The Journal of Environmental Education, 17*(2), 31–40.

Simpson, P. (1990, April). *The effects of an extended STS case study on citizenship behavior and associated variables in fifth and sixth grade students.* Paper presented at the annual convention of the National Association for Research in Science Teaching, Atlanta, GA.

Stapp, W., Bennett, D., Bryan, W., Jr., Fulton, J., MacGregor, J., Nowak, P., Swan, J., Wall, R., & Havlick, S. (1969). The concept of environmental education. *The Journal of Environmental Education, 1*(1), 31–36.

Tbilisi Intergovernmental Conference on Environmental Education, FICE Subcommittee on Environmental Education. (1978). *Toward an action plan: A report on the Tbilisi conference on environmental education.* Washington, DC: U.S. Government Printing Office. (Stock No. 017–080–01838–1)

Waks, L. J., & Prakash, M. S. (1985). STS education and its three step-sisters. *Bulletin of Science, Technology and Society, 5*(2), 105–116.

Wiesenmayer, R. L., & Rubba, P. A. (1990, April). *The effects of STS issue investigation and action instruction and traditional life science instruction on seventh grade students' citizenship behaviors.* Paper presented at the Annual Convention of the National Association for Research in Science Teaching, Atlanta, GA.

Afterword

Immediate Needs for STS as Reform

The re-education of teachers must take place at the schools where they teach. School-directed programs have been shown to be more effective at dealing with complex behaviors than programs conducted at colleges. Hart and Robottom (1990) fear that the STS paradigm shift may be hampered by failure of advocates to practice the tenets which they embrace in STS as they deal with all those involved in the reform—foremost the teachers. Teacher education must be improved; teachers must experience STS and learning in a constructivist environment.

Educational, government, industrial, and other leaders need to understand STS as reform and conceptualize the changes with statements of goals, curriculum frameworks, instructional strategies, and ways of assessing the degree goals are realized. Without attention to all these critical incidents for learning, little real improvement can occur.

The ties between STS and the Constructivist Learning Model must be strengthened via testing, analysis, and communication. Many of the features of constructivist teaching actually characterizes the STS approach to instruction.

The following components of today's education system must be carefully prepared to accept and welcome reform. Hopefully the research reviewed in this volume can help in each arena, including:

- Teacher education
- Curriculum planning
- Continuing education
- Instructional techniques
- School restructuring
- Community expectations
- Parent involvement

Some degree of consensus is needed to provide a focus for reform efforts such as Project 2061 and Scope, Sequence, and Coordination (SS&C). Elizabeth Culotta (1990) has reviewed the basic tenants of 2061 and SS&C and has defined an emerging consensus for the reforms and restructuring that the two huge and well-funded projects provide. Certainly the research available to support STS approaches is far greater than for those two projects—perhaps because STS efforts have been underway for ten years in the United States. Project 2061 and SS&C have been reform efforts centering on schools for only two years. Almost no research currently exists to indicate how 2061 and SS&C reform efforts offer improvements and correctives to the problems in science education which have been so widely deplored.

Culotta has identified the following six points of consensus. Certainly STS approaches invariably accept the same beliefs. In fact, the emerging research concerning STS provides evidence that Culotta's consensus points are supported by assessing successes with STS approaches.

• **Less is more.** It's time for students to stop memorizing the difference between a type I and type II level and the names of all the molecules involved in photosynthesis. One study (Yager, 1983) estimated that students encounter more new words in a high school biology book then in two years of instruction in a foreign language. "We still live with the Victorian view of school, with minds trained like dogs to memorize things," says Timothy Goldsmith, chair of the committee that wrote a recent report on biology education for the National Research Council. New programs have students doing less memorizing and more projects.

• **Teacher power.** Post-Sputnik reforms sometimes took the tone of academic highbrows telling teachers what to do, and teachers have taken much of the blame for education's ills. But the new goal is to boost teachers, not bash them, giving them time to learn science themselves, rather than berating them for their backgrounds.

• **Science without walls.** Sixth graders in rural Elbert County, Georgia, don't take science, math, social studies, or reading. Instead they take one all-encompassing course—200 minutes run by four teachers—that incorporates all four subjects. A trial instigated by members of Project 2061, the course illustrates the push for integrating subjects. Real-life problems rarely come labeled as "chemistry" or "math." How far should such course integration go? Each program seems to have a different answer. Meanwhile, Georgia teachers are still seeking a good moniker for their mega-course.

• **Do it yourself.** At the end of the school day in inner-city Philadelphia, teachers gather to learn how to separate salt from pepper using static electricity. They're being trained to use an elementary science kit, doing all the experiments their students will do. A staple of the 1960s reforms, hands-on activities are back and better, with a new emphasis on quality—"minds-on" as well as hands-on. Teachers are being trained more carefully and given the logistic support they need.

• **Two-way traffic.** Children haven't understood much of what we've been telling them, in part because we haven't listened to the ideas they already have. For example, research shows that many youngsters don't understand the concept of temperature. They think putting on a sweater keeps you warm because a sweater always exists at a higher temperature. By listening to children, teachers can get clues on how to change such misconceptions.

• **Science for everyone.** It's vital to widen the science career pipeline, especially to include more women and minorities. Reformers now also recognize a second goal: producing scientifically literate citizens. Even students who will never become scientists need to understand more about how the world works. New programs are aimed at all students, not just the gifted.

Reference

Culotta, E. (1990). Can science education be saved? *Science, 250*(4986), 1327–1330.

Hart, E. P, & Robottom, I. M. (1990). The Science-Technology-Society movement in science education: A critique of the reform process. *Journal of Research in Science Teaching, 27*(6), 575–588.

Yager, R. E. (1983). The importance of terminology in teaching K–12 science. *Journal of Research in Science Teaching, 20*(6), 577–588.